Turning Sweden Around

Turning Sweden Around

Assar Lindbeck,
Per Molander,
Torsten Persson,
Olof Petersson,
Agnar Sandmo,
Birgitta Swedenborg,
and Niels Thygesen

The MIT Press
Cambridge, Massachusetts
London, England

© 1994 Massachusetts Institute of Technology

All rights reserved. No part of this book may be reproduced in any form by any electronic or mechanical means (including photocopying, recording, or information storage and retrieval) without permission in writing from the publisher.

This book was set in Palatino by DEKR Corporation and was printed and bound in the United States of America.

Library of Congress Cataloging-in-Publication Data

Nya villkor för ekonomi och politik. English
  Turning Sweden around / Assar Lindbeck . . . [et al.].
    p. cm.
  Translation of: Nya villkor för ekonomi och politik :
Ekonomikommissions förslag (SOU 1993: 16).
  Includes bibliographical references and index.
  ISBN 0-262-12181-6
  1. Sweden—Economic conditions—1945–   2. Sweden—Economic policy.
3. Sweden—Politics and government—1973–   I. Lindbeck, Assar.
II. Sweden. Ekonomikommissionen. III. Title.
HC375.N93813 1994
338.9485—dc20   94-842
                                                                            CIP

Contents

Preface   vii

1 The Swedish Crisis   1

2 Stability   23

3 Efficiency   75

4 Growth   137

5 Democracy   171

6 Recovery   205

References   229
Index   237

Preface

On December 10, 1992, the Swedish government appointed a commission of independent academics to analyze the economic crisis in Sweden and suggest ways to solve it. The commission was asked to deal with short-term as well as medium-term problems.

The commission's members were: Assar Lindbeck (chairman), the Institute for International Economic Studies, Stockholm University; Per Molander, the Expert Group on Public Finance (ESO), Stockholm; Torsten Persson, the Institute for International Economic Studies, Stockholm University; Olof Petersson, Department of Government, Uppsala University; Agnar Sandmo, Norges Handelshøjskole, Bergen; Birgitta Swedenborg, Center for Business and Social Studies (SNS), Stockholm; and Niels Thygesen, University of Copenhagen.

The group took the name "Ekonomikommissionen"—the Economics Commission. Its final report, "Nya Villkor för Ekonomi och Politik, Ekonomikommissionens förslag," was presented as a 200-page, printed volume on March 9, 1993, three months after the appointment of the commission.

The commission asked a large number of experts to write background papers on specific topics. Twenty-seven of these papers were subsequently published in two volumes, accompanying the report. It is no exaggeration to say that the report created an exceptionally intense discussion in Sweden about the economic and political problems of the country.

We translated the report into English in the belief that many of the economic problems in Sweden already exist or may emerge in other highly developed countries. Only very minor—mostly editorial—changes have been made to the original report. Here and there we have added a few sentences describing Swedish institutions for the benefit of foreign readers; we have also added a number of references to the literature. We have extended the time series used in some of the tables and figures by a few quarters, or in some cases by a year. Moreover, we have added a few observations, in brackets, about developments after the publication of the original report.

It is our hope that the report, even though it deals with a country of eight million inhabitants on the periphery of Europe, will be of some interest to readers in other countries. After all, foreign observers have often regarded with interest both Sweden's macroeconomic policies and the Swedish version of welfare-state policies.

We are grateful to Berthill Munkestam and David Strömberg for assistance with data and figures, and to Kerstin Blomquist, Maria Gil, Molly Åkerlund, and Lotta Änggård for typing and editorial assistance.

Stockholm
August 18, 1993

1   The Swedish Crisis

At some rare moments a nation pauses to reflect on its future. Such moments usually occur in periods of decline and crisis. The ability of a nation to reconsider past decisions and rejuvenate itself is then put to the test. Today Sweden is experiencing its most serious crisis since the 1930s. How Sweden works to overcome the crisis will mark the country for decades to come. The form the solution will take is still an open question.

Certain conditions are favorable: Sweden is an affluent society; the democratic system is well anchored; and the citizens have in the past proved able to combine common sense with common visions about the future. But other conditions are unfavorable. The basic problems became apparent many years ago and have grown worse over time. They reflect a complex mixture of acute cyclical problems and chronic structural problems. It is therefore not possible to solve the crisis solely by the application of short-term measures. Furthermore, the economic problems have their origin to a large extent in political decisions of the past, which makes it necessary to analyze both economic and political systems.

In this light, the commission has set three overriding tasks for itself:

1. To identify basic weaknesses of the Swedish economic system and to suggest improvements, in particular, of those rules and institutions that are politically determined. It is our ambition to suggest reforms that contribute to increased economic stability, efficiency, and growth—respecting commonly accepted goals of maintaining a social safety net, and with due concern for income distribution.

2. To suggest changes in the political system, aiming at stable rules and a good general economic environment for firms and households.

3. To propose ways to turn the current crisis situation into a more satisfactory state of affairs, minimizing various transition problems.

The commission's time horizon, as set by the government's initial directives, is medium term, which we interpret as about ten years ahead. The suggested policies should, however, also be sustainable over an even longer-term perspective. The cost of today's consumption should not be pushed into the future, limiting the options of future generations: our generation should not pass on a large public-sector debt, a heavy pension debt, or a welfare-reducing environmental debt.

The Economic Dimensions of the Crisis

International observers have often made positive statements about the Swedish economy during the postwar period, emphasizing the low unemployment rate, the high and evenly distributed incomes, the high degree of economic safety of the citizens, and the rich supply of public-sector services to households. Disturbing signs in the Swedish economy emerged, however, in the 1970s and the 1980s. Obvious examples are the slow rate of productivity growth, the recurring public-sector budget deficits, and the high rate of inflation, leading to repeated cost crises in the tradable sector and frequent exchange rate devaluations.

Stiffer competition in world markets has, moreover, created problems for Swedish firms in the tradable sector. In the 1970s this was particularly evident in labor-intensive industries as well as in certain basic industries such as steel and shipbuilding; but parts of the engineering industry also felt the pinch. To ease the difficulties, the state provided huge subsidies, partly to protect jobs in response to public demands. The restructuring of Swedish industry was postponed by these policy actions, but not evaded. In the future, increased competition from low-wage countries, including the neighboring former socialist countries, is a new challenge to the tradable sector in Sweden.

Stability Problems

The recurring macroeconomic crises experienced during the last two decades may largely be seen as a collision between attempts to keep a fixed exchange rate on the one hand, and a strongly inflationary system of wage formation on the other (see chapter 2). Domestic inflation has time and again raised production costs and product prices to levels where Swedish firms—at the going exchange rate—have lost market shares and experienced a drastic profit squeeze. This phenomenon has repeatedly threatened employment in the tradable sectors of the economy.

One explanation for this collision between the exchange rate and domestic inflation is simply that macroeconomic policy has not been consistent with the attempts to maintain a fixed exchange rate. Fiscal policy has often been expansionary also during economic booms. It has therefore contributed to, or passively accepted, an overheated labor market, with domestic wage costs rising faster than those in the outside world. Political declarations that the exchange rate parity should be maintained, and warnings of economic decline if wages and prices soar, have been repeated in one government budget proposal after another. These declarations were not credible, however, and they were therefore not able to prevent inflationary developments (see chapter 2).

The immediate background to the acute macroeconomic crisis was the inflationary policies following the huge devaluations in 1981 and 1982; during the rest of the 1980s, wage costs per hour increased about 2% more per year than inflation in competing countries. This inflationary development was accentuated by the pronounced credit expansion in the wake of financial market deregulation in the 1980s—stimulated by low real after-tax interest rates due to rapid inflation and high marginal tax rates against which interest costs could be deducted. One important consequence was a drastic fall in the household saving rate from about 4% to about −4% of disposable household income, and hence a huge increase in private consumption. Another consequence of the explosive credit expansion was the dramatic real estate and building boom, with skyrocketing real estate prices. Because the fixed exchange rate regime tied monetary policy to the task of upholding the exchange rate, the central bank could not do much to prevent the drastic credit expansion.

The international business slowdown during the first years of the 1990s made the cost crisis acute in Sweden: high-cost countries, such as ours, were particularly badly hurt by stagnating or falling world demand for goods and services. Between 1990 and 1993 industrial production in Sweden fell by 17%–18%, that is, by about the same

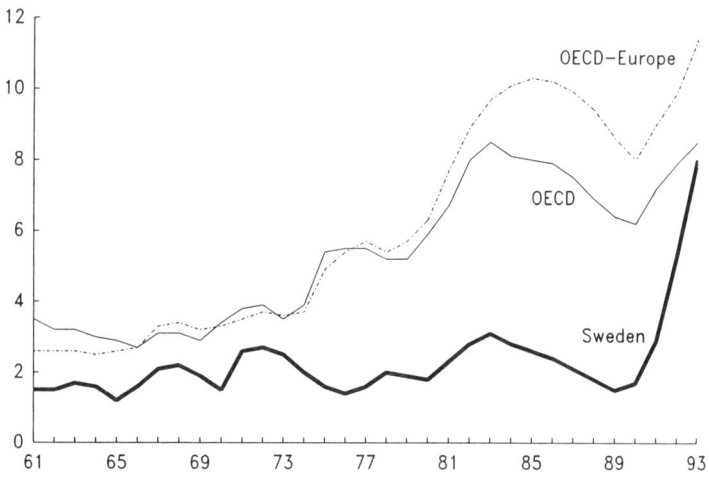

Source: Konjunkturinstitutet.

Figure 1.1
Unemployment in OECD and Sweden (percent of labor force)

magnitude as during the depression in the 1930s. As a result, open unemployment has reached levels previously unthinkable during the postwar period: about 9% in September 1993 (figure 1.1), and 5% of the labor force engaged in various types of active labor market programs. "Total unemployment" therefore reached about 14% in the fall of 1993.

The insistence on upholding the exchange rate until November 1992, when the krona was allowed to float, also contributed to the drastic fall in inflation: from 8% in 1990 to about 2% in 1991; core inflation has continued at about that rate recently. Low inflation was, in fact, formally announced as "an overriding goal" for economic policy by the (social democratic) government in its budget proposal in January 1991. This policy was subsequently confirmed by formally but unilaterally tying the exchange rate to the ecu (the European Currency Unit) in May 1991.

Low inflation combined with the 1991 tax reform, which reduced the tax rates on capital income to 30%, and high international interest rates caused real after-tax interest rates to rise dramatically. This contributed not only to a deeper recession, but also to the most severe real estate and financial crisis in Sweden during this century—a backlash to the previous boom in financial and real estate markets. Beside the dramatic fall in inflation and the huge increase in unemployment, the real estate and financial crisis is the most characteristic feature of the contemporary macroeconomic situation.

The recurring cost problems, and related tendencies to increased unemployment, cannot be blamed solely on economic policy. A complementary explanation is the institutional setup of the labor market. Wage formation in Sweden has for a long time involved wage bargaining on two or three levels: firm, branch, and economywide. The system has also been used by the unions to drastically squeeze wage differentials, the so-called solidaristic wage policy. This bargaining system emerged during a period of rapid labor productivity growth (about 5% per year in the private sector) and steady inflation in competing countries (at about 4% per year). Wage bargaining adjusted neither to the slower productivity growth after the mid-1970s nor to the slowdown of inflation abroad; the bargaining system therefore contributed to the recurrent cost crises.

The dramatic rise in public sector spending—from 25% of GDP in 1950 to 70% in 1992—may similarly be regarded as a result of institutions unable to adjust to slower productivity growth. (The size of public-sector spending in Sweden is not strictly comparable to that of many other countries, because several types of transfers in Sweden are taxed, while in many other countries they are not.) Public-sector spending continued to expand at about the same rate a decade after the slowdown of productivity growth; from the early 1970s to the early 1980s total government spending rose by 20% in relation to GDP (see figure 3.4). This contributed both to the overheating of the economy during boom periods and to recurring budget deficits (figure 1.2).

It is tempting to conjecture that the years of rapid economic growth, when there was much to distribute, formed long-lasting spendthrift political attitudes. The ever higher levels of public spending, and ever higher tax rates, may also have created a vicious circle of rising public spending and falling productivity growth, because of the disincentives created by ever wider tax wedges.

Thus we have identified four potentially serious stability problems: (1) the strong inflation bias in the Swedish economy, apparent in wage formation; (2) the recurrent budget deficits; (3) the severe financial and building crises; and since the early 1990s, also (4) high unemployment.

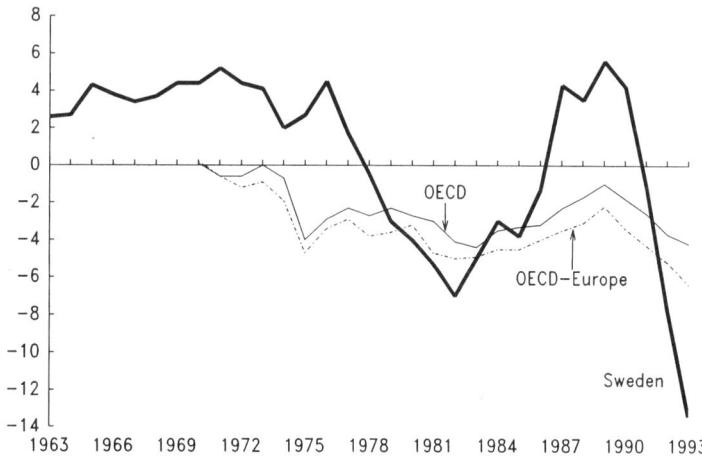

Source: Konjunkturinstitutet.

Figure 1.2
Financial surplus in the public sector (percent of GDP)

In the commission's view, high unemployment is the most serious consequence of the present economic crisis. During the 1970s and 1980s, long-term unemployment became a serious social problem in most Western European countries. There is now an obvious risk that Sweden will go the same way. Although Sweden's total unemployment, including people in various labor market programs, has recently reached European levels, long-term unemployment of the same magnitude has not yet emerged. It should be an overriding task of economic policy to prevent creating a large group of permanently unemployed citizens—without giving up the ambitions of low inflation, an efficient use of economic resources, and satisfactory economic growth.

Efficiency Problems

Low efficiency in production and restricted variety in service consumption are more difficult to document than macroeconomic instability. It is, however, quite clear that a number of important markets in the Swedish economy function poorly, such that resources are used inefficiently and hence impose considerable costs on the economy (see chapter 3). An important explanation for this lack of efficiency, according to the commission, is the restrictions on competition. Prices of a large number of goods in Sweden have been consistently higher than in other countries, to an extent that cannot be fully explained by an occasionally overvalued currency, high indirect taxes, or the specific Swedish wage structure. Other indicators of inadequate competition are government regulations, cartel agreements between firms, and the monopoly-like market structure in several sectors of the economy.

Limited competition constitutes an obvious example of how special (producer) interests may dominate the general (consumer) interest. Interaction between the regulatory authorities and special interest groups also helps the latter to avoid competition—so-called regulatory capture. Continued integration of the Swedish economy with the rest of Europe may enhance competition in many product and service markets, but it is mainly up to domestic policies to restore competition within Sweden.

High production costs and constrained consumer choices are even more pronounced where personal "social" services are supplied mainly by public-sector monopolies: in medical care, education, child care, old age care, etc. Today the social-service sector accounts for about 28% of Swedish GDP, slightly more of total labor hours, and about 35% of the employees.

The costs of many public-sector services seem to be considerably higher in Sweden than comparable services in several other developed countries. Where comparisons are possible, costs are also often higher than in corresponding private service production in Sweden. The most likely reason is simply that public-sector services are produced outside the market system, and that private production is discriminated against or even prohibited.

Competition is severely restricted not only in product and service markets, but also in the labor and financial markets. In the labor market it is mainly wage formation and the legal rules for hiring and firing of labor, that is, the labor legislation, that is problematic. In particular, wage formation tends to conflict with the need for a flexible labor market, because relative wages have to a large extent become tools for redistributive ambitions. Existing labor legislation springs from a society with less heterogeneous workers and jobs than today, and with less need for flexibility.

Serious problems are also tied to the tax and social security systems. Following the tax reform of 1991, the problem is not mainly the design of the tax system, but rather the level of public spending and hence the general level of taxation. In the social security system, by contrast, both the design of the system and the general level of benefits are problematic.

Serious transition problems are bound to occur as soon as we try to do something about these various efficiency problems. Cutting public-sector transfers or raising the efficiency of public-sector service production in today's deep recession would surely increase unemployment still further, at least temporarily. It is therefore important to adjust the timing of such reforms, so that the recession is not aggravated. As public-sector monopolies have hampered private and cooperative initiatives, there is also an obvious risk that certain services will temporarily disappear after abrupt cuts in public-sector service production.

Serious transition problems may also arise in connection with reforms of the social security system. Because many citizens have built their lives on expected benefits, they have neither saved enough nor bought ample private insurance. A sudden reduction in benefits may thus create severe hardships for many citizens. Moreover, appropriate timing is again important, because a reduction of promised future benefits can be expected to stimulate private saving. While this is favorable in a long-term context, it would accentuate the present recession.

Growth Problems

Deficiencies in the economic environment of firms and households may not only waste resources at every point of time; they may also hamper the accumulation of resources, and hence productivity growth (see chapter 4). Even though the precise figures are subject to debate, it is by now well documented that Sweden has had serious problems with productivity growth during the last two decades. While labor productivity for the economy as a whole (GDP per employed), increased by about 3.3% per year during the 1950s and 1960s, the corresponding figure since 1970 is about 1.1%. This is a serious problem regardless of whether productivity growth has fallen more or less than in other countries, and regardless of whether the slowdown of productivity growth is caused by the same or different

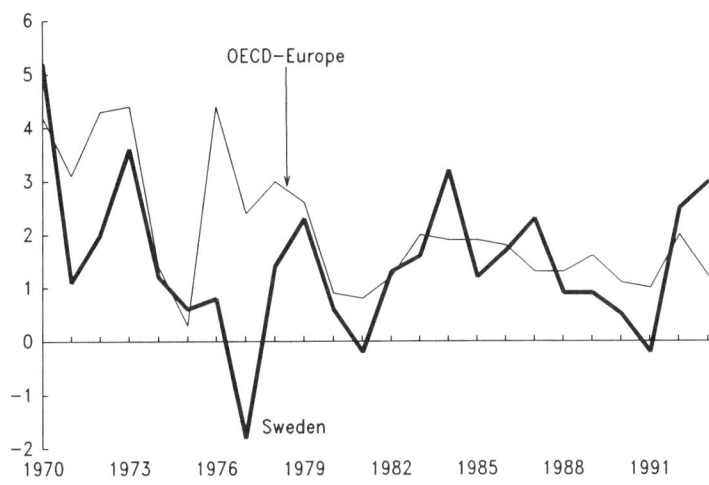

Source: Konjunkturinstitutet.

Figure 1.3
Change in productivity—GDP per employed—OECD-Europe and Sweden (yearly change in percent)

factors in Sweden and in other countries. It is, however, quite clear that overall productivity growth (GDP per employed) has been slower in Sweden than the average for the OECD during the last two decades (1970–1992)—about 0.6% slower per year (figure 1.3). Moreover, aggregate manufacturing production has increased about 1.5% more slowly per year than the OECD average, and labor productivity in that sector about 0.3% more slowly (2.4% as compared to 2.7%). It would also seem that total factor productivity (value added per factor input) in manufacturing has grown more slowly in Sweden than in any developed country for which comparable statistics are available. Hansson and Lundberg (1991), for instance, estimate total factor productivity growth at only 0.6% per year during 1970 to 1985, while figures in the 1.2%–2.5% interval were typical for most other countries in the study.

As a consequence, Sweden has lost its previously high position in the ranking of the world's richest countries. While GDP per person in Sweden was 8% above the (weighted) OECD average in 1970, by 1991 it had slid down to a level 6% below the weighted average, implying a drop from a shared third place to a fourteenth place in the OECD ranking (table 1.1). It should then be noted that 1991 was

Table 1.1
GDP per capita in PPP terms (percent of OECD average, 1970 and 1991)

1970 Rank		Index	1991 Rank		Index
1	Switzerland	145	1	USA	125
2	USA	141	2	Switzerland	122
3	Luxembourg	108	3	Luxembourg	120
3	**Sweden**	**108**	4	Germany	110
5	Germany	105	5	Canada	108
6	Canada	102	5	Japan	108
7	Netherlands	101	7	France	103
8	Denmark	100	8	Denmark	99
8	France	100	9	Belgium	98
10	Australia	99	10	Austria	97
11	New Zealand	98	10	Iceland	97
12	UK	93	12	Italy	95
13	Belgium	90	12	Norway	95
14	Austria	86	**14**	**Sweden**	**94**
15	Italy	85	15	Netherlands	93
16	Finland	82	16	Australia	91
17	Japan	80	17	Finland	90
18	Norway	33	18	UK	88
19	Iceland	75	19	New Zealand	78
20	Spain	64	20	Spain	72
21	Ireland	50	21	Ireland	65
22	Portugal	42	22	Portugal	52
23	Greece	41	23	Greece	44
24	Turkey	17	24	Turkey	20

Source: OECD national accounts.

not a particularly bad year from the cyclical point of view (2.9% unemployment).

What has been the role of economic policy in this development? When discussing this issue, we start with some "proximate sources" of growth: the accumulation of physical capital, human capital, and technology. Behind these proximate sources lie, in turn, the general economic, social, and political environment of firms and households in Sweden.

Available studies indicate that the return on physical investments in Sweden has been relatively low as compared to other countries during several decades; (see, for instance, various studies by the OECD, and Jakobsson 1992). The return on physical investments has often been even below the return on government bonds. One explanation is the recurrent cost crises that have, from time to time, kept down the return on capital in sectors exposed to foreign competition. This may not have hurt Swedish investment activity too much, as long as Swedish capital was "locked in" by capital control before the late 1980s.

If we want not only high GDP but also high national wealth and national income, considerable national saving is also necessary. In a macroeconomic context it may be tempting to regard private and public-sector saving as good substitutes: the greater the public-sector saving, the less private saving is necessary to achieve a given accumulation of national wealth. However, when it comes to the functioning of the economic system, private- and public-sector saving cannot really be regarded as perfect substitutes. In particular, private saving is important in order to keep and develop domestic private entrepreneurship; small entrepreneurs have to depend on domestic private saving because of informational asymmetries in the capital market. This means that government policy should take responsibility not only for safeguarding a reasonable return on capital, after tax, but also for not discriminating against private saving.

Empirical studies indicate that slower accumulation of physical capital can only explain the Swedish fall in productivity growth during the 1970s and 1980s to a limited extent; the drastic fall in measured total factor productivity growth also supports this interpretation. Other explanations are necessary. It is then tempting to pinpoint the accumulation of human capital, in the form of formal education and on-the-job training. The private return on education and on-the-job training has indeed been quite low in Sweden for a long time. Part of the problem is policy induced: the government is largely in charge of the education system, and the after-tax return on investment in human capital is strongly influenced by the tax system. Moreover, the government is responsible for the wage structure in the public sector.

Explaining the diffusion of technology is much more difficult. It is, for instance, unclear which role public policy has played, and can play, in this field. It is our understanding that it is important for technological progress to facilitate the entry of new firms, and to provide a good general environment for entrepreneurship and invest-

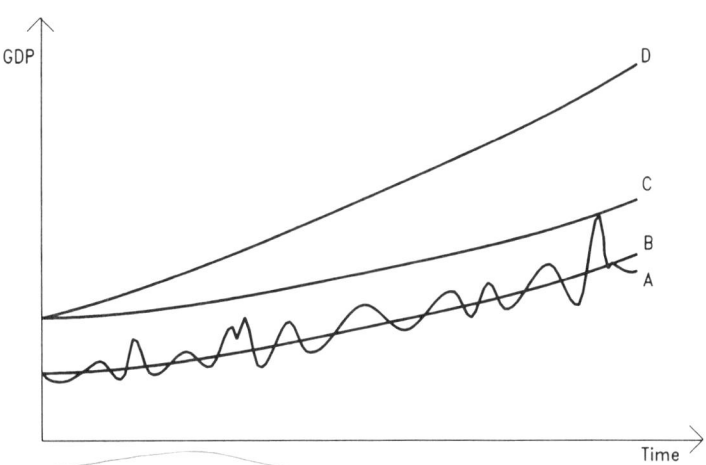

Figure 1.4
Efficiency, stability, and growth: an outline of principles

ment in physical and human capital, as well as for research and diffusion of technology. However, we argue that government initiatives may also have a more specific role to play in stimulating the development and transmission of "generic" technologies where the incentives both of universities and production firms may be lacking.

Three Basic Economic Problems

In the discussion above we divided the economic crisis in Sweden into problems of macroeconomic stability, efficiency, and growth. We organize our report in a similar way, even though the three aspects are strongly interconnected.

The three problems are illustrated in figure 1.4. The uneven curve, A, illustrates schematically the actual development of GDP, while the smooth curve, B, expresses its growth trend. The deviations of the A curve from the trend curve, B, illustrate macroeconomic instability ("the business cycle"). Curve C depicts the hypothetical level of GDP that could be achieved at different points in time with more efficient use of available resources, while the steeper curve D depicts the GDP trend with a higher growth rate.

The purpose of our proposals is to enhance macroeconomic stability, that is, to even out short-term macroeconomic fluctuations; to raise the level of the entire growth path by way of a more efficient use of given resources; and to increase the slope of the growth path. GDP is of course a very incomplete welfare measure. The GDP calculations are nevertheless a good starting point for identifying macroeconomic problems such as macroeconomic instability, inefficiency, and slow economic growth—as well as unemployment and inflationary tendencies.

The Political Dimensions of the Crisis

Several of today's economic problems may be traced to political decisions and institutional change of the past. The expansion of the welfare state during the 1970s and the 1980s weakened economic incentives and contributed to public-sector deficits. Labor market legislation favored short-term job security rather than flexibility and dynamism in the economy. It hampered the ability of firms to adjust and rejuvenate, and hence create higher long-run living standard for employees. The institutions of wage bargaining impaired macroeconomic stability. Labor market legislation and institutions neglected economic incentives and efficiency by emphasizing distributional aspects in a rather one-sided way.

The economic crisis in Sweden is therefore also a crisis of politics and institutions. By this we do not only, or even mainly, mean to blame a number of specific policy mistakes. Rather we want to emphasize some basic weaknesses in the political system. Certain crisis-triggering factors, such as the global energy crisis and the recessions of 1975–76, 1980–82, and 1990–93, originated of course outside Sweden. But the difficulties experienced by the Swedish economy in adjusting to these disturbances are homemade. For instance, shorter election periods (three years) after the constitutional reform of 1970 made it more difficult for a government to establish and implement a long-term strategy. The abolition of the first chamber in parliament, and the shift to a strictly proportional election system, probably increased the instability in the political system by making it harder to form strong cabinets. At a time when it became particularly important for politicians to take firm action, their ability to do so was reduced.

From an economic point of view, the Swedish political system has one particularly serious bias: it seems to be much easier to decide about higher spending than to cut benefits or raise public-sector revenues. Public-sector spending once expanded mainly to create a social safety net for the citizens and to even out living standards between different population groups. Swedish politicians often relied on centralized and standardized approaches to these tasks. The original goal has to a large extent been achieved. But today the weaknesses of the solutions also show up quite clearly. Both the scope and form of public-sector activities in Sweden have hampered economic efficiency. The public sector, therefore, has tended to undermine its own foundations.

The system of wage bargaining is also, as noted above, poorly adapted to contemporary conditions. It was once constructed to make it possible for unions and employers' associations to agree about wages without government intervention. Government incomes policy has been regarded as inconsistent with Swedish traditions in wage formation. In practice, however, wage formation has been increasingly tied to political decision-making. With a rapidly expanding public sector, taxes and social security fees became ever more important for real, after-tax wages, and this tempted the government to intervene with incomes policy (for instance, by inducing unions to accept lower wage demands by way of tax concessions). At the same time, the government became increasingly important as an employer. Public-sector employees emerged as an important pressure group, whose power was strongly accentuated by liberal rights to strike. The fruitless search for new forms of wage formation in Sweden illustrates the weakness of the old system and the difficulties in finding new rules of the game.

Basic Responsibilities of the State

A serious problem with the present organization of Swedish society is the confusion of roles and the unclear division of responsibility. It is characteristic that no distinction is usually made in Swedish discussions between the state (public sector) and the society (including also the "civic," voluntary society). We believe—and this is of course a value judgment—that the basic role of the state is to set the framework for the civic society, and to contribute to favorable general conditions for households and firms.

How then should the responsibility of the state be specified? First, it is important that the irreplaceable "classical" tasks of the state are performed well. No other organization in society is able to provide collective goods such as legal rules, including guarantees of the civil rights of individuals. It is also unavoidable that the state assumes the main responsibility for dealing with various economic externalities, since many of these are not automatically taken care of by voluntary contracts. This holds both for positive externalities, such as those tied to education and research, and for negative externalities, such as those tied to environmental damages. There is also general agreement that the state should assume the basic responsibility for large parts of the physical infrastructure, including roads, harbors, and telecommunication networks.

It is, however, impossible to argue that the state today performs these classical tasks particularly well—either in Sweden or in other countries. The safety assured to life and property has hardly kept pace with increased income safety. Public-sector contributions in the fields of education and research also leave a lot to be desired. Several environmental problems remain unsolved, even though a more active environmental policy has been pursued during recent decades. Investment in and maintenance of the physical infrastructure have often been neglected. The legal framework for firms has not been particularly conducive to economic efficiency; for instance, the government has hampered rather than facilitated competition in the Swedish economy.

The dominating public-sector activities today do not of course reflect these classical functions of the state. Rather, they reflect the ambitions to enhance individual income safety, in particular by way of the social security system; to influence the distribution of income by way of taxes and transfers between individuals and socioeconomic groups; and to influence macroeconomic variables, such as unemployment, inflation, and economic growth (this may also be seen as a method to increase the economic safety of the individual and to influence the distribution of income). These are, of course, as legitimate tasks as the classical functions of the state.

The reason for emphasizing macroeconomic stability, efficiency, and economic growth is that the contemporary economic crisis is reflected in precisely these aspects. It is, however, important to consider also income safety and distribution. One reason is that the desire of politicians to influence the distribution of income has contributed to some of our recent economic problems; another reason is that attempts to improve efficiency and productivity growth are bound to have consequences also for the distribution of income and wealth.

One further aspect of the role of the state in the economy should be mentioned. Traditional recommendations for government intervention are implicitly based on the assumption that the government is willing and able to act as an instrument of the general interest. This assumption has been increasingly questioned. Public-policy decisions are made in the context of a political process, in which political parties compete for votes, and hence for power. What is actually done by a government is also the result of conflicts between different interest groups in society, many of which try to use the state for their own purposes. Today it is well understood that governmental decisions reflect not only attempts to promote the general interest, but also various special interests. This is an important insight, because the general interest often conflicts with special interests. Measures that satisfy special interests may shrink total resources and harm most citizens in the long run.

Economic policy recommendations are hazardous in these circumstances. One reason is that it is difficult to predict the effects of a particular recommendation on actual policy. This means that it is not enough to make policy recommendations; it is also necessary to discuss appropriate rules according to which decisions are taken in the political system.

The Crisis of the Swedish Model

Both foreign and domestic observers agree that Swedish society since the 1930s has had certain distinct features. The specific Swedish way of decision-making has been called "the Swedish model." The centralized and peaceful way of solving conflicts in the labor market, the full-employment policy, the centralized organization of society, and several other aspects of Swedish society, once proudly shown to visiting observers, are now breaking up.

We may say that the Swedish model mirrored the structure and distribution of power in an industrial society, which was characterized by a strong and well-organized working class represented by the confederation of Labor Unions (LO), and a unified group of industrial employers, represented by the employers' confederation (SAF). The model has been described as a historical compromise between labor and capital. During the first twenty-five years after World War II the model was no doubt consistent with rather rapid economic growth and rising, and ever more equally distributed, material welfare. But it also resulted in institutions and structures that today constitute an obstacle to economic efficiency and economic growth because of their lack of flexibility and their one-sided concerns for income safety and distribution, with limited concern for economic incentives.

The crisis of the Swedish model is, for these reasons, largely a crisis of institutions. It has several causes. One is that organizations have a tendency to preserve themselves even when the original reasons for their existence have weakened or disappeared. Another cause is the natural tendency of organizations to take a narrow view, that is, to partly ignore the consequences for the economy as a whole. Behavior that is beneficial to individual actors or subsystems may have negative consequences for the system as a whole if there is no mechanism for efficient coordination. The many special interests favored by the present system are in fact important obstacles to economic change.

The conflict between special interests and the general interest is apparent also to the individual citizen. In the role of recipient of benefits, producer, employee, or member of a voluntary organization, the individual may derive short-term benefits from the present system. But the flip side may be negative long-run consequences for all citizens.

Our society also experiences a legitimacy crisis. Established powerful groups have been challenged by new opposition groups in a "red wave" directed against private business, a "blue wave" against the public sector, and a "green wave" against productivity growth, technology, and large-scale activities. These successive waves have eroded the citizens' confidence in established organizations and institutions.

The legitimacy crisis is also related to a management crisis. Gradually, the political system has taken on so many difficult tasks that the quality of decisions has been impossible to sustain. The gulf between expectations and results has widened. In Sweden, as well as in several Western European countries, concepts such as nonmanageability and overload of the political system were discussed as early as the 1970s. Old organizational models and conventional management methods have proved inefficient. The powerlessness of people in power has become increasingly obvious. After an age of increased expectations, demands have grown for more freedom of choice and more personal integrity. Collective and uniform systems based on standardized solutions have great difficulties in satisfying increasingly differentiated demands. The management crisis has been accentuated by the conflict between an increasingly international economic system and nationally based political systems.

A New Social Contract

With a metaphor common in the social sciences, the Swedish model may be seen as a social contract, analogous to individual contracts. Such a social contract may be of longer or shorter duration, it may cover larger or smaller parts of social life, and it may be more or less unique to a certain country. A social contract does not have to be a formal, written document, but can be interpreted metaphorically. It may always be debated who agreed to the contract, when it was agreed upon, and what its content really is.

Several interacting changes in society imply that at least parts of the social contract in Sweden have been terminated. Sweden is therefore in a contractless state. This holds not only for the system of wage formation, with strong disagreement between unions and employers' associations about the proper bargaining system, but also for the social security system, and indeed for the former dominance in society of the public sector.

The deep economic crisis indicates that Sweden is in acute need of institutional change. The question is not if, but when and how this change is going to occur. Well-documented historical experience suggests that an economic crisis may turn into a democratic crisis. Indeed, the demands placed on the political system are very strong. The economic crisis lowers the living standard for large groups of citizens, at least temporarily. This may foster discontent, apathy, and lack of confidence in the political system, even in the democratic system. The crisis can be solved only through a determined policy that aims at the long-term general interest. Today's political decision-making process tends instead to favor short-term special interests. It is therefore not enough to take specific short-term economic policy actions. Basic changes in institutions and decision rules are necessary.

It is a test of the vitality of Swedish democracy whether it will be able to bring about a new, functioning social contract. This contract requires both constitutional change in political life and structural change in economic life—with broad support across party lines.

Perspectives for the Future

Basic Principles

A theme running through the entire report is the need for institutional change. The paramount task is simultaneously to move Sweden out of the economic crisis and to reform the Swedish political system. There is no necessary conflict between these two goals. On the contrary, we believe that it is possible to bring about increased economic stability, efficiency, and growth and at the same time strengthen democracy. Economic and political reforms may therefore support each other.

The type of social organization that the commission advocates—on the basis of our explicit value judgments—rests on three basic principles: active citizenship, pluralism, and a clear division of responsibility (see chapter 5).

Active citizenship means self-determination. Representative democracy implies that a collective of citizens exercises self-determination within a nation, or a municipality. But democracy also presupposes individual self-determination. A system of active, full-fledged citizens presupposes a high degree of personal responsibility. Many of our proposals are designed exactly to strengthen the freedom of choice and the self-determination of individuals.

Pluralism means that society is based not on a single but on several different mechanisms of social coordination. In a pluralistic society, markets, voluntary organizations, the judiciary, religious organizations, universities, cooperatives, and local governments all operate by their own rules within their respective spheres of interest. In Sweden pluralism has been restrained by state interventions in area after area. For us, to strengthen pluralism means to redefine the role of the state and to liberate both markets and private organizations. In this way the responsibility of the state becomes more well defined, in particular to represent the common long-term interest of all citizens.

Clear division of responsibility means that different agents and organizations in society have clearly defined tasks and clear incentives. Responsibility presupposes a close connection between contribution and result. The confusion of roles and the diffuse division of power has tended to blur accountability. Exercise of accountability requires clearly stated objectives and effective methods of scrutiny. Publicity and debate are of crucial importance.

The Goal and How to Get There

To the extent that it is possible to learn from previous mistakes, the future is bright for Sweden. A major difficulty lies in keeping a critical distance on recent developments, however. Judgments about the actual situation are colored by ideology and short-term special interests.

Foreign experiences is also a crucial source of information. It is hardly advisable to copy solutions from other countries mechanically; conditions in individual countries are often too different. It may, however, be possible to avoid some mistakes by studying the outside world. As Sweden can hardly be expected to lead progress with regard to all aspects of society, a certain openness toward other countries may be in place, even though this insight seems to be hard to absorb for some Swedes. The experiences of our Nordic neighbors, in economics as well as politics, are perhaps of particular interest.

The commission has in its work tried to learn from the theoretical and empirical insights in the social sciences, particularly in economics and political science. Common to these two fields is a growing interest in the role of institutions. This report seeks to diagnose the economic crisis in Sweden on the basis of recent research in both economics and politics. Since research rarely tells the full story, we must also use our accumulated experience as observers of society. Moreover, policy recommendations often require value judgments, and we try to state ours openly.

The following three chapters deal with the three basic problems in the Swedish economy, which we defined above: stability (chapter 2), efficiency (chapter 3), and growth (chapter 4). The chapters describe the problems, discuss possible solutions, and put forward proposals—sometimes alternative proposals. Each chapter starts with an attempt to specify the long-term goals. The next step is to discuss the road from here to there, since the desirable long-term policy usually is connected with difficult transition problems. This is particularly true in the current crisis, in which long-term system changes often tend to worsen acute short-term problems. Several European countries have started a similar process of change under more favorable circumstances. The transition problems in Sweden are also likely to be especially pronounced because the adjustments have been postponed for so long.

With respect to long-term systemic and structural issues, we outline changes that we consider particularly urgent. Often we put forward concrete proposals, which conform with our basic principles. In the case of the acute economic crisis—manifest in high unemployment, a large budget deficit, and serious financial crisis—we are particularly concrete and specific.

In chapter 5 we suggest how to change the political system so as to strengthen democracy. The starting point is the principles of active citizenship, pluralism, and clear division of responsibility. Our proposals somewhat alter the role of the Swedish state. We deal specifically with the cabinet, the parliament, the budget process, the administrative authorities, local governments, nongovernmental organizations, and the mass media.

Chapter 6 summarizes our most important conclusions and proposals.

A shift toward the type of economic policy, rules, and institutions that we propose requires an open attitude and a willingness to experiment and learn. Profound public discussion is necessary to solve Sweden's present crisis in a sustainable way. We hope that our report will contribute to this discussion.

2 Stability

Deep recession and high unemployment have hit Sweden with a force that has surprised everybody. The depth of the crisis is a consequence not only of acute macroeconomic shocks; it also reflects several decades of neglect and the inability to correct deficiencies in the economic and political system.

We start by sketching the macroeconomic trends over recent decades, paying special attention to the cost crises, the inflationary process, and the dramatic consequences of the reduction in inflation. We outline the way monetary and fiscal policies function under fixed and floating exchange rates. Against this background we recommend measures aiming at low and stable inflation, and high and stable employment. A main thesis, as in other chapters, is that reaching these objectives requires reformed rules and institutions. The damaging effects of inflation and unemployment are well known and will not be further described in this study.

Proposing measures to avoid future crises is not enough. We must also get out of today's serious crisis, without sliding back to the previous inflationary economy. It is therefore important to formulate policies that address the acute crisis in a long-term perspective.

The Exchange Rate, Inflation, and the Present Crisis

The Fixed Exchange Rate as a Nominal Anchor

Except for the period after November 1992 and two short periods in the interwar era, Sweden has maintained a fixed exchange rate for the past 120 years. To peg the exchange rate against one or more foreign currencies is—for a country like Sweden—identical to formulating a medium-term target for the domestic inflation rate. A small nation heavily dependent on trade can only temporarily depart from the inflation rate in those countries against which it has pegged its currency. The average inflation rate of these countries implicitly defines a target for the domestic inflation rate. As long as the exchange-rate commitment remains credible, this target will function as a guidepost, or an anchor, for the inflationary expectations in the economy.

Inflationary expectations are reflected in millions of economic contracts into which households, firms, and organizations enter each year. Agreements on wages, prices, and interest rates are typically expressed in terms of current kronor or a percentage, but they must be assumed to aim at a desired real outcome. A wage contract that aims at 2% higher purchasing power requires an increase of nominal wages of 4% if the expected inflation rate is 2%, but an increase of 10% if the expected inflation rate is 8%. A well-defined and generally accepted nominal anchor is extremely important, because it coordinates the inflationary expectations reflected in all these contracts. Such coordination reduces the risk of an accelerating inflationary process, where the content of earlier agreements influence the inflationary expectations of those who are currently negotiating, and where earlier expiring agreements are renegotiated at a higher level to compensate for erroneous expectations.

The Fixed Exchange Rate of the 1950s and 1960s

At the end of World War II, most industrial countries agreed to maintain fixed exchange rates among themselves; these rates were only to be realigned in exceptional cases. This arrangement, the so-called Bretton Woods system, had other elements as well. It included, for example, common arrangements for the financing of current account deficits—a valuable insurance system, because few international credit markets existed during the first two decades after the war. The Bretton Woods system also comprised sanctions against countries that broke the rules. Altogether, the arrangement strongly committed individual countries to their exchange rate policy.

Wage formation in Sweden worked well during this period, in the sense that nominal wages stayed very much in line with the "room" for wage increase, as defined by the inflation target plus the increase in labor productivity (output per hour worked). During the 1960s, this room was indeed regularly taken as a basis for wage negotiations;

Stability

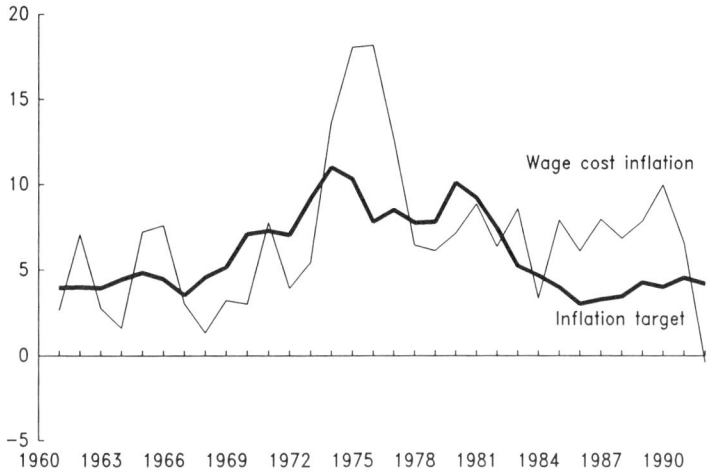

Sources: Konjubkturinstitutet, Statistiska centralbyrån, Bergman and Hansson (1991), Riksbanken, and own calculations.

Figure 2.1
Wage-cost inflation (unit labor cost) and the inflation target implied by the fixed exchange rate

formally the reasoning was expressed in the so-called Scandinavian model of inflation (Aukrust, Holte, and Stoltz 1967; Edgren, Faxén, and Odhner 1973). The fixed exchange rate and inflation abroad thereby came to operate as an anchor for domestic wage and price formation.

Figure 2.1 illustrates the successful role of this anchor during the 1960s. The thicker curve shows the inflation target defined by the exchange rate commitment. During the 1960s this target was around 4%. The thinner curve shows the increase in labor costs per unit of output in industry (wage-cost inflation): the percentage increase in nominal hourly wages minus the percentage increase in output per worker-hour. This is a realistic way of comparing domestic cost inflation with the inflation target. Figure 2.2 illustrates that the inflation target was compatible with average nominal wage increases per hour of as much as 9% during the 1960s; labor productivity went up by as much as 5% per annum on average.

Strict regulations of the capital market set the stage for macroeconomic policies. Monetary policy tried to achieve two domestic functions: to maintain a low interest rate and to channel credit to the

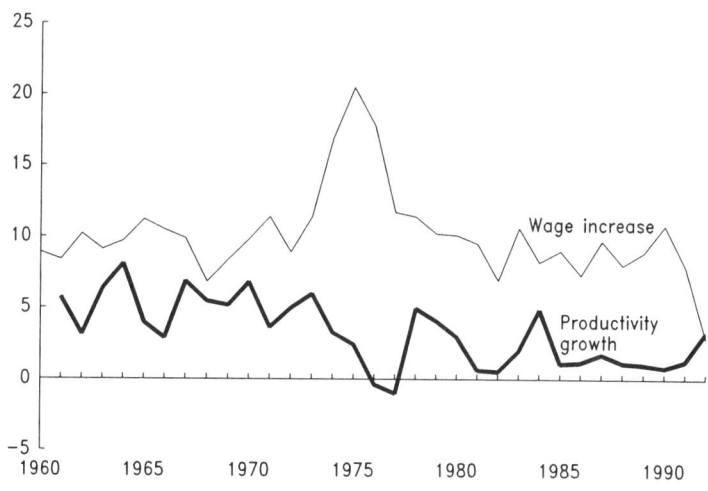

Sources: Konjunkturinstitutet, Statistiska centralbyrån, Bergman and Hansson (1991).

Figure 2.2
Increase in hourly wages and in productivity

government and the housing sector. Low international capital mobility, and hence difficulties in borrowing abroad, meant that the current account outcome strongly constrained fiscal policy.

Another characteristic of these decades was a stable political situation in Sweden, which facilitated a responsible budgetary policy with a rather long-term perspective.

The Fixed Exchange Rate of the 1970s and 1980s: New Conditions

At the end of the 1960s, the Bretton Woods system was exposed to major tensions; it finally collapsed in 1973. Many countries, especially large industrial countries, allowed their currencies to float and still do so, even though their central banks, to a smaller or larger extent, intervene to influence the exchange rate. Initially, Sweden participated in the exchange rate cooperation within the so-called snake in the European Community. But Sweden left that system in 1977 to unilaterally peg the value of the krona, initially against a basket of trading partners' currencies and from May 1991 against the synthetic EC currency, the ecu. The commitment to a fixed exchange rate became weaker than before 1973.

Recycled surpluses of the oil-exporting countries, after the oil price hike in 1973, triggered rapid evolution of the Eurocurrency market. Just a few years later the international credit market, which had been dormant since World War II, woke up again. The new possibilities for borrowing abroad were used increasingly by Swedish corporations, and the leaking foreign exchange regulations were gradually dismantled in the course of the 1980s. The domestic credit market regulations were also dismantled; an especially important step in that direction was taken in 1985, when the quantity controls of bank credit were lifted. Both the expansion of international capital markets and the lifting of capital controls created more room for maneuver in fiscal policy.

The framework for stabilization policy was, in other words, transformed in a radical way. The Swedish macroeconomic situation approached the stylized assumptions of the textbook model, which describes how monetary and fiscal policy operate under fixed exchange rates, high capital mobility, and an unregulated domestic credit market—the so-called Mundell-Fleming model (see, e.g., Krugman and Obstfeld 1991). Under these conditions the interest rate policy of the Riksbank had to balance foreign exchange flows so that the exchange rate commitment could be maintained. The only remaining degree of freedom for monetary policy, in this kind of situation, is to realign the unilaterally fixed parity—that is, to devalue or revalue the currency. Fiscal policy measures, by contrast, have important effects on aggregate demand. An expansionary fiscal policy, for example, will boost the demand for goods and labor. This boosts the demand for liquidity, which the Riksbank has to accommodate at an interest rate that is consistent with the fixed parity. For that reason, the short-run expansion of the economy is not attenuated. Nor is the hike in prices and wages that remains once prices and wages have adjusted fully to the higher level of demand. In this situation, fiscal policy has to take on the main responsibility for keeping aggregate demand under reasonable control and for avoiding unacceptable inflation (or unemployment) due to overheating (or contraction) of the economy.

The stability in the political system that had marked Sweden since the 1930s was replaced by a situation of changing majorities, a more diversified Riksdag, and weak minority or coalition governments—all of which increased the difficulties of conducting a responsible fiscal policy. The new constitution (from 1970) also shortened the time horizon in fiscal policy by abolishing the bicameral system and shortening the mandates for parliament (from four to three years).

The slowdown of productivity growth in the early 1970s complicated the task of controlling inflation. As shown in figure 2.2, average yearly productivity growth in private business fell to 2% from 5%. This diminished the room for nominal wage increases for any given inflation target by about 3%. As we discuss further in chapter 4, Sweden has also lost competitiveness at unchanged relative wage costs per unit of output. The room for wage increases was therefore reduced even more, because the trendwise worsening of underlying competitiveness required still lower relative wages to avoid losses of market share.

Figure 2.1 shows how the international rate of inflation first increased in the 1970s, changing the Swedish implicit inflation target to about 8%, and then in the 1980s gradually fell to about 4%, that is, to the same level as in the 1960s.

The Cost Crises

All these economic and political changes date back to the beginning of the 1970s. Monetary policy, fiscal policy, and wage formation were thus faced with new and tougher challenges than in previous decades. In retrospect, it is easy to see that these challenges were too strong to keep a lid on inflation. Unemployment was, however, kept low, though a certain upward trend in both open and total unemployment can be detected during this period (see figure 2.3).

Sweden's macroeconomic problems culminated in three cost crises—periods of rising relative wage costs, which led to losses of competitiveness and lower activity and employment in the tradable sector. The cost crises—which peaked in 1977, 1981, and 1992—have a number of elements in common. Each crisis was preceded by a few years of high nominal wage growth; especially in the mid-1970s, the hike in wage costs was also accentuated by policy-induced increases in indirect labor costs. Rapid wage growth largely reflected high labor demand, manifest in very low unemployment and high vacancies (see figure 2.3).

Excessively expansionary fiscal policy contributed to overheating domestic demand. Efforts to conduct hard-currency policy deepened the crises. In the mid-1970s the krona was, via the snake, linked to

Stability

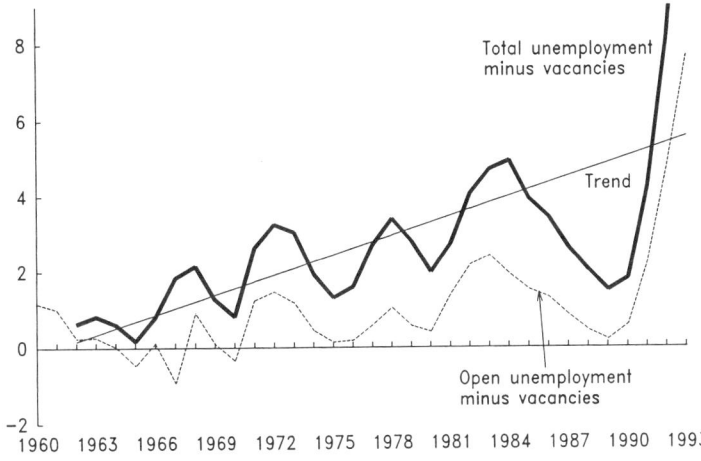

Source: Statistiska centralbyrån.

Figure 2.3
Unemployment less vacancies (percent of labor force)

the D-mark, which was rising in value. But the ecu linkage from 1991 also strengthened the commitment to a fixed exchange rate. Each cost crisis ended with a massive depreciation of the krona, offering accommodation to the previous dose of inflation. The order of magnitude of the (effective) depreciations was similar: 19% through the three devaluations of 1976–77, 26% through the two devaluations of 1981–82, and approximately 20% through the depreciation from November 1992 to September 1993.

The commitment to a fixed exchange rate obviously collided with strong domestic wage inflation and an expansionary, or insufficiently contractive, fiscal policy. Figure 2.1 vividly illustrates this collision. It is evident how wage-cost inflation during several years in the mid-1970s was far above the inflation targets. Despite the devaluations of 1976–77, and very limited wage-cost inflation in the years thereafter, employment problems emerged at the beginning of the next international recession around 1980 (see figure 2.3). Wage-cost inflation was 3%–4% above the inflation target (i.e., inflation abroad) throughout the second half of the 1980s. During this period, the overheating of the labor market became especially pronounced. In the second half of the 1980s, the number of unemployed minus the number of vacancies was far below its trend line. It was this overheating that laid the foundations of the 1990–92 cost crisis.

Repeated devaluations since the middle of the 1970s, and insufficiently restrictive fiscal policy, deprived the unilaterally declared fixed exchange rate of its credibility. The anchor for inflationary expectations, and thereby for prices and wages, was pulled up. Similar devaluation spirals also characterize Finland and Norway (Honkapohja et al. 1993; Steigum 1993). Figure 2.1 indicates that these credibility problems continued during the period after the 1982 devaluation, as domestic cost inflation did not fall below the inflation target until 1992. Recent research has also produced more direct measures of the credibility of exchange rate policy; these clearly demonstrate that there were devaluation expectations in the financial markets throughout the period from 1982 (Lindberg, Svensson, and Söderlind 1993).

The banking crisis is strongly related to mistaken expectations among agents in the real estate and financial markets. Purchasers of real estate, and those who were lending to them, seem to have expected real estate prices to continue rising faster than the nominal interest rate. No doubt these expectations were nourished by confidence in strong demand for office space, high inflation, and a tax system that would continue to offer incentives to borrowing and the purchase of real assets. The deregulation of the credit market in the mid-1980s suddenly made it possible to operate on the basis of such expectations, that is, to borrow for purchases of old or new real estate.

When these expectations had to be drastically revised at the beginning of the 1990s, a crisis in the real estate and financial markets was unavoidable. Suddenly it became apparent that the authorities took inflation fighting seriously and also that the tax system was indeed going to be reformed. Moreover, real estate taxes were increased just as the real estate market began to falter. The collapse of economic activity drastically shrank the demand for office space and real estate.

Today's crisis in the real estate and financial markets hence depends strongly on economic policy. But a contributing factor was certainly also limited experience among market participants about how to operate in an unregulated capital market; above all, financial institutions seem to have lacked appropriate management and information systems.

The Present Crisis

In the two earlier cost crises substantial increases in industrial subsidies and public sector hiring held up employment. When production and employment began to decline in 1990 and 1991, there was no such accommodation, however. Instead, the decline in industrial employment produced reduced labor force participation and increased unemployment; only gradually did the Labor Market Board step up employment-creating activities. Another difference between the present and the earlier cost crises was that devaluations came relatively early in the mid-1970s and in 1981–82. During the cost crisis after 1990, the Riksbank instead maintained a firm exchange rate policy.

This strategy of nonaccommodation on several fronts finally checked inflation, while capacity utilization and employment fell drastically. The Swedish economic trends from that point onward closely resemble the earlier developments in Norway and Finland (Honkapohja et al. 1993; Steigum 1993). The Swedish crisis, like that in Finland and Norway, was intensified by the drastic increase in the household savings rate, in the wake of falling asset prices and increased uncertainty among households about jobs and income; tax reforms were made not only in Sweden but also in Norway.

As a consequence, the cost crisis in industry was transformed into a general economic crisis. What is unique about the crisis in the early 1990s is that all sectors contracted at the same time, which explains why the crisis became so deep. Employment fell by 8%–9% in just two years and still shows no signs of recovery—an incredible deterioration from the perspective of earlier experience. Sweden thereby, for the first time since the 1930s, experienced a genuine unemployment crisis. The number of business failures rose and the prices of real estate fell in a way that also had not been observed since the interwar period; this is the background to the financial sector crisis. Public sector finances deteriorated very rapidly: public sector saving fell by an incredible 180–200 billion kronor, corresponding to 13%–14% of GDP, in only three years. This public finance crisis is historically and internationally extreme (OECD 1992).

Following the turmoil in European currency markets in the late summer and fall of 1992 and massive Swedish currency outflows, stubborn resistance from the Riksbank and two packages of drastic budget improvements put together by government and opposition overcame the pressure on the currency, for a while. But on 19 November 1992 the Riksbank announced that the krona had been left to float. The problems of an overvalued currency were solved, and the economic crisis was transformed into a domestic demand contraction. We will return to this demand crisis.

The Floating Exchange Rate

Our recommendation is that the Swedish krona should continue to float for quite some time, for reasons we shall explain. This will leave considerable room for short-term maneuver in monetary policy. The Riksbank has the option to set short-term rates and influence aggregate demand. The question is how this room for maneuver is to be used. A fixed exchange rate is a clearly formulated intermediate target for monetary policy. The rationale behind this target is to contain domestic inflation at the rate that prevails abroad. With a floating exchange rate, by contrast, one has to specify some other objective for monetary policy to discuss stabilization policy in a concrete way.

A single thought experiment can illustrate the problem: what would the macroeconomic outcomes have been if Sweden, from the beginning of the 1970s, had allowed the krona to float? For this experiment to be meaningful, we assume that the economic and political environment in other respects would have been the same as it actually was. In particular, we assume that the ultimate objective of monetary policy would have been an inflation target like the one implied by the fixed exchange rate: about 8% in the 1970s and 4% in the 1980s.

Under what conditions would these targets have been reached? To achieve a given inflation target over a long period definitely requires a nonaccommodating monetary policy, in the sense that liquidity growth has to correspond with the inflation target. This is certainly true over a time span of a few years, even though short-term departures to accommodate occasional disturbances of the economy are possible. Such a nonaccommodating monetary policy is indeed implicitly assumed in the textbook model of stabilization policy with a floating exchange rate and high capital mobility (Krugman and Obstfeld 1991). In large measure this has also been the monetary policy design in Germany and Switzerland (Genberg 1993).

With a nonaccommodating monetary policy under floating rates, fiscal policy has much weaker effects on demand than with a fixed exchange rate. The higher demand for liquidity resulting from an expansionary fiscal policy cannot be satisfied by the Riksbank, which results in higher real interest rates. This in turn produces a stronger exchange rate. Higher interest rates and the strengthening of the exchange rate both dampen domestic demand and counteract the expansionary effect of fiscal policy in goods and labor markets.

If an overheating of the labor market nevertheless occurs for some other reason, and wages begin to rise faster, the increased rate of inflation will subsequently weaken the currency. A nonaccommodating monetary policy implies in this case that the Riksbank has to raise interest rates to tighten policy, offset the depreciation, and reduce inflation.

More specifically, such a monetary policy would have required the Riksbank to meet the expansionary fiscal policy and wage inflation during 1974–76 and during the second half of the 1980s with higher interest rates, implying an appreciation of the krona. If the policy of the Riksbank had been credible, an understanding that no accommodation was forthcoming would have anchored inflationary expectations and contained wage increases. In this successful scenario, we further have to assume that fiscal policy would have been different: the perception that expansionary policies would drive up real interest rates ought to have limited the quest to raise government spending.

The Role of Institutions

How credible is this successful scenario? It is easy to point to several questionable conditions. The first is the credibility of an anti-inflationary monetary policy. Would the governors of the Riksbank and the members of parliament who served on its board of governors have had the courage to conduct a monetary policy in conflict with an expansionary fiscal policy and wage inflation arising from an overheated labor market? Our judgment is that in a collision between interest rate policy and the inflationary trend, the Riksbank leadership would have found it extremely difficult to push through the necessary increases in interest rates. If that is true, the inflation target would soon have lost credibility and the krona would have depreciated. It is likely that the credibility problem would have been even worse with a floating exchange rate, because the political pressure on the Riksbank to reduce interest rates would have been stronger in a floating-rate regime with more short-term discretion over monetary policy.

Let us nevertheless, for the sake of argument, assume that the Riksbank had indeed maintained credibility, so that inflationary expectations were in line with the inflation target. Would employers and union leaders at different levels of negotiation have had the authority to maintain annual wage increases at 6% during the 1980s, even at the low prevailing unemployment levels? We are far from confident that the Swedish process of wage formation—with its strong, conflict-ready, and competing trade unions, and with negotiations taking place at several levels—would have managed to conclude agreements with aggregate nominal wage increases at those levels, even with low inflationary expectations.

The third question mark is about fiscal policy in a different policy regime. Would political parties and individual politicians in minority and coalition governments have had the strength to constrain increases in public expenditures so that systematic overheating of the economy could have been avoided? Also on this point we find reason for doubt. As we shall explain in the next section, the Swedish budgetary process is particularly ill-suited to resist political pressure for more expenditures.

The krona would thus probably have lost as much of its value during these last twenty years with a floating exchange rate as it did with a fixed exchange rate—and probably more. Given productivity growth, the trend of production and employment would no doubt have been much the same, even though the cost crises would probably have been less dramatic, and the recessions perhaps somewhat milder.

This discussion of a counterfactual scenario corresponds well with the academic literature, which has had great difficulties in empirically identifying systematic differences in real economic outcomes under different exchange rate regimes.

The thrust of our argument is that the Swedish inflationary process has been maintained by certain fundamental institutional features—in wage bargaining and in the decisionmaking process for monetary and fiscal policy—and by the prevailing incentives of individuals and organizations. As we have explained, the economic and political environment changed at the beginning of the 1970s in a number of respects. Existing institutions were faced with new challenges that they could not handle. Thus institutional deterioration and rigidity in the face of altered conditions is, in our opinion, a very important factor behind the macroeconomic problems experienced over the past two decades.

Institutions and Rules for Better Stability

Stabilization Policy in a Long-Term Perspective

Summarizing the message of the past section, we may say that Swedish institutions have failed to provide a suitable framework consistent to containing inflation at reasonable cost. If this is right, one may be tempted to conclude that we have only had the inflation we "deserve." Then it is just as well to allow inflation to roll on and minimize its damaging effects on production and employment through a policy of continuing depreciation. This is roughly the policy that the U.S. economists in the so-called Brookings Report recommended for Sweden some years ago (Bosworth et al. 1987). We regard this conclusion as unnecessarily defeatist. In addition, the costs connected with the recent reduction of inflation would then have been wasted; we might have to incur similar costs once more in the future. There was an emerging political consensus in the early 1990s on the importance of low inflation. It was, in fact, the previous Social Democratic government that formulated and introduced the policy of nonaccommodation, which the new center-right government of 1991 subsequently followed up. These two political groups also found it possible to agree on two far-reaching budget packages in the fall of 1992 with the purpose of defending the fixed exchange rate. And in January 1993 the governing board of the Riksbank—with members from both political groups—unanimously formulated a long-term inflation target of 2%.

If we take the objective of low inflation seriously, the conclusion from our discussion is that we need to change the institutions to permanently keep down inflation and at the same time maintain high employment.

According to the general procedure employed in our study, we first discuss the requirements for a successful long-run stabilization policy; the urgent and difficult problems linked to phasing in such policies in today's serious situation are postponed until the next section.

Wage Formation and Inflation

We have shown how monetary and fiscal policy are instrumental in achieving favorable macroeconomic outcomes. The conclusion was that major responsibility rests upon those institutions in charge of monetary and budgetary instruments: the Riksbank, the cabinet, and the Riksdag. But these bodies cannot assume sole responsibility for either inflation or unemployment. Wage formation, as noted above, is strategic to both. It is important to recall that wage income constitutes about 80% of GDP. Empirical research indicates that domestic costs spill over into price increases even in the sector competing with the rest of the world (Calmfors and Herin 1979; Myhrman 1979; Gottfries 1987). Moreover, contrary to a common misperception, a large part of the Swedish economy is sheltered from international competition (see chapter 3). In this sheltered sector the resistance to higher prices is weak, and wage costs are more or less automatically passed on to prices through cost-plus pricing.

We have already hinted that lower wage growth requires not only that inflationary expectations conform with the inflation target. Heavy demands are also placed on how wage negotiations are organized, above all on the number of levels (centrally, by sectors, and by individual firms). In the literature, it is a controversial point whether nominal wage increases tend to become larger or smaller with central or with local negotiations (Calmfors and Driffill 1988; Holmlund 1993). It is, however, likely that negotiations at two or three levels give rise to larger total wage increases than negotiations at only one level, because negotiations at each level lays a floor for the next. Some support for this idea may be found in figure 2.2. Wages rose by 8%–9% in most years in the 1960s as well as in the 1980s—despite the major difference in productivity growth between the two decades. It is difficult to imagine that no negotiations will take place at the firm level. Therefore it is natural to assume that negotiations at two levels, in practice, has to include negotiations within firms. Germany (and Austria) has a special variant where the firm has the main responsibility for outgoing wages without formal bargaining, once negotiations have taken place at the sectoral level.

The government does not have—and in our judgment should not have—more than indirect instruments to influence the negotiations in the private labor market. Nevertheless most governments in Sweden have often encouraged parties to negotiate at a central level, in conjunction with various attempts at incomes policy.

A shift to more decentralized wage formation is well in line with the current reorganization of firms. Delegation of tasks to the individual employee plays an increasingly important role within the firm. When command is replaced by incentives, wages have to be differentiated, which can only take place in a rational (well-informed) way inside the firm.

The government can facilitate decentralized wage bargaining by avoiding attempts at incomes policy. This is hardly a cost to society: Swedish and international research unanimously point to incomes policy as an ineffective means of containing inflation in the long term. Moreover, decentralized public-sector wage bargaining can facilitate decentralized wage bargaining in the private sector. However weak this effect, we still believe it is desirable to change public-sector wage negotiations in the direction of general appropriations for the total wage bill for each public authority, leaving the detailed negotiations up to the individual authority. Such a reform may succeed better than the experiments of the 1980s in setting cash limits for the total wage bill in parity with the inflation target. Decentralized and strict cash limits for public-sector employees—as well as for the transfers from the central government to the local authorities—can simulate a demand curve for labor at the level of the individual public authority, because high wage increases will not leave enough funds for an unchanged number of employees.

Wage Formation and Employment

Wage formation is a main determinant of employment; after all, wages are the price of labor, and the demand for labor falls as real wages go up. Under normal conditions, the partners in the market therefore have a decisive responsibility for employment.

The government has, however, a major responsibility for the legal framework (the labor law), which influences wage formation and unemployment indirectly. A problem with the present legislation is that the respectable ambition of boosting job security tends to strengthen the negotiating power of those who already have jobs—the so-called insiders in the labor market—relative to those who do not have jobs—the so-called outsiders. It becomes easier for insiders to push up wages without losing their jobs, which makes it more difficult for outsiders to get jobs.

The government is also responsible for unemployment benefits and compensation to individuals in public works programs or labor market training. Higher unemployment benefits and compensation for retraining and public works tend to push up wages because the cost of becoming unemployed is lower. Reducing unemployment benefits and compensation levels in Labor Market Board programs, therefore, contributes to lower unemployment (Calmfors 1993; Holmlund 1990).

To mitigate the unemployment effects of wage formation, one may also let wage earners and employers themselves bear a larger share of unemployment costs through employer and employee contributions to unemployment insurance. With negotiations at the branch level, it should be possible to limit unemployment-creating wage hikes by differentiating insurance contributions with respect to the area negotiated. The idea is to increase the resistance among labor market parties to excessive wages by conditioning insurance fees on the risk of unemployment (Calmfors 1993). Such an arrangement obviously does not preclude some distributional considerations when setting the fees. If wages are negotiated at the firm level only, one has instead to rely on the firm's resistance to wages that threaten its competitiveness, and on the employees' fear of losing their jobs.

In the long term, one might imagine a comprehensive reform that covers both the unemployment insurance system and labor market policy. Different competing insurers could then play an important role, in particular when it comes to bringing the unemployed back to work. The idea is that insurers would have an interest in training the unemployed in order to improve their chances of finding new employment. However, this assumes that the present monopoly of the unemployment benefit system comes to an end (Calmfors 1993). We believe that these proposals are worth considering.

Long-Run Monetary Policy Design

Low long-run inflation requires that monetary policy is designed for that very purpose. Other long-term objectives for monetary policy are impossible anyway. Even though a sudden, unanticipated change in monetary policy may have real effects on production and employment that remain for a few years, through various so-called persistence mechanisms, the effects of systematic and expected monetary policy are confined to prices and wages. More specifically, under a floating exchange rate, systematic expansions of liquidity beyond what is warranted by long-run economic growth and the inflation target should be avoided. In the same way, a systematic (and expected) policy of recurring devaluation should be avoided in a fixed exchange rate regime. But this is easier said than done, because such policies require a credible anchor for inflationary expectations. As we showed earlier, the efforts to introduce low-inflation policies in Sweden via a fixed exchange rate ran into serious credibility problems during the last two decades. The difficulties of pursuing a credible anti-inflation policy with floating exchange rates is even greater. To avoid such problems in the future, the natural route is stronger commitment to a long-run low-inflation policy.

One possibility for strengthening the commitment is to participate in a multilateral exchange rate agreement. After the devaluations of 1981–82, the debate focused on participation in the monetary cooperation of the European Communities (European Monetary System); the possibility for nonmember states to participate in this system was in principle open in the EMS agreement of 1978. The advantage, relative to a unilateral exchange rate peg, would be a double one. First, it would be a mutual undertaking; realignments would have to be discussed with other EMS participants, who in turn would have been obliged to support the Swedish krona in the short term. Second, entering the EMS parity grid would force an adjustment of the Swedish inflation rate and nominal interest rates toward the lower level prevailing in the EMS countries, especially in Germany. During the 1983–87 period, interest rates and inflation rates of the non-German EMS participants did indeed converge toward the German level (Svensson 1989).

Some skeptics in the international debate (for instance, Giavazzi and Giovannini 1989) did point out that stability in a monetary arrangement, where realignments remained possible, assumes regulated capital flows. Evolution of the EMS after the deregulations that occurred in the 1980s—especially after 1988—appeared instead to warrant another conclusion: free capital movements worked to make a commitment to fixed exchange rates stronger. When, from 1990, prospects emerged of monetary union in the course of the second half of the 1990s, interest rate differentials narrowed further among EMS countries.

The turmoil in the exchange markets in the fall of 1992 finally gave support to the skeptics. After five and a half years without parity changes, the price levels in the EMS countries had become so divergent that it was no longer credible to argue that realignments could be resisted. The recession of 1991–92 made it increasingly costly for several member states to adjust their interest rates to high and rising German levels. At the same time, financial markets began to doubt that a monetary union was in the cards, as a result of the difficulties of ratifying the Maastricht Treaty; speculation against many European currencies followed. [Between the publication of our report and the English translation in August 1993, the EMS disintegrated almost completely.]

Pegging the krona to the ecu in May 1991 was one further effort by Sweden to build credibility for the fixed exchange rate policy. But this effort backfired and credibility received a final blow when the monetary union became still more uncertain in the course of the summer of 1992. Following the exchange rate crisis in September of that year, when the Swedish krona had to be defended by extreme (500% overnight) interest rates, pegging became even less credible because one-fourth of the currencies in the ecu were no longer bound by any obligations to intervene. The ecu anchor started to drift.

Against the backdrop of this discussion, we do not propose further efforts to link Swedish monetary policy through a unilateral Swedish peg to one or more currencies, without accompanying institutional changes. It is true that Austria has succeeded in a policy of linking the schilling to the D-mark. But the institutional conditions in Austria—as far as the position of the central bank and the wage formation process are concerned—are different from those prevailing in Sweden (Genberg 1993). The advantages of a unilaterally declared fixed exchange rate today are probably small or even negligible, as the risk of recurrent exchange rate crises in the EMS remains. Such crises can, as we have learned, result in extreme interest rates and incur large costs to the national economy. Given the present instability of the EMS, it is difficult to claim that there exists today a stable intermediate position between floating exchange rates and full monetary union. As long as national autonomy in monetary and fiscal policies remains, there is always a risk that these policies will become incompatible with the fixed exchange rate, and then speculation may easily arise. In the case of real disturbances, when there is actually a strong case for a realignment, it may, however, be difficult to reach agreement. This was illustrated dramatically in the EMS when no agreement could be reached to revalue the D-mark following German unification. (The French experience in the summer of 1993 illustrates once again how domestic macroeconomic ambitions easily undermine the credibility of a fixed exchange rate, even with strong fundamentals and a strong multilateral exchange rate agreement.)

It is also questionable whether participating in an exchange rate arrangement with fixed but adjustable rates is a useful preparation for full monetary union. This doubt is especially relevant for a country that has been forced to give up its fixed exchange rate several times and that has not yet modified the institutional conditions that contributed to these events.

It is in this perspective that one has to view our proposal that Sweden should in the future try to recreate credibility for its currency—and its economic policy in general—through domestic economic and political reforms, rather than to try the short-cut of once again pegging the krona to the other currencies.

Monetary Union?

The possibility still remains that the monetary union outlined in the Maastricht Treaty will be brought about, perhaps by a smaller group of EC countries such as Germany and the Benelux countries, maybe also France, Denmark, Ireland, and Austria (still an EFTA country). All of these countries have converged considerably in terms of inflation and interest rates, even though they do not meet the budgetary convergence criteria of the Maastricht Treaty. Such a smaller union of well-established low-inflation countries may enhance the credibility of a low and stable inflation rate. On the other hand, the advantages of lower transaction costs and the elimination of currency risk recede the fewer countries participate in the union. For Sweden, which has only about 40% of its foreign trade with this smaller group of countries, it would be an advantage that a monetary union—if it is formed—becomes as comprehensive as possible.

If a monetary union at some point is brought about and Sweden participates—an outcome that this commission's proposals in other areas is likely to facilitate—monetary policy will of course completely lose its autonomy. To lock exchange rates definitively by introducing a common European currency means that all participants subject themselves to the common monetary policy of a European Central

Bank. This would bring potentially large gains of credibility and eliminate transaction costs and currency risks. However, it would also remove monetary autonomy, which may be a problem when large disturbances hit Sweden, but not the other participants. Opinions are divided among economists as to whether the gains outweigh the losses; the answer hinges largely on how one evaluates the risks for strong *domestic* disturbances. Our proposals for reforming Swedish rules and institutions would, however, reduce the risks of serious domestic disturbances.

We are therefore inclined to believe that participation in a European monetary union would in principle be favorable, as compared to our present situation—at least from a narrow monetary perspective. But the links to other aspects of Sweden's relations with the European Community turns participation in an eventual monetary union into much more than a monetary question. The decision would be part of a larger package. Since considerable uncertainty remains about the realization of the monetary union, the number of participants, and the timetable, it may still be advisable to postpone taking a stance on monetary union until a late stage of Sweden's membership negotiations.

A strategy that aims chiefly at establishing credibility for an anti-inflationary policy by reference to future participation in monetary union has one major weakness, however. Since Sweden does not control the realization of the union, the conditions may suddenly change. Sweden's pegging to the ecu in 1991, in connection with its application for EC membership, is one illustrative example. That step could be seen as an effort to put on a straitjacket: the entry requirements to the future economic and monetary union would make devaluations appear extremely costly. But as the union became less likely, the straitjacket was subsequently untied.

Central Bank Reform

The proposals for reforming the statutes of the Riksbank represent efforts to strengthen domestic institutions rather than to build credibility through external measures. A government committee on central bank reform has recently put forward a specific proposal along these lines (Riksbanksutredningen 1993). The basic idea in this proposal is to delegate monetary policy to a central bank that is more independent than now and to legislate an objective for the bank's operations that gives priority to price stability. But the independence of the central bank comprises many aspects: the composition of the governing board, the power to nominate, adaptability, length of mandates, control of monetary instruments, the government's scope for borrowing in the bank, etc. In several of these respects the Riksbank already has an independent position compared to other central banks.

In other respects, however, its independence is more limited than that of central banks in other countries. That is particularly true with respect to the short mandates for members of its board of governors, which are also fully synchronized with the three-year election periods for the Riksdag. During much of the postwar period the board functioned, in fact, more or less as a department of the ministry of finance or as a standing committee of the Riksdag. Available information indicates that several important monetary policy decisions were taken with short-term motives in the process of party politics (Jonung 1993). A certain depoliticization has occurred recently in connection with the deregulation of credit markets, as well as the break with past traditions of nominating only members of parliament for the central bank board and the change in statutes from 1989 (the governor is no longer nominated by the government, but by the governing board, and for a period of five rather than three years). We agree with the committee's special report that it is desirable to further the possibilities for more continuity and a longer-term perspective in monetary policy—in other words, to help the Riksbank operate at some distance from day-to-day politics. This could be achieved by a considerable lengthening of the board's mandates and with overlapping periods of nominations.

We also support other points in the report. It is important to reach political agreement on low inflation, and legislate that this be the overriding objective of the central bank, that is, to safeguard the value of the currency. A large and growing public debt will fuel inflationary expectations, due to the suspicion that the government sooner or later will try to resolve the problem through inflation. To reduce this risk, it would be useful to eliminate the government's present borrowing possibilities in the Riksbank, thereby reducing the risk of an inflationary monetary policy. Accountability of the Riksbank leadership should be strengthened by regular and public hearings on the motives and the design of monetary policy before the Riksdag and its specialized committees.

Our proposals on this issue are based both on recent economic theory and international evidence. Theory emphasizes how discretion in monetary policy, together with political pressure on the central bank to stimulate the economy, may generate an excessively expansionary policy—both on the average and at the wrong point in time (Persson and Tabellini 1990 and Cuikerman 1992 survey this theory). According to this theory, the political principal of the central bank can strengthen the long-term commitment to an anti-inflationary policy by delegating monetary policy to an institution removed from day-to-day politics. The leadership of that institution need a well-defined target for their activities, and must be held accountable as to how well they succeed in meeting the objective.

Evidence, particularly from the past two decades, suggests that those countries that have succeeded at containing inflation also have independent central banks that emphasize price stability (see Cuikerman 1992 and Grilli et al. 1991). These countries have not done worse than others in terms of output or employment. (The central bank's reform report and its appendixes contain an exhaustive exposition of both theory and evidence.)

Delegation to an independent central bank with a clear formulation of its objectives is, of course, fully compatible with the basic principle of bringing about a clearer division of labor between the government and its various agencies, as discussed in chapter 1 and further in chapter 5, but the notion of a more independent central bank can only be realized if firmly anchored in political and public opinion.

Short-Run Monetary Policy Design

All of the above relates to the institutional framework for monetary policy and its long-run goals. Another important question is how short-term autonomy in monetary policy should be used to promote a stable macroeconomic development. As we argued earlier, the question of short-term policy design is, strictly speaking, only relevant under a floating exchange rate.

A more specific question is to what extent the Riksbank should take account of employment, international competitiveness, and other real economic variables when the economy is hit by various disturbances. Among the likely disturbances are exchange rate fluctuations resulting from occasional capital flows, speculative bubbles, or other changes in financial markets. Assume for instance a strong appreciation of the krona that worsens competitiveness and threatens employment in the tradable sector. Such a recessionary impulse tends to reduce inflation in the economy, an effect that is accentuated by the decline in prices of imported goods. In this case, concern for the real economy leads to the same policy prescription as the concern for maintaining low inflation: easing monetary policy by lowering short-term interest rates in order to avoid further appreciation. But this strategy may be difficult to implement if a very strong policy action is required to restore competitiveness. Switzerland, for instance, has been faced with this type of dilemma (Genberg 1993).

Other types of disturbances may create more substantial conflict between different objectives. Let us assume that competitiveness worsens for the same reason as during the 1970s—faster wage growth than warranted by the productivity trend and the inflation target. Then the inflation target requires the Riksbank to refuse accommodation via lower interest rates and depreciation, and instead raise interest rates to check emerging domestic inflation. If it does not, the inflation target loses credibility, which increases the risk of new wage disturbances, creating new demands for expansionary policy, etc. This example once again underlines how important it is that wage formation work properly. The example also illustrates the importance of a stable nominal anchor for medium-term inflationary expectations. Experience shows that countries like Germany and Switzerland, with strong domestic institutions and a good track record for low inflationary policies, can take short-term real economic objectives into consideration without losing their long-term credibility. For example, the Bundesbank has cut the short-term interest rate by 4–5 percentage points in each recession since the 1960s. Countries like the United Kingdom, without a strong central bank and with a history of strongly variable inflation, has had much less scope for such maneuvers (Bernanke and Mishkin 1992; Genberg 1993).

Government Debt and Inflation

It is important that long-term fiscal and monetary policies be compatible. Stable macroeconomic development requires that the sudden recent deterioration of public finances be checked. Rapid accumulation of government debt diminishes the room for maneuver in fiscal policy; it has already done so in a destructive way. But rapid debt accumulation also increases the risk that future governments will choose the politically simplest solution to the government debt problem: to erode the real value of debt by high inflation. It is sufficient that domestic and foreign observers begin to suspect such a development looming in the future for long-term inflationary expectations to jump, something that shows up in higher long-term interest rates. The Italian situation in recent years shows how worrisome a situation a high public-debt country can be trapped in.

However, Sweden is far from a debt crisis at the present time. Especially if one looks at the consolidated public sector (central government, local government, and the social insurance sector), Sweden is still among the OECD countries with the lowest ratio between public debt and GDP. It was not until the period 1991–92 that the consolidated public sector experienced financial net indebtedness (OECD 1992). But with deficits corresponding to 13%–14% of GDP, the situation is rapidly deteriorating. It is therefore an absolute requirement to stabilize the public debt well before the turn of the century so that it stops growing faster than GDP. Such a fiscal stabilization requires a surplus in the total government budget exclusive of interest rates—the so-called primary budget balance—which offsets the interest payments on the outstanding debt, adjusted for economic growth. Assume that we want to stabilize the debt ratio at 45% of GDP. At a 5% real rate of interest and 2% real growth in GDP, this requires that public revenues exceed expenditures net of interest rates by about 20 billion kronor in today's prices, which corresponds to 1.35% of GDP (1.35 = 45 × 0.03). This year (1993) revenues are estimated to fall some 160 billion kronor short of expenditures, exclusive of interest rates. The whole gap of 180 billion kronor does not have to be closed by discretionary long-run budget improvement, because the budget balance will improve significantly—at a rough estimate by at least 100 billion kronor—in the coming economic upturn.

At what level one should aim to stabilize the debt ratio is essentially a question of intergenerational equity (see chapter 4). The composition of budget cuts is a political question, but decision on this issue should rely on a careful analysis of different public expenditure and revenues (see chapter 3). The rate at which one should aim to reduce the public deficits is one of the most pressing and important problems of current stabilization policy. We soon return to this question.

We also recommend a two-way restructuring of public debt. The purpose is to diminish the government's future incentives to inflate away the public debt and thereby reduce long-term inflationary expectations today. First, we suggest more borrowing in foreign currency, which has already started; the rationale for this proposal is that it is only the real value of public debt in kronor that can be diluted by domestic inflation. We do not share the view that the Swedish government presently would have any major difficulties in borrowing significant amounts in international capital markets. Admittedly, some credit rating agencies have recently downgraded the Swedish government, but this implies only a very marginal increase in borrowing costs.

Second, we propose that the public-debt office finance part of its borrowing requirements by issuing indexed debt. Indexed government bonds protect investors against any real loss via inflation. For a number of actors in the Swedish market, like pension funds and insurance companies, long-term investment in indexed bonds would be a very attractive portfolio investment. Considerable volumes could, no doubt, be issued. There are certain technical problems related to indexed bonds under the current Swedish tax law, but these could surely be handled (Lindgren 1992).

Both these forms of borrowing would reduce the government's nominal interest payments in the immediate future. They ought to be relatively cheap for the government—and thereby for the taxpayers—if the markets take an excessively pessimistic view of the ability of the government and the Riksbank to maintain low inflation. By borrowing in foreign currency or by issuing indexed government bonds, and by succeeding in maintaining low inflation, the government will avoid paying the entire premium related to expected depreciation and inflation, as reflected today in long-term nominal interest rates.

Fiscal Policy Design

It is important that fiscal policy is not allowed either to overheat the economy, as it did several times during the 1970s and 1980s, or to cause large-scale unemployment.

In our judgment, fiscal policy, particularly with a fixed exchange rate, should also be used to offset major changes in overall demand, regardless of whether these changes depend on previous government policies, disturbances from abroad, or large fluctuations in the domestic savings rate. An interesting example of the latter is the sharp fluctuations in the household saving ratio (the ratio between household saving and aggregate household disposable income) since the middle of the 1980s: initially the savings ratio diminished by about 6%, subsequently it increased again by about 10%. This cycle in the savings ratio contributed both to the overheating of the Swedish economy in the second half of the 1980s and then to the deep recession in 1992 and 1993. The falling savings ratio in the 1980s was caused by a combination of government measures—deregulation of credit markets without an adequate simultaneous change in the tax rules—and other changes such as rising prices on a number of important assets (which in turn depended on the deregulation of credit markets). Similarly, government policy—above all the 1991 tax reform—contributed to the rising savings ratio in the early 1990s; the effects were accentuated by falling asset prices and precautionary household saving in the wake of dramatically rising unemployment and increased doubts about the viability of the social security systems.

We would like to underline that the possibility of successfully fine-tuning aggregate demand by means of fiscal policy is very limited. This difficulty is linked, inter alia, to the problem of making reliable forecasts. It is easier to adjust fiscal policy to extreme overheating (as in the second half of the 1980s), or to extreme declines in demand (as during 1992–93). In such situations the risk is much less that public measures will have their effect in a wrong phase of the business cycle. Difficulties in fine-tuning do not constitute a strong argument against "coarse-tuning" aggregate demand—if it is possible to find a majority in parliament for such policies.

Reform of the Budget Process

Long-term consolidation of the currently weak public finances, and responsible fiscal policies under more normal conditions, do not occur by themselves. Budgetary policy played a part in overheating the economy during the emergence of each cost crisis. During the 1980s, a certain understanding of the problem developed. However, the political conditions for appropriate actions were not present. Minority governments and short electoral periods weakened the executive. Over time, the gap between the letter and the reality of the constitution has become increasingly evident; according to the letter the government has a responsibility for running the country, but in reality it has often lacked the power to implement the necessary measures.

International evidence demonstrates that actual budget discipline depends critically on the design of the budgetary process. Countries with a strict budget procedure normally have healthy public finances (von Hagen 1992). In chapter 5 we suggest a number of changes in the procedures of the Riksdag and of the cabinet. Although the general purpose behind these changes is to improve the general functioning of parliamentary democracy, a more specific purpose is to strengthen the political responsibility for public finances.

We recommend a stronger position of the cabinet relative to that of the Riksdag, so that the cabinet has a larger scope for fulfilling its executive role. The prime task of the Riksdag is to give general guidelines for policy and to actively and critically monitor the cabinet's work.

Today's budgetary problems are aggravated by an obsolete organization of the cabinet office. We suggest therefore that the organization of and coordination between ministries be adjusted for the current need for effective political action. The cabinet must set firm limits at an early stage of the budgetary preparations; the prime minister's office and the ministry of finance must be strengthened relative to the spending departments. The annual budget presentation must be modified so that actual revenues and expenditures appear more clearly.

It is essential that the work of the Riksdag be preoccupied less with details and more with general principles. The division of labor between different standing parliamentary committees should be changed so that they become less prone to following narrow sectoral interests and instead become more sensitive to broader areas of responsibility. The role of the standing finance committee should be strengthened. The Riksdag should either accept or reject the budget as a whole.

PROPOSALS

Long-Term Stabilization Policy

1. Let the Swedish krona float while awaiting possible adaptation to a currency union in Europe. A return to a fixed exchange rate is not advisable for the time being.

2. Assign a long-term price stabilization goal to the Bank of Sweden. Make the bank more independent, but at the same time more accountable to the parliament.

3. Stabilize the public-sector debt in relation to GDP. The debt (mainly nominal debt in domestic currency) should be transformed into indexed bonds and bonds in foreign currency. To make this program credible, important institutional changes are called for.

4. Fiscal policy should be used for coarse-tuning (rather than fine-tuning) in situations with severe deviations from normal capacity utilization.

5. Liberalize labor market legislation and reduce unemployment benefits so as to create a more flexible labor market that can handle structural and regional change, as well as respond swiftly to economic recovery.

6. The government should abstain from incomes policy initiatives, and decentralize wage negotiations in the public sector.

7. To increase the probability of low inflation, we advise the parties in the labor market to limit wage negotiations to one level (sectoral or firm level), even if other working conditions may be negotiated at a higher level.

How to Overcome the Acute Crisis?

Policy Trade-offs

Section 2.1 described how a domestic cost crisis, aggravated by an international recession, rapidly developed into an overall domestic demand crisis, materializing in falling investment and consumption. Figure 2.4 shows how different components of demand contributed to yearly changes in GDP. Exports began to weaken in 1990, and declined outright in 1991. But the strongest effect of the cost crisis was that investment fell very sharply, both in 1991 and 1992, and is falling further in 1993; in 1991 declining inventory investment also contributed to the fall in GDP. Consumption fell in 1992 and even more sharply in 1993.

The depreciation of the krona since November 1992 means that exports are likely to increase sharply over the next few years; those

Stability

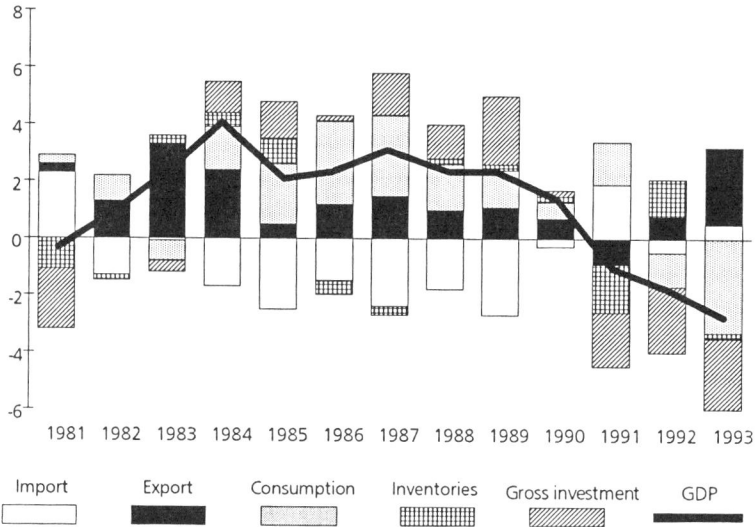

Source: Konjunkturinstitutet.

Figure 2.4
Contributions to GDP growth (percent of GDP)

sectors of Swedish industry that compete with imports will also be stimulated. Sweden thereby comes close to being a dual economy, where the internationally competing fifth of the economy expands strongly, whereas the remaining four-fifths contract strongly, particularly in the construction sector.

This situation may appear to be the perfect starting point for a more expansionary monetary or fiscal policy to stimulate depressed domestic demand. Because the country has plenty of idle resources, an expansion of investment and consumption should not harm sectors that compete internationally. Moreover, the risk of high inflation is small in the short run. A stimulus to domestic demand is, however, far from unproblematic for two related reasons: the budget deficit and the risk of a relapse into high inflation after a few years.

A fiscal expansion that further raised the budget deficit would fuel long-term inflationary expectations. A short-term fiscal stimulus, if implemented, should therefore be designed to have minimal negative effects on the budget deficit. We have structured our proposals under this constraint.

Monetary policy also faces serious trade-offs. If the Riksbank lowers interest rates aggressively from their 9%–10% level (in early 1993), the krona will fall further, which would strengthen the inflationary impulse already hitting the Swedish economy from the depreciating krona since November 1992. This would accentuate the duality of the economy: competitiveness would improve further for the tradable sector, while domestic demand would decline even more. This would be unfortunate, because the acute problem today is low domestic demand. An aggressive reduction of short-term interest rates might also push up longer-term rates if expectations regarding future inflation go up. This does not mean higher expected long-term *real* rates of interest. But higher long-term nominal rates could create liquidity problems in many firms and households, for example, if they have loans with floating interest rates or old loans to be renegotiated. This could dampen or remove the intended stimulus to demand. Against these risks, one must weigh the risk that continued high short-term interest rates further depress the Swedish economy and sharpen the crisis in the real estate and financial markets. This would not only worsen unemployment—it might also further increase the budget deficit; such a policy could thus also push up long-term interest rates.

The depressing conclusion is that there are no simple solutions in the present context. Every policy entails substantial risks that the situation could get worse. What measures can we suggest, then, to alleviate the acute economic crisis and put the Swedish economy on the track toward acceptable inflation and employment levels? This requires a difficult judgment about which is the more important of several serious risks: the risk of inflation in a medium-term perspective, or the risk of even deeper and prolonged unemployment in the direction of a Finnish situation, with a combination of larger deficits with risks of increased inflation in a longer-term perspective.

We believe that the unemployment risk is the more severe risk today. We base this judgment not only on the observation that today's high unemployment is an extremely serious social and economic problem (Janlert and Meidner 1992). We may also become trapped in high long-term unemployment, with all the problems linked to this phenomenon. The question is then how the unemployment problem could be relaxed—and in the long term resolved—without compromising the important objectives of stopping the galloping public debt and avoiding a relapse into high inflation in the 5%–10% interval, or even higher.

Stability 53

Steps to Widen the Scope for Expansion

Expansionary policy is easier to pursue if one can simultaneously restore credibility in future cuts of the budget deficit. Various steps could be taken in this direction. One is to reform rules in budget making. Another important step would be to decide now on budget improvements in future periods; we return to this issue below. Our proposals for changing the composition of public debt might in the same way improve the scope for short-term action.

The maneuver room in monetary policy would, similarly, be enlarged today with increased confidence in long-term policy. As we pointed out in the previous section, the Bundesbank has typically been able to lower interest rates effectively in each business cycle downturn without being suspected of giving up the fight against inflation. Wide political support for a reform to increase the Riksbank's independence may not only contribute to long-run macroeconomic stability; it may also increase short-run credibility, hence creating more scope for lowering interest rates. Particularly in combination with a Europe-wide lowering of interest rates, the Riksbank would be in a better position to help Sweden out of the deep recession.

The Way Out of the Crisis: Monetary Policy

What can monetary policy do to mitigate the acute crisis? We propose that the Riksbank continue its strategy of successively lowering the short-term (overnight) interest rate while monitoring the exchange rate, the term structure of interest rates (the so-called yield curve), wage and price inflation, and inflationary expectations. In order not to deepen the recession further, this strategy should be continued as long as nothing dramatic and unfavorable happens either to long-term interest rates or to the exchange rate.

So far, this strategy has been successful: expected future short-term interest rates appear to have been reduced. This is illustrated in figure 2.5, which shows a number of implicit forward interest rates at different points in time. These rates can be interpreted as expected future short-term rates. It is obvious that markets have expected lower short-term rates over the coming twelve months; this is illustrated by the downward-sloping portion of the curve. In the left part of the figure we also see that the curves corresponding to later

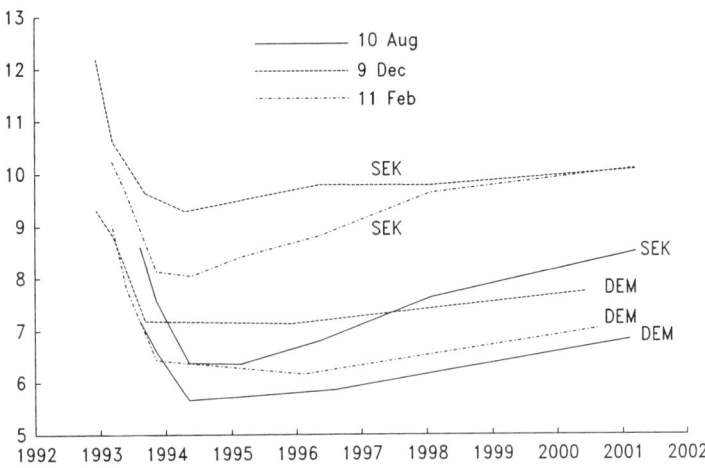

Source: Calculations by Lars Svensson.

Figure 2.5
Implicit forward interest rates

observation dates are systematically below the curves of earlier dates. This shows that the Riksbank actually proceeded more rapidly toward lower rates than financial markets expected in December 1992 or in February 1993. But the curves also indicate that higher short-term rates are expected some years into the future; from about 1998 expected rates have edged up just above 9%. This is an indication that markets expect an adjustment of the interest rate to higher inflation in a few years' time. [We have added a recent set of observations from August 1993 in this English translation of the original report; these observations (figure 2.5) confirm that the central bank has been able to continue its strategy of gradual cuts in interest rates.]

The lower German implicit forward rates are shown in the bottom part of the figure. Here, there is a parallel movement of the curves from different dates. The Bundesbank has gradually adjusted rates downward approximately at the pace anticipated by markets. The difference between the Swedish and German curves may be interpreted as an expected future depreciation of the Swedish krona and thereby, of course, also higher expected inflation in Sweden than in Germany. Implicit in the curves from February 19 is an expected yearly depreciation of the krona vis-à-vis the D-mark of between

2.5% and 3.5% per annum from about 1994. (Since then, the rate of expected depreciation seems to have fallen; while the krona–DM exchange rate has not changed much.)

It is not easy to decide which strategy is better: the Swedish (and German) strategy with successive, cautious reductions of interest rates, or the British strategy with an aggressive lowering of rates (initially from 10% to 7% and subsequently lower still). Because the Riksbank has chosen an experimental strategy of gradually lowering the money market rate, it would, however, be unwise to shift suddenly to a British strategy with a cut in the short-term rate to, for example, 6%, the U.K. rate at the time of writing (February 1993). Such a change of strategy in Sweden could be interpreted as the Riksbank having given up, under political pressure, its long-term struggle against inflation. It may also become difficult to turn policy around if the krona fell sharply as interest rates were cut aggressively. We agree therefore with the Riksbank's experimental strategy of gradually lowering short-term interest rates.

The most damaging interest rates today are, however, to be found in the lending rates of banks, rather than in money market rates. Therefore it is necessary to solve the financial crisis by methods that make lower bank lending rates possible. We return to that point later in the chapter.

The Way Out of the Crisis: Fiscal Policy

Our main proposal for immediate fiscal policy action is to increase *the leverage* of the large government expenditures, which relate to high unemployment—in 1993 about 90 billion kronor (about 6.5% of GDP). The purpose is to allow more openly unemployed persons to take part in productive and meaningful activity. Higher leverage could be brought about in two ways. One way is to shift government spending toward less costly activities. This means a shift from expensive labor-market programs, such as conventional training programs, public works programs, and university education for people living on unemployment benefits, toward, for instance, low-paid practical vocational training for youngsters, adult education, and normal high-school training.

The other way of increasing the leverage of public expenditure is to reduce the cost per person in expensive activities. This means in effect lower levels of compensation—say, about 20% lower. This would, however, require legislation prescribing lower wages than in prevailing collective agreements. To retain incentives for the unemployed to take on such jobs, rather than to live on unemployment benefits, the latter would have to be reduced to a lower level, for example to 70% of normal wages, though not below the social welfare levels. Lower unemployment benefits will also be necessary to induce those who have lost higher paid jobs to work for a significantly lower wage.

Against these proposals one may object—and such objections will surely be made—that it is not equitable to impose the costs of fighting unemployment on these who have lost their jobs. We have sympathy for this objection. It is reasonable that those who have work assume a larger share of the burden for today's unemployment. In our view, however, the natural method for doing that is not to increase taxes on households, as has been proposed, but instead to let those who have jobs help cover the deficit in the unemployment insurance system through higher fees. Here is a further argument for our proposal for shifting to actuarially fair fees. In chapter 3 we also propose—as part of the consolidation of public finances—higher fees for firms by about 1.5% of the wage bill for employees by kronor 2,500 ($300) per person and year.

In the same spirit, we also propose that some funds today used for unemployment compensation—and especially for expensive labor market programs—be redirected to the repair and maintenance of public buildings such as schools. This could be done by stimulating local government public works with central government subsidies for labor costs—but not capital costs—again, with wages below those of collective agreements to generate as much employment as possible for each krona spent.

Efforts to squeeze more employment out of each government krona need not be confined to the public sector. It should also be possible to mobilize the large financial saving surplus in the private sector (currently as large as the government deficit) and redirect some of these funds towards labor-intensive activities.

In stimulating higher employment along these lines, it is desirable to chose general measures with a minimum of administrative red tape. The measures should be easy to start, simple to administer, and possible to discontinue. These arguments all speak in favor of using the tax system, for instance, by giving tax deductions for certain labor-intensive investments. But the tax system should not be overburdened by new permanent deductions that erode the principle of the 1991 tax reform, which was to create a large tax base and symmetry in taxation. It is therefore important that these measures be clearly limited in time. It is also important to set a definite time limit for the measures to obtain maximum effect; only temporary measures will offer a strong incentive to invest now rather than later.

The tax incentives should be designed to affect areas that use labor intensively, relative to capital, and where unemployment is high and rising. Repair and maintenance of buildings is a prime example of such an area. For households, it would be natural to allows tax deductions for home repairs; indeed, such efforts are already under way. For firms, it should also be possible to use tax allowances to encourage expenditures now rather than later.

We further suggest that infrastructure investments that have already been started be speeded up. To obtain higher employment effects, work on such projects should be carried out in double or triple shifts, instead of the single shift that prevails today. Finally, public investment projects should be speeded up. This should lower costs, as there is no shortage of labor and machines today, and shorter completion times imply lower interest costs.

We might also envisage the start of some additional infrastructure projects. By building now, when the costs are moderate, certain savings could be made—relative to building later—even if today's budget deficit is increased. We want to underline that it is an absolute condition that investment projects are selected so that the outcome is to advance the socially most profitable projects. As we explain further in chapter 4, the results of social cost-benefit analyses are often neglected, at least in the building of roads. In today's very difficult employment situation, pressures from regional or sectoral interests may push forward projects with a low or negative return. The decision-making process for heavy infrastructure investments therefore should be examined critically.

Domestic demand falls in 1993 as a result of declining private consumption and investment (see figure 2.4). If these components of demand, which together amount to some 70% of GDP, fall more rapidly in the near future than what is foreseen in most forecasts, further stimulation may become necessary to avoid the free-fall of demand that has occurred in Finland (Honkapohja et al. 1993).

The most effective way of maintaining private consumption is no doubt to temporarily lower the VAT, making it attractive for households to buy more goods and services, especially durable goods, at relatively low prices (intertemporal substitution). A lowering of the VAT rate would obviously increase the budget deficit for some time; each percentage point of the VAT rate is worth on the order of 5 billion kronor (0.3% of GDP). The discomfort one might feel in making such a proposal has to be weighed against the concern that private consumption and employment might otherwise deteriorate further. If a short-term increase in the cyclical budget deficit is unacceptable, it might be possible to reverse the "internal devaluation" that was carried out in the second crisis package in the fall of 1992. Temporarily lower VAT would then be financed by temporarily higher payroll taxes. The rationale for this proposal is that today a collapse of domestic demand presents the most severe threat to the economy.

The method we recommend in a situation with collapsing investment is similar. By means of a significant but temporary tax credit for all investments, except for investment in housing, it should be possible to create incentives for firms to move up investment projects. In that case one might imagine methods similar to the earlier system of investment funds, that is, some form of first-year write-off for investments. A possibility is to let firms use reserves from the old tax system—which are now supposed to be taxed in the course of 1993–94—and allow depreciation against these reserves.

We do not take a position as to the exact techniques. The main point is that there is a possibility of transforming some of the large excess financial saving in the private sector (12% of GDP) into investment of different kinds, and in this way avoid a disastrous slump similar to the one currently observed in Finland.

The Way Out of the Crisis: How to Consolidate Government Finances

Even if one is worried about the present domestic demand situation, it is extremely important to formulate a long-term stabilization program of government finances. To restore confidence in the Swedish economy in the medium term, and increase the scope for short-term expansion, it is not enough to approve a vague plan for unspecified public budget improvements at a later time. The Riksdag must at once take the decisions necessary for consolidating the budget in future. In practice, agreements have to be made across traditional political boundaries to make the decisions credible, even after the next election (in 1994). Even though some increases of public revenues might be feasible, we strongly argue that the main effort be on the expenditure side. To balance different special interests against each other, we favor a comprehensive expenditure reform, similar to the 1991 tax reform (see chapter 3).

In this section we discuss the macroeconomic aspects of the issue: what is the order of magnitude of the necessary expenditure cuts and how should they be distributed over time if one aims at stabilizing the public sector's net debt at some prespecified level? We present a number of alternative scenarios to illustrate this question. Because we are concerned with the medium term, it is necessary to see the issue in a growth perspective. We describe the path of public-sector debt up until the turn of the century under different assumptions about macroeconomic variables and budget policy. In our calculations we allow the assumed macroeconomic trends to influence both revenues and expenditures of the public sector. It would have been desirable to allow also for reverse causation. But in the short time at our disposal it was not possible to solve the complicated task of making convincing interactive scenarios that capture the medium-term interplay between demand and supply forces. Our calculations should therefore be regarded as illustrative examples, not as detailed projections. Our "pessimistic" scenario may, however, be interpreted as an attempt to consider how restrictive policies may influence macroeconomic variables.

Our calculations start from a baseline scenario (at "unchanged policies"). As far as GDP is concerned, we assume—like most available projections—that real GDP declines by 1.5% in 1993 and subsequently rises at the same rate in 1994. Over the four years 1995–98 we assume that GDP grows at an average rate of 3%. This is admittedly a high figure in the perspective of the last two decades. However, because of the huge present capacity slack, there is substantial scope for expanding production at existing capacity simply through higher capacity utilization. In addition, we do see some encouraging signs in the Swedish economy, which could increase productivity growth. For that reason we do not regard a growth rate of 3% over a few years as unlikely.

For unemployment, we start from the fact that about 12% of the labor force is without regular jobs in 1993 and find themselves either in open unemployment or in various labor market programs. Total unemployment is likely to become somewhat higher in the course of 1994, but later the trend may reverse so that some of the growth of GDP in the 1995–98 period can take the form of higher employment. We assume in the baseline scenario that open unemployment and labor market programs in total will amount to about 5% of the labor force in 1998. This is based on the assumption that we can avoid long-term unemployment. As explained later in this chapter, this will require a more flexible labor market, brought about by liberalization of labor market legislation, at least temporarily, to minimize the risk of ending up in a European-type trap of high long-term unemployment.

This scenario for employment, in combination with a GDP growth rate of 3%, implies that labor productivity for the whole economy and real wages before tax will rise by 1%–2% per year in the 1995–98 period.

It turns out that our calculations are not very sensitive to variations in the rate of interest or in the rate of inflation, as long as these two variables vary within reasonable intervals. In our scenarios we assume that inflation will be 5% in 1993, 3.5% in 1994, and 2% in subsequent years, while the real rate of interest will be steady at 5% throughout the period.

The starting point for our baseline scenario is the 1993 government budget as laid out in the preliminary national budget proposal. Starting from 1994, we assume that public revenues grow in step with GDP. This is reasonable because the Swedish tax system after the 1991 tax reform is broadly proportional.

As far as public-sector consumption and investments are concerned, we assume that they too follow the trend in GDP. As is evident from figure 3.4, this assumption corresponds closely to actual developments; since the beginning of the 1980s the GDP shares for public consumption and investment have been virtually steady around 28% and 3%, respectively. As far as transfers are concerned, we assume that they grow at a constant rate of 2% in real terms (1993 prices). This assumption too corresponds to the observations over the most recent decade. The bulk of pensions grow in proportion to past real wage growth, which amounts to just over 2% per year. Most other systems of transfers (except child allowances) are linked to real wages, which are assumed to rise by 2% in the latter part of the period. Because the time path of transfers is fixed in our analysis, each extra percent of GDP growth reduces the public deficit as a share of GDP. In terms of 1993 prices, a growth rate of 3% rather than 2% reduces the deficit by about 6 billion kronor.

The extreme unemployment has pulled up public consumption and transfers. With an unemployment rate of 12% and unemployment-related spending of over 6% of GDP, a percentage point reduction of the unemployment rate, at a given production level, improves public finances by more than half a percent of GDP (7 billion kronor). This, however, is a gross figure. Because wages and transfers are both taxable, the net figure is smaller, about 5 billion kronor, according to our estimates. If higher employment is associated with higher GDP growth, the total net budget improvement will be larger, to be sure, since we have assumed that gross public revenues grew in step with GDP.

A large and highly uncertain item in the 1993 budget is the support for failing banks, but that is a temporary expenditure item. We have assumed that the associated strain on public finances will be around 30 billion kronor in 1993, about 15 billion kronor in 1994, and nothing from 1995 onward. This implies that the deficit shrinks, ceteris paribus, up to 1995. Another uncertain item is the potential cost of membership in the European Community.

Higher employment and faster growth, which we have assumed for the 1995–98 period, improve the public finances over these years. In discussions of budget deficits a distinction is often made between a cyclical part, which diminishes when business conditions improve, and a structural part, which remains. In our opinion, such a distinction between cyclical and structural deficits raises a number of irrelevant questions. We have, furthermore, emphasized that it is the public-sector debt (a stock) and not the deficit in any particular year (a flow) that has to be stabilized. Rather than taking a detour via calculations of a structural deficit, we find it simpler and more direct to concentrate on the time path for the public sector's debt.

Figure 2.6 shows how the total public debt grows over time in some alternative scenarios. The lowest dashed curve illustrates what would happen in our baseline alternative (unchanged policies as of January 1993). Evidently the financial position slides out of control: at the turn of the century the public-sector debt has risen to about 70% of GDP (and central government debt to nearly 100% of GDP), and it continues to grow rapidly.

The second curve from below shows what happens if we take into account the future effects of those expenditure cuts that have been

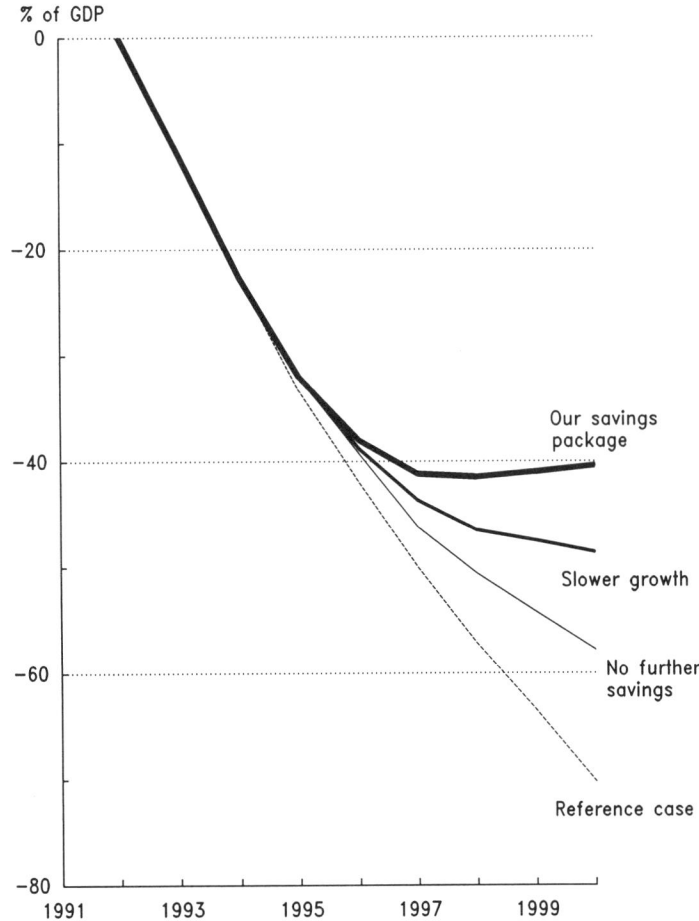

Source: Own calculations.

Figure 2.6
The path of public sector debt (percent of GDP)

decided by the Riksdag or are included in the two crisis packages of 1992. This time path also looks like a ski slope without an end; the debt ratio reaches 60% of GDP at the turn of the century and continues to grow by 4 percentage points a year.

A strengthening of the budget is thus necessary to stabilize the debt-to-GDP ratio. We have looked at several different alternatives. The one we recommend is to phase in a number of budget improvements over a four-year period (1994–97). There are several reasons for choosing this period: (1) For decisions about future expenditure cuts to be credible, these decisions must be implemented relatively soon. (2) The period coincides with the present three-year election period and the next one, which is important for similar reasons. (3) Those European countries that did carry out budgetary consolidations of a similar order of magnitude in recent years all did so over a four-year period. This is true for Denmark (1982–86), Belgium (1981–85), and Ireland (1985–89). In Belgium and Ireland, however, efforts were postponed to such a late stage that the interest payments on a very sizable debt made it extremely hard to stabilize government finances despite draconian measures.

We have made two alternative scenarios for stabilizing the debt-to-GDP ratio. The first alternative implies expenditure cuts and a total reduction of the deficit, relative to the baseline, corresponding to 100 billion kronor (in 1993 prices about 7% of GDP). Relative to the expenditure cuts in the crisis packages and in the 1993 budget, this requires a further 60–70 billion kronor of savings. Taking into account the present deep crisis, we propose that only one-tenth of this budgetary improvement be made in 1994. Remaining savings have been equally distributed over the years 1995–97, but the outcome is not particularly sensitive to the precise timing. The upper thicker curve in the figure shows this alternative, where debt is stabilized at a little over 40% from 1997 onward. Forty percent is close to the 1993 average for the OECD area, but below the predicted OECD average later in the 1990s (OECD 1992). As is further explained in chapter 4, the deterioration of public finances from the end of the 1980s in this alternative implies that higher taxes are imposed on future generations corresponding to just under 4,000 kronor ($500) per employed and year.

These calculations may be regarded as fairly optimistic, as we have assumed total unemployment in 1998 to be 5%; let us therefore call this "the optimistic scenario." We have also made experiments with less optimistic macroeconomic assumptions; let us call this "the pessimistic scenario." Above all, the results depend on the assumptions about the growth rate and the level of unemployment. The second curve from the top in figure 2.6 shows what would happen with the pessimistic evolution of growth and employment. In this second scenario we assume that growth over the 1995–98 period will be 2% per annum rather than 3%. We further assume that this is reminiscent of the "Danish" unemployment situation: total unemployment gets stuck at the high level of 10% in 1998. In this case, reducing the public sector deficit by 100 billion kronor cannot prevent public debt from rising relative to GDP. To stabilize the debt ratio under these assumptions, further expenditure cuts of 30 billion kronor will be necessary also in 1998. With this combination of assumptions, public debt is stabilized between 45% and 50% of GDP by the turn of the century.

These various scenarios illustrate that growth by itself cannot solve the problem, as suggested by some observers. It is simply not possible to find any shortcut that avoids the need for major savings in the near future. Although we have not chosen to formulate the problem of debt stabilization as a question of structural versus cyclical deficits, we may note that the necessary budget savings of 100–130 billion kronor is of the same magnitude as several calculations of the structural budget deficit.

The discussion has so far left open the particular content of the expenditure cuts. Although this is essentially a question of political priorities, we do find it useful to illustrate by concrete examples what might be done. Obviously, radical budget cuts cannot be decided upon with a view to macroeconomic considerations only. The question will be dealt with in the following chapter, when public sector expenditures and revenues are discussed also from the viewpoint of economic efficiency. At the end of that chapter we present a number of concrete budgetary measures that in the aggregate meet the requirements outlined here.

The Way Out of the Crisis: Restoring the Health of the Financial Sector

It is not enough to agree on demand management policies to take Sweden out of its present deep recession. It is also necessary to ease supply-side bottlenecks. Therefore, measures to improve the work-

Table 2.1
Operating results and capital base in banking system. Figures before government contributions (about 45 billion kronor in 1993–1994).

	1991	1992	1993	1994	1995
Result before nonperforming interest	32	44	50	40	35
Nonperforming interest payments	−5	−15	−12	−8	−5
Result before credit losses	27	29	38	32	30
Credit losses	−36	−73	−47	−30	−20
Net result	−9	−44	−9	−2	10
Total capital base	*117*	*69*	*58*	*55*	*65*

Source: Calculation by Gabriel Utwitz.

ings of both financial markets and the labor market are required. Let us start with financial markets.

Toward the end of the 1980s the bulk of new bank credits was directed to real estate. The recent free-fall of real estate prices, and related bankruptcies in a number of financial companies, have left heavy marks on the balance sheets of banks. Table 2.1 shows profit and loss results, as well as the capital base, of the aggregate Swedish banking system in 1991 and 1992 and some projections for subsequent years.

The table reveals that banks continue to make quite good cash flow on their ordinary activity (first line), although nonperforming interest payments on bad debts reduce the results significantly (third line.) But the huge credit losses, whether realized or expected, have driven down the overall result strongly into the red (fourth line). The dominant part of the credit losses are directly or indirectly related to the crisis in the real estate market.

The table also shows how the negative overall results gradually tend to erode the capital base of the banks (fifth line). Without new capital of about 45 billion kronor from the government, three banks, in particular the government-owned bank (Nordbanken), would have been unable to meet the 8% capital requirement in 1992. Without government injections of capital, the total capital base of the aggregate banking system would have fallen from 117 billion in 1991 to 69 at the end of 1992. It is today an open question to what extent other banks also need assistance from the government, or rather, from the new Bank Rescue Fund. [In our calculations above regarding public debt, we assumed these injections to be 30 billion kronor in 1993 and

15 billion kronor in 1994; at the time of the English translation of the report, these figures look fairly realistic.] Before we outline how the situation could and should be handled, we would like to point to the important macroeconomic risks inherent in the situation.

One serious macroeconomic risk is that banks that fail to meet the capital requirement will be obliged to reduce their lending, such that new lending becomes totally inelastic with respect to the interest rate. Earlier credit losses may also make the banks excessively risk averse. The demand for loans is admittedly low in the current business situation, but an inadequate capital base and the unwillingness to take on risks may dampen or even break an otherwise possible economic upturn. It may become difficult to finance new investment, start new firms, or make bankrupted firms viable.

Another serious risk—indeed a realistic one—is that banks try to correct their capital position by keeping up the margin between deposit and lending rates, which are at historical and international record level (somewhere around 8% in the spring of 1993).

One may view part of the wide interest margin and the high lending rates as a natural risk premium in the present depressed economy, where lending is more risky than normally. But the high lending rates are also a consequence of inadequate competition, due to the cartelized market structure in Swedish banking. (On the deposit side, competition is tougher because households have access to good substitutes for deposits such as money-market instruments and deposits with mortgage companies, though no substitutes are available for checking accounts).

The cartelized situation, in combination with tight enforcement of capital requirements, can easily produce high lending rates. If several banks are close to the point where they fail to meet the capital requirement, they cannot expand their lending. Then it becomes tempting to charge the highest possible interest rates to borrowers, regardless of the marginal cost of funds. This implies that lower money-market rates will not necessarily yield lower lending rates in banks; they may only produce a wider interest rate margin.

The macroeconomic consequences of the present interest margins could prove highly destructive for the Swedish economy. Indebted households and firms may face severe liquidity problems. But primarily, it becomes difficult to find projects yielding a return above 15%, a typical lending rate in 1992 and 1993, with an inflation rate of only 2%–5%. These consequences in turn threaten the future recovery from recession.

It is important to keep these macroeconomic threats in mind when considering how to design the support to banks. Specific decisions on this matter require detailed knowledge of the portfolios held by banks, which we do not have, but which the new Bank Rescue Fund must acquire. We do have some general principles to suggest.

The government owns some banks: Nordbanken has been owned mainly by the government for a long time, and Gotabanken has recently been taken over to prevent bankruptcy. With these banks the first effort, which has already begun, must be to split up the banks into viable and nonviable parts. The viable part should be sold as soon as possible to domestic or foreign buyers. It is important to bring in new actors and owners in the Swedish banking sector to sharpen competition and put downward pressure on interest rate margins.

In the case of cooperative banks in need of public support, a guarantee by the government is a natural method of meeting the capital requirement. The guarantee might either be linked to specific assets—real estate mortgages or loans—or be of a general nature. A specific guarantee may be applied to good or bad loans (Johansson 1993). The government obviously runs less risk in the former case. Even a failing cooperative bank should be split up into a viable and a nonviable part.

The guarantees method might also be used to meet the capital requirement in a privately owned bank forced to ask for government support. Guarantees of bad loans imply that losses will only show up in the balance sheet when they are realized. The effect is largely that losses are smoothed out over time. Loans from the government, conditional on future profits, imply instead that some revenue is advanced in time.

But a second and supplementary method of restoring the capital base of banks is to inject new capital. The traditional method of share issues is to offer new shares on the stock market. In today's crisis situation that would imply that a bank that turns to the government for help is asked to issue government-guaranteed shares in the bank. If the former shareholders and others in the private sector are prepared to buy the new shares, the capital base of the bank will grow in this way. If instead the private sector is unwilling to inject enough capital in the banks, the government will, in practice, buy the larger part of the new shares. The voting rights of the existing owners will be diluted and the state becomes the main owner of the bank.

The government then splits up the bank into a viable and a nonviable part. The viable part is sold in the market, which enables the government to recover part of its expenses. The assets of the nonviable part are sold later on. It is obviously very difficult to know how much the government might recover in the future from the nonviable part of the bank.

What are the advantages and disadvantages of the guarantee method as compared to the method of share issues? One point in favor of the former method is that the government does not have to make any immediate payments. The government pays out only to the extent that banks realize losses or have a negative operating result. As was already pointed out in connection with table 2.1, the average bank continues to show a substantial positive profit before credit losses.

But this method also has obvious drawbacks. Banks will have to show very good operating results for a number of years in order to come out of the guarantee in the future, unless of course real estate prices rise rapidly and early. The only way for the banks to do this in practice is to maintain high interest margins, which may prevent an economic upturn. Weak competition in the Swedish banking system makes these high lending rates possible.

A new share issue implies that banks receive new funds immediately. New share capital will enable owners with a long horizon to manage with lower present interest margins than otherwise. Competition from new (foreign or domestic) banks would oblige all banks to accept such behavior.

The major advantage of the share-issue method is that it is compatible with intensified competition. A reconstructed bank is not obliged to maintain high interest margins to restore its capital base. It becomes possible to establish a more normal relationship between deposit and lending rates and reduce the risk of negative macroeconomic consequences. But the method also has its drawbacks. Those banks that, with high interest margins, do not need to turn to the Bank Rescue Fund might eventually be obliged to do so if new banks enter the market and squeeze the interest rate margin. Furthermore, the early strain on the government budget will be larger. Compared to the guarantee method it is not self-evident, however, that the overall long-term costs will be higher. That depends primarily on how quickly and strongly the real estate market recovers.

Another difference between the two methods lies in the treatment of former bank shareholders. The guarantee method places, in principle, the risk of future losses on the taxpayers, while the shareholders in the banks retain the possibility of future gains. New share issues, by contrast, leave only limited possibilities for the existing shareholders, as their shares may be expected to lose value when the group of owners is widened. It is therefore more of a "capitalist" solution, while the guarantee method for the weaker banks operates as a safety net for shareholders. The method of issuing new shares is easier to reconcile with our general principle of clear and explicit rules and responsibilities.

Our most important point is that the crisis in financial markets has to be resolved rapidly and with methods that enable lending rates to come down and lending to increase. New share issues, wherever they can be applied, is thus the preferred method. In spite of our sympathy for this method, however, we would like to impose a definite condition on its application. The government should carry out the operation of buying and selling banks rapidly—for example, within half a year—to avoid a Norwegian situation with a governmental banking system of a more permanent nature (Steigum 1993). If this were to occur, large Swedish enterprises might lose their loyalty to the Swedish banking sector and transfer a large part of their business to foreign banks. A rapid operation is possible because most of the bad loans in each bank have been extended to a limited number of large real estate companies. As the viable part of the bank is sold off, there is of course a possibility of initially turning to Swedish investors and only later to foreign investors.

A special advantage in getting new owners into the Swedish banking sector is that there will be several countervailing interests to watch keenly whether support to the crisis banks are in fact extended on market-like conditions. This may become important in order to save money for the taxpayers because negotiations between the Bank Rescue Fund and the banks in crisis will definitely be very tough: a bank that has taken the difficult decision of approaching the Bank Rescue Fund may try to extract the best conditions possible. Increasing the number of actors in financial markets is something we discuss in more detail in chapter 3.

The Way Out of the Crisis: How to Avoid Long-Term Unemployment

In our view the most severe problem of the present crisis is the risk that the high unemployment develops into high long-term unemployment. Economic research has recently identified several mechanisms that may lead to persistence in unemployment. It is therefore important to prevent the emergence of high unemployment in the first place (for surveys, see Layard, Nickell, and Jackman 1991; Lindbeck 1993).

Sweden by now already has high unemployment, because of many years of deficient economic policy and a poorly functioning system of wage formation. What can be done? The answer hinges on the mechanisms that underlie long-term unemployment. One mechanism may be that the physical capital stock has become too small to employ the entire labor force at existing real wages—that is, a so-called physical capital shortage. Another possible mechanism may be a shortage of skilled labor, that is, a so-called human capital shortage. In both of these cases, real wages have to fall, at least for part of the labor force, to increase employment at the existing stock of physical and human capital. Investment in new physical or human capital may of course improve the situation after some time.

Labor-market legislation is another factor of importance for employment. When looking at hiring legislation, the focus has been on the possibilities of temporary employment, including a trial period. Theoretical and empirical analyses suggest that legislation that increases the costs of hiring labor reduces employment fluctuations. Such an effect may be regarded as an advantage in normal business cycles, because employment is thereby stabilized. Following a deep recession, however, such rules may instead become an impediment to new jobs, because firms do not know for how long they will need a larger labor force (Holmlund 1993; Lindbeck and Snower 1988).

Rules on firing of labor, which normally include rules for notification and compensation on departure (severance pay), may also make it more difficult to come out of the employment crisis. Because such rules increase the costs to the firm of firing labor, the rules also make it advantageous to hoard labor as fluctuations in production occur. But increased firing costs also mean increased hiring costs, because any firm must allow for the possibility that in the future it may not need everybody who is hired now. Both theory and experience suggest that the fluctuations in employment are reduced also by these rules. But increasing employment may also in this case become more difficult after a deep recession. This effect may have been limited in Sweden because firing costs are paid through a collectively organized insurance system set up by the labor-market parties and not by the firms themselves (Holmlund 1993).

The legal framework for hiring and firing can be expected to influence the possibilities to a return to normal employment levels in other ways as well. The costs of hiring and firing labor give insiders the possibility of driving up wages in a recovery without risking their own jobs, which reduces the possibilities for outsiders to obtain new jobs.

Mandatory rules for hiring and firing are probably especially burdensome for small and medium-sized enterprises, which have a low labor turnover and may have an uneven age structure among their employees. Smaller firms cannot, in general, assume that their problem disappears through natural retirements, unless they happen to have a number of employees approaching pension age. Such firms will therefore be reluctant to hire labor early in a business upturn unless they are strongly convinced that they will need more labor in the future and regard the new employee as suited for the job.

It would appear that existing rules were better adjusted to the limited and regular business cycle fluctuations during the first two decades after World War II than they are to today's high and possibly persistent unemployment. The rules did not of course cause the present serious unemployment, but they do increase the difficulties of getting out of it. We argue, in short, that there are employment motives for—at least temporarily—modifying or abolishing this legislation. We wish in particular to point to the need for liberalizing the rules for temporary employment.

Conclusion

In this chapter we have shown how the institutional setup in the political system and in the labor market failed to adjust to new conditions from the early 1970s. Instead of resolving the fundamental problems, policymakers opted for temporary "solutions" through inflation, increased public-sector employment, and repeated devaluations. When efforts were finally made to reduce inflation through a strict adherence to a fixed exchange rate—despite accumulated cost increases, the onset of a banking crisis, and growing budget deficits—the economy plunged into the deepest recession of the postwar period.

We have argued that the best way to avoid similar situations in the future is to reform various rules and institutions now, both in the political system and in the labor market. Such reforms would also increase the possibility of attacking the acute unemployment crisis. No rapid and easy fix can solve today's serious macroeconomic problems. We have, however, outlined a program that may help to end the crisis without increasing the budget deficit and letting inflation loose again.

Proposals

Short-Term Stabilization Policy

8. Increase the scope for successful monetary and fiscal policy in the short run by trying to raise the credibility of government policies in the long run. This calls for institutional changes concerning the status of the Bank of Sweden and the budget process.

9. Decide now on a concrete program to stabilize the public-sector debt within five years, using a combination of expenditure cuts and revenue increases. Start with limited measures only in 1994 and proceed with more substantial measures in 1995 through 1997, possibly also in 1998. Depending on the development of key macroeconomic variables, the gap to be closed is between 60 billion and 100 billion Swedish kronor (US$ 8–13 billion) in addition to deficit reductions already decided on (up to January 1993); this will stabilize the debt at 40%–50% of GNP. EC membership would call for additional expenditure cuts or tax increases.

10. The Bank of Sweden should continue its policy of stepwise reductions in short-term interest rates, as long as nothing dramatic happens to the exchange rate or long-term interest rates.

11. Given that the high borrowing rates in the commercial banks currently pose a greater problem than money-market rates, the financial crisis has to be solved swiftly and in such a way as to stimulate the credit supply and force down interest differentials. Issues of new shares is the best way to accomplish this in private banks.

12. If the government temporarily becomes the principal owner of a private bank, the good and the bad portions of the bank should promptly be separated, and the good portion should be sold back to the market as soon as possible (within a year). The previous owners have to accept the fact that their shares will lose most of their value in the process.

13. To increase competition and force borrowing rates down, try to attract new agents (domestic and foreign banks) to the market.

14. When liberalizing labor-market legislation (point 5), moderate the law regulating temporary employment in firms, at least for the time being, to facilitate increased employment when the economy starts to recover.

15. Increase the leverage of the unemployment measures of the Labor Market Board by reducing compensation levels and shifting to less costly programs (education, inexpensive and labor-intensive public work programs, etc.), to bring down open unemployment at lower cost.

16. Firms and employees should bear a larger part of the costs of unemployment through increased employers' and employees' fees to the Unemployment Benefit Fund.

17. Allow temporary tax deductions for labor-intensive investments, such as repairs, maintenance, rebuilding, etc., in the private sector. Intensify such activities in the public sector as well (schools renovation, etc.).

18. Speed up the process of infrastructure investments by working in double or triple shifts, to increase labor intensity and reduce capital costs.

19. If private consumption or investment should fall drastically as compared to prevailing forecasts, we suggest a temporary reduction in the VAT or a temporary increase in the investment tax credit.

3   Efficiency

The living standard in Sweden is held down by high production costs and limited consumption variety. This is another way of saying that Sweden has efficiency problems. Many of these problems can be traced directly or indirectly to policy decisions in the past. Although the problems are long run and structural, they need to be attacked now to improve the functioning of the economy and to raise future living standards.

The first part of this chapter deals with efficiency problems in the private sector, specifically in product markets, labor markets, and financial markets. The focus is on problems created by government regulations and private restriction on competition. The second part of the chapter deals with problems in the public sector, where we discuss taxes, transfers, and public consumption from an efficiency point of view.

An important theme in our analysis is that severe efficiency problems in the Swedish economy largely result from distorted market mechanisms. In some cases, mainly in the public sector, market mechanisms have been eliminated altogether. We conclude, as in other chapters, that solutions require new rules and reformed institutions. At the end of the chapter we present a number of alternative concrete proposals of how to solve the crisis in government finances, that is, to reduce the deficit and stabilize the debt-to-GDP ratio by 1998.

The Private Sector

Sweden's Efficiency Problems

Policy measures that have weakened market mechanisms and impaired the functioning of the economy explain many of the efficiency problems in the Swedish economy. The motive behind those policy measures has often been to attain other politically desired objectives. In fact, however, these objectives rarely justify the loss in efficiency: the reason is that they could be achieved at a much lower cost to society.

The problems exist both in the public and private sector. A number of recent public-sector reforms have aimed at solving the efficiency problems by widening opportunities for consumer choice in government-provided services (such as health, schools, child care, old-age care) and by increasing competition between different providers. Despite these reforms, consumer choice is still quite limited and these services are still mainly provided by government monopolies. Hardly any use is made of the price mechanism, and no gains accrue to more efficient producers.

Sweden's efficiency problems are by no means limited to the public sector, however. In the private sector, an important cause of inefficiency is government regulation of different markets, which inhibits competition, raises costs, and redistributes incomes in a way that is often inconsistent with commonly accepted principles of income redistribution. Typically, redistribution is from consumers to producers.

In many cases it is private collusion and cartel agreements between firms that limit competition. This is partly a reflection of weak antitrust legislation and supervision in Sweden. All this means that lack of competition is a major problem in large parts of the Swedish economy.

Sweden's efficiency problems, then, are sometimes due to the government intervening too much or in the wrong way, sometimes to the government doing too little. Obviously the political process does not work as well as many would think. Ideally the government should provide a legal and institutional framework ensuring adequate competition. It should also correct market failures and choose taxes and transfers so as to minimize the conflict between efficiency and redistribution. But that does not seem to be the case.

To understand the problems one must adopt a more realistic view of the political process. One reason why political intervention in practice often conflicts with the general interest is that special interests have a disproportionate influence on policy. Citizens who want to attain something through the political process find that voting for a political party is not always an efficient way to express their views on specific issues. Political parties represent packages of views. To express the intensity of their specific interests and preferences, citizens form interest groups to lobby on their own behalf. Such interest groups tend to represent narrow interests, usually producer interests. They rarely represent the general consumer or taxpayer.

The general interest is something other than the sum of all special interests. Indeed, there is often a conflict between special interests and the general interest (Joskow and Rose 1990). We can compare the relationship between special interests and the general interest with the relationship between monopoly and competition. In a monopoly situation, self-interested producers do not produce socially efficient outcomes. The government thus has a task to set rules that ensure competition. Similarly the government has to create an institutional framework for the political process that strengthens the general interest. In practice it is difficult to induce the government to perform either of these tasks.

A realistic view of the political process makes it possible to explain both why there are efficiency problems in the economy and—even more important—why it may be difficult to get rid of them. The same forces that have led to a specific policy measure in the past are likely to block a reversal in the policy.

The Role of Competition

The State of Competition
"Sweden is a small open economy" is a worn expression used to describe the Swedish economy. It suggests that Sweden, through its large dependence on foreign trade, is subjected to fierce international competition, something that guarantees that prices of goods and services cannot diverge very much from those abroad. This view implies that one need not be overly concerned with competition issues in Sweden, because international competition can be expected to do the job. However, the picture of Sweden as a highly competitive economy needs to be considerably modified.

It is true that Sweden is a small and relatively open economy, but that is not enough to guarantee adequate competition within the country. Not all goods and very few services are traded internationally, which means that only a very small part of the economy is exposed to international competition. Together tradables amount to a little over 20% of GDP (expressed as value added). The rest of the economy is sheltered from international competition. In the nontradable sector domestic costs determine prices, which makes domestic competition crucial for efficiency and prices. Here the small domestic market is a limiting factor, as a small market normally has fewer firms than a larger one.

Small countries, then, need to be particularly watchful of domestic competition. That has not been true of Sweden. On the contrary, antitrust legislation in Sweden has been more permissive than in many other countries; certain cartels have not only been legal, but enforced by government organization (such as the dairy sector). This will be changed as of this year (1993), when Sweden moves to conform to the competition rules of the European Community.

How do we know that Sweden suffers from inadequate competition? The degree of competition can not be measured directly. Barriers to international trade, regulatory policies that inhibit competition, entry barriers and price controls, price collusion, cartel agreements, and concentration all signal potentially weak competition, but they do not reveal how weak it is, or what the consequences are in terms of reduced efficiency. Because lack of competition often means higher prices, a consistently higher general price level in Sweden than in comparable countries can be used as a rough measure of weaker competition.

Sweden has extremely high prices in international comparison, measured over a number of years. This has puzzled many observers, because prices—at least over longer periods—should tend to converge between countries. Sharp fluctuations in exchange rates make prices deviate temporarily. But sustained disparities should be due to structural differences between countries. Important structural determinants include real incomes per capita (which affect the wage level in the nontraded sector), value-added taxes (which tax domestic sales and create a wedge between prices in different countries), and perhaps also wage structures (a more compressed wage structure tending to result in relatively high wages in low-skill domestic service production). In addition, the degree of competition in the domestic market can be an important factor. The role of competition may then be inferred from price differences when we control for other structural differences between countries.

Available data indicate that the high Swedish price level is indeed a long-term phenomenon. According to OECD's surveys of purchasing power parities, which measure the price of a common basket of

Efficiency 79

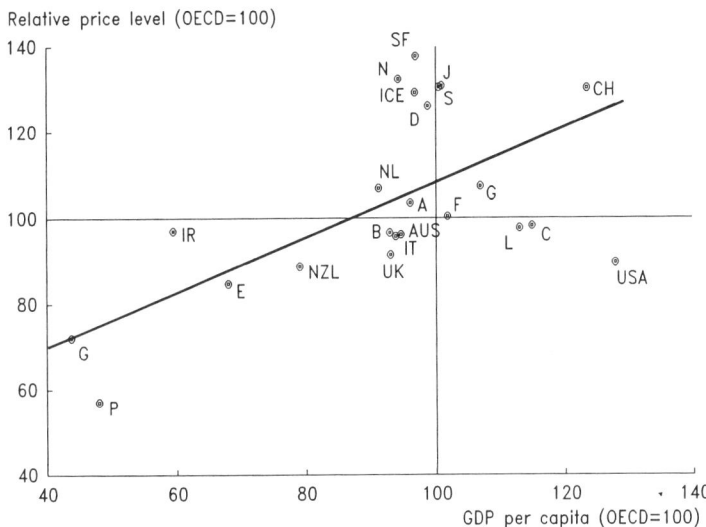

Source: OECD.

Figure 3.1
Real income and price levels in OECD countries 1990 (relative price level; OECD = 100)

goods and services in a common currency, the Swedish price level has been 20–40% higher than the OECD average during most of the 1970–90 period. Structural determinants such as the level of real per capita income and the relatively high value-added tax in Sweden can only partly account for this price difference (Bolin and Swedenborg 1992; Lipsey and Swedenborg 1993). As seen in figure 3.1, Sweden's per capita income in 1990 was equal to the OECD average—since then, of course, it has fallen—but its price level was considerably above the average for the OECD. Sweden shares this extreme position with the other Nordic countries and Japan.

The price comparison becomes more informative when broken down by commodities. Figure 3.2 shows Swedish prices relative to prices in the European Community: for some commodities Swedish prices are actually lower, but for many they are up to 60% higher. They are lower for investment goods such as machinery (which weigh heavily in Swedish exports) and some consumer goods such as clothing and furniture. They are much higher for food, housing,

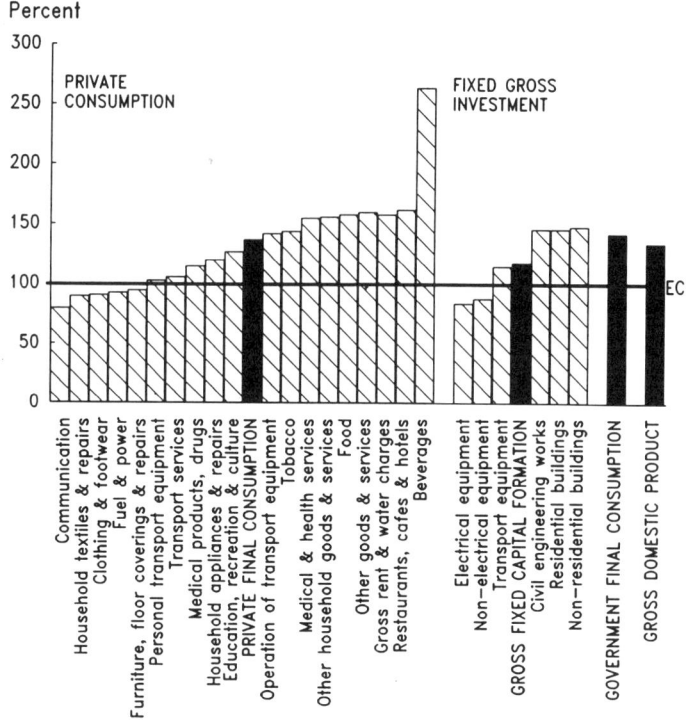

Source: OECD.

Figure 3.2
Prices in Sweden relative to EC, 1990

hotels, and restaurants. (Beverages are most extreme, largely due to heavy taxation.)

It is reasonable to view at least the larger price differences for individual goods and services as reflecting efficiency problems in Sweden. They cannot be explained by general country characteristics, including an occasionally overvalued exchange rate, but show that prices and costs (rather than profits) in many sectors are higher in Sweden than in other comparable countries. Indeed, the price differences underestimate the absolute efficiency problems in Sweden, because the EC, too, has efficiency problems. A stated purpose of the EC's internal market reforms is to increase competition and enhance efficiency.

Price comparisons roughly indicate the costs of limited competition. Even though Sweden had a lower per capita income in 1990 than Germany and the United States, it had almost 30% higher prices than Germany and almost 60% higher prices than the United States. Part of that reflected an overvaluation of the Swedish krona and has been eliminated since the krona started floating in the fall of 1992. (In August 1993 the krona has depreciated by around 25% vis-à-vis the D-mark and around 30% vis-à-vis the U.S. dollar.) A large unexplained price divergence still remains, however. If that price difference could be eliminated through increased competition, it would mean a considerable increase in Swedish real incomes.

Causes of Inadequate Competition
It is well known that businesspeople and producers generally favor free competition in all markets except their own. Firms seek monopoly profits ("rents"). One way for an industry to seek rents is to enlist the help of the state to regulate competition. Popular arguments hold that the industry needs protection against "disloyal foreign competition," "dumped world market prices," or "cream skimming" in regulated industries. Government regulation is therefore an important source of inadequate competition. Cartels not supported by government regulations are not as effective or as long lived as cartels that have such support (Demsetz 1989).

Figure 3.3 shows the myriad of regulations and "spontaneous" business practices used to restrain competition. It also illustrates how regulation can reinforce cartelization. It is, for example, remarkable how often public regulation and/or trade barriers are associated with concentration and an oligopolistic market structure. The figure gives a snapshot of the state of competition in large segments of the Swedish tradable sector. A number of Swedish studies confirm that concentration, regulation, and the absence of international competition all have negative effects on productivity and growth (cf. Productivity Delegation 1991; Bourdet 1992).

The effects of weak competition may be divided into the following components: smaller output and higher prices; unnecessarily high costs and a low propensity to innovate; lobbying costs of special interest groups. A side effect is a politically undesired income redistribution in the form of excess profits (rents) in sheltered activities.

The role of regulation practice can be illustrated by reference to the two sectors that stand out as extreme in figure 3.3, namely, the food sector and the construction and housing sector. Together they account for almost half of private consumption in Sweden, and in

Chapter 3

	Few dominant firms	Little import competition	Public regulations	Vertical integration	Vertical recommended price lists	Vertical agreements	Horizontal integration	Horizontal recommended price lists	Horizontal agreements	Entry barriers — economies of scale	Entry barriers — other	Import barriers — technical	Import barriers — other
THE FOOD SECTOR													
Dairy products	●	●	●	●		●		●			●		●
Oils and fats	●	●	●	●							●		●
Meat	●	●	●	●		●			●		●		●
Bread and cereals	●	●	●	●									
Brewery products	●											●	
Canned and frozen products	●		●									●	
Food retail	●	●		●		●	●	●			●		
Agricultural fertilizers	●	●	●	●			●		●			●	
Agricultural machinery	●					●	●		●	●		●	
CONSTRUCTION													
Building contractors		●	●	●									
Building consultants		●	●										
Building material retail		●		●		●		●					
Cement	●	●		●						●		●	
Reinforcement steel	●	●								●		●	
Mineral wool	●	●		●		●					●	●	
Building boards	●	●		●								●	
Flat glass	●			●						●			
Door	●	●		●								●	
Windows	●	●		●	●							●	
Interior fittings, carpentry	●	●		●	●							●	
Floors	●			●				●					
Paints and varnishes	●	●				●		●					
Heating, ventilation, sanitation products	●	●										●	
Heating, ventilation, sanitation wholesale	●	●											
Heating, ventilation, sanitation installation		●						●					
Electrical material wholesale	●	●		●			●	●					
Electrical installation		●		●				●					
ENERGY													
Petroleum products	●		●	●	●	●					●		
Natural gas	●	—	●	●		●				●	●		
Electrical power	●	—	●	●		●	●		●		●		

Source: Konkurrensverket.

Figure 3.3
The state of competition in some industries

Efficiency

	Few dominant firms	Little import competition	Public regulations	Vertical integration	Vertical recommended price lists	Vertical agreements	Horizontal integration	Horizontal recommended price lists	Horizontal agreements	Entry barriers — economies of scale	Entry barriers — other	Import barriers — technical	Import barriers — other
PACKAGING MATERIAL													
Glass containers	●	●	●							●	●		
Plastic packaging material													
Aluminum cans	●	●	●							●	●		
Wood packaging material													
Heavy paper packaging	●	●		●					●				
Cartons	●	●		●		●	●				●		
PAPER AND PULP													
Pulp	●	●		●						●			
Paper for newspapers, magazines	●	●				●				●	●		
CONSUMER GOODS													
Apparel													
Eyeglasses					●								
Pharmaceuticals	●		●				●	●			●		
Newspapers	●	●	●		●								
Tissue paper	●	●									●		
Textbooks	●	●	●						●				
Electrical household appliances													
Automobiles and parts					●	●	●	●				●	
Auto repairs		—				●			●				
PRIVATE SERVICES													
Landry services		—	●					●					
Hotels		—											
Funerals	●	—									●		
Repairs of electrical appliances		—											
Repairs of/service on home electronics		—											
Service on computer equipment		—		●		●			●				

— = not relevant

both cases prices to consumers are very high in international comparison. Both sectors, too, have been subject to extensive government regulation for a long time. Originally the regulations were designed to favor well-defined interests, but in both cases they have had unanticipated and widespread side effects.

In the food sector the foundation was laid in the 1930s by regulating agriculture and raising import barriers in an attempt to protect farm incomes. In practice the regulation also served to protect suppliers of farm inputs (such as fertilizers and agricultural machinery) as well as the food industry, where farmers' cooperatives obtained a dominant position. (Their market share is 50%–100% in regulated food sectors.) The vertically integrated wholesale and retail industry for food had their purchasing prices determined through official discussions with a government body (the Consumer Delegation) followed by legislation in parliament. Considerable concentration of producers in the distribution sector and, as a consequence, weak competition followed. Entry barriers for new food stores under the municipal zoning authority (used to favor established stores) reduced competition further.

In the housing sector the foundation for government regulation was laid in the 1940s by introducing rent controls. The original purpose was to prevent soaring rents during wartime conditions, but it turned out to be politically impossible to remove controls after the war. That, however, made it necessary to introduce new regulations and subsidies. Artificially low rents led to a housing shortage and made subsidies a prerequisite for new construction. Subsidized construction, in turn, made it necessary to regulate in detail how one should build in order to qualify for subsidies, etc. (Meyerson, Ståhl, and Wickman 1990).

The inner logic of market regulations has over time made both of these sectors thoroughly regulated and subject to detailed planning with a cabinet minister and a ministry at the top (the ministry of housing was, however, recently abolished), inefficient production at the bottom, and an extensive regulatory bureaucracy in between. The system has also sustained influential special-interest organizations, which devote considerable resources to maintaining the system and squeezing out additional favors. Their rent-seeking activities are at best socially wasteful insofar that they only achieve redistribution; typically, however, they impair the functioning of the economy in the process.

In this kind of environment consumer interests come last. A telling example was given by top managers in producer cooperative food companies, who were asked in a study to rank the different "interested parties" that they took into account. Consumers came last—after the owners, regulatory authorities, administrative and political bodies, retailers and suppliers, competitors and opinion makers (Wikström 1993).

Consumers and taxpayers bear the costs of regulation. For the food sector the OECD has estimated the cost of regulation in Sweden at approximately 18 billion kronor in 1990. This corresponds to 8,500 kronor per family (of four). It corresponds to 300,000 kronor per full-time farmer, which may be compared to an average Swedish industrial worker wage (before tax), which in the same year amounts to 150,000 kronor. These are large sums, but they are nonetheless underestimated. The reason is that the costs are measured at the semimanufactured stage, where agricultural products are tradable, and therefore do not include direct and indirect costs at later stages of processing and distribution. According to a recent study of agricultural protection in the OECD countries, the total costs in Sweden amounted to around 18,000 kronor per family, or a little more than twice that estimated by the OECD (Bolin and Swedenborg 1992; Lipsey and Swedenborg 1993).

It is highly unlikely that parliament had approved cash transfers of this size, if they had been presented openly. It is even less likely that they had been approved if it had been known that most of these transfers do not accrue as income to farmers but instead become dissipated in higher costs at different stages of the production process. Agricultural regulation is—from a social point of view—a very inefficient method of income redistribution.

In the housing area, the market is distorted partly as a result of tax-financed housing subsidies—currently around 35 billion kronor (2.5% of GDP), and partly as a result of rent control. There are no comprehensive estimates of the total social cost. However, it is worth noting that rising construction costs have caused controlled rents to catch up with potential market rents in most of the country. It is mainly in central Stockholm that rent control is still effective. Otherwise, there is no longer excess demand for housing. That means that the whole regulatory apparatus could be dismantled without significantly raising average rents, except in Stockholm and perhaps a few other cities (Ståhl and Wickman 1992).

The above examples illustrate how regulations can impose substantial social costs. One set of regulations leads to further regulations. They create a distorted market structure and breed cartelization and higher costs, and in the end almost everyone is hurt. Initially regulations create capital gains for favored groups, for example, high farm values, low rents, and high (illegal) prices for rental contracts. That makes it difficult to deregulate, because deregulation would cause capital losses in the regulated sector—either for producers or consumers. The special interests supporting continued regulation thereby become substantial. A policy reversal creates other problems as well. Today's crisis in the Swedish construction sector is a particularly dramatic example of what may happen when an industry has to adjust to a lower level of subsidization and a more realistic market situation.

Conclusions

In the view of the commission, one of the most important tasks for economic policy is to restore a well-functioning market economy in Sweden. The welfare gains will be considerable. The ongoing integration with Europe will contribute to enhancing competition in Sweden. But it is mainly up to Swedish policy to create conditions for freer competition through deregulation and stricter antitrust legislation. To pursue such a policy forcefully, parliament ought to give the Competition Board extended authority under clear guidelines as well as strengthen the board's competence.

Two pending changes will significantly alter the state of competition in Sweden (Flam et al. 1993). One is the new antitrust legislation effective as of mid-1993. The other is the agreement on the European Economic Area (EEA), under which the reforms of the EC internal market will apply also to Sweden. In many areas these reforms—depending on their application—may be sufficient to restore vigorous competition in the Swedish economy. The new Swedish antitrust law is much stricter than the old law in that it actually forbids certain activities that reduce competition. Under the old law such activities were forbidden only if the competition authority could prove that they had harmful effects. The EEA agreement removes certain barriers to entry and to trade between the European countries, which will lead to increased specialization and more intensive competition. Important elements are the removal of nontariff barriers to trade as well as barriers to competition in services in the enlarged European market. There will also be new legislation requiring open competition in public procurement.

These changes will lay a foundation for a better-functioning market economy. But we also need to start a process of deregulation and, where possible, speed up the expected positive effects of internationalization. EC membership for Sweden may take a long time yet. Therefore there is a case for overhauling existing regulations and in some cases deregulating immediately. For example, we should consider introducing the new requirements for competition in public procurement unilaterally. We might also consider deregulating the transportation sector unilaterally by allowing foreign trucks to compete freely on domestic routes. Such deregulation is being planned in the EC.

Agriculture is an area in which future EC membership will entail a less desirable policy for consumers than what we might achieve on our own. Sweden has started to deregulate its agricultural sector. EC membership will mean re-regulating it. Today—because of both deregulation and the depreciation of the krona—Sweden is actually in the historically unique situation that we could allow free trade in some products (notably wheat) without adverse effects on farmers.

For reasons of both equity and efficiency, we suggest that rent control and most of the detailed building code regulating construction be abolished. Naturally one should take account of the income distribution effects of such changes, and there are several ways to remove various undesired side effects (see Ståhl and Wickman 1992). There is often a good case for safety regulations (such as protection against fire), but these can be designed so as not to hamper innovation, limit consumer choice, or raise costs as much as today. Some regulation can probably be replaced by rules for private liability.

One could argue that aggressive deregulation and increased competition would further aggravate the current recession and the crises in different industries. In some cases that might motivate gradual deregulation. But most policy changes take time to prepare, decide, and put into place, and their effects will be even further delayed. Therefore deregulation should be prepared and decided on as soon as possible so that it can be pursued vigorously when the economy recovers.

When it comes to the new antitrust legislation, there are good reasons to specify how one plans to apply it in practice and extend the area of application. The new law is a potentially powerful instrument. It allows the authorities to consider special circumstances in individual cases, which is an advantage, since it is impossible to establish beforehand which activities are harmful from an efficiency point of view. However, this also means that special interests could influence the way the law is applied, so-called regulatory capture. To reduce that risk and to make legal enforcement more predictable, we suggest that the antitrust legislation be specified in the form of guidelines, which are nonbinding but nevertheless spell out under what conditions a particular action is allowed and how the law will be applied. An interesting model is the official U.S. merger guidelines (Flam et al. 1993).

"Natural monopolies" require government regulation. Public natural monopolies should therefore not be privatized before one has determined whether and how they should be regulated.

We particularly want to stress the importance of free entry. Actual or potential entry by new firms in an industry is perhaps the most important factor disciplining firms' market behavior. Destruction of old firms and creation of new firms are indispensable features of a dynamic market economy. Officially sanctioned barriers to entry, such as licensing requirements and permits to set up a business, should therefore be avoided.

Several political reforms should serve to strengthen the general interest. One such reform would be to reexamine existing regulation at regular intervals (as with so-called sunset laws) and when doing so make its redistribution effects transparent. If parliament were to base its vote on an open account of the actual regulatory costs to taxpayers and consumers, they would probably be less prone to favor special interests at the expense of the general interest.

Another important reform would be to require that norms justifying income redistribution be openly presented. The same norms should ideally be applied to redistribution via regulation (and public consumption) as to redistribution via taxes and transfers. In taxation it is hard to enlist support for the principle that low-income earners should be taxed at a higher rate than high-income earners, that one professional group should be taxed differently than another, and that one category of home dwellers should be taxed differently than another. But this is exactly the kind of discrimination that takes place through regulatory policy.

A third reform that would have similar effects would be to diminish the influence of special interests in various public bodies (standing parliamentary committees, administrative bodies, etc.). One method that is sometimes advocated is to introduce stricter rules regarding conflicts of interest (e.g., farmers should not serve on the agriculture committee in parliament) or limitations on the length of time one can serve on parliamentary committees so as not to identify with special interests. A better method, however, to neutralize special interests is probably to give standing parliamentary committees a broader area of responsibility, for example, a general committee for industry including housing and agriculture along with other private industry. These kinds of institutional problems have not been analyzed much by economists, but the economic problems under consideration demand that they be addressed.

Proposals

Competition Policy

20. Abolish remaining officially sanctioned obstacles to competition in commerce and industry, including entry barriers.

21. Implement those aspects of the EEA agreement that will enhance competition, ahead of the established time schedule.

22. Do not adjust prematurely to those aspects of EC policy that inhibit competition, for instance by reintroducing export subsidies to the agricultural sector and the food industry.

23. Deregulate the housing and construction markets by dismantling rent controls and parts of the building code.

24. Codify, in the form of public guidelines, the new antitrust legislation, in order to increase predictability and to avoid "capture" from special interests.

25. Adapt the pace of deregulation so as not to aggravate the current recession, but take the necessary decisions immediately.

26. Increase the authority and competence of the Competition Board, allowing it to monitor competition in the entire economy, including the public sector.

27. Make regulations subject to reconsideration in parliament at regular intervals; on such occasions, the costs of the regulations to consumers and taxpayers should be clearly exposed.

Regulations in the Labor Market

The labor market is one of the most regulated markets in Sweden, as in many other countries. Regulations include some ninety laws and ordinances. In addition, there are numerous rules determined through collective bargaining. Such negotiated agreements are binding whenever the employer or the employee is organized. Extraordinarily high unionization in Sweden—80%–90% of the labor force—means that such rules apply to most of the labor force.

The purpose of this extensive government regulation is multifold: to increase the job security and general safety of the individual; to allow time for the individual who loses his job to find new employment; to increase the influence of employees in their workplace; to satisfy the desire of individuals for recreation and education; to make it easier for employees to stay home and take care of small children and sick family members, etc.

The regulations in the labor market may be well intended. Nevertheless, they entail considerable costs—like the regulations in goods markets. In fact, the pervasive role of the labor market means that these regulations affect the whole economy. The Swedish debate, as well as modern research, has focused on five kinds of legislated rules, namely, rules regulating temporary employment contracts (for example, in connection with trial employment periods or during peak periods), layoffs, seniority rules, contracting out, and labor-market disputes (Sigeman 1991). The first two were discussed in chapter 2, as they may have profound effects on unemployment and therefore are relevant for finding a way out of the current unemployment crisis. Here we will discuss the remaining three sets of rules, as they may be expected to affect the efficiency of the labor market.

Rules regulating layoffs and seniority have to do with when and why an employee may be fired, which workers may be laid off when the workforce is reduced ("last in, first out"), as well as the right of laid-off workers to reemployment if and when the employer rehires. Unfortunately there is not much reliable empirical research on the effects of such rules (Holmlund 1993). However, one would expect that the rules would increase the short-term security of an individual in his job, because the rules specify who runs the highest risk of losing his job. This is, of course, the intended effect. A worker who loses his job because of low seniority may also find it easier to get a new job than a worker who is fired because he is not so attractive to the firm; the "stigmatization" of a fired worker may be smaller in the first case.

However, the rules also make it easier for those who have been employed for a long time, and hence have seniority, to demand large wage increases without risking their jobs. This is similar to the effect of severance pay. As a consequence, aggregate labor demand may be kept down.

The rules can also make it difficult for employers to retain those employees that they consider most valuable when they have to reduce the workforce. It is true that seniority rules may be set aside, but only if employers and unions can reach agreement on this in collective bargaining. This, clearly, is a cumbersome and costly method. Also, many small firms are not covered by the collective bargaining agreements. Many firms may therefore find it difficult, even prohibitive, to retain their most valuable workers (perhaps younger and better educated) when forced to cut down. The requirement that laid-off workers with the highest (previous) seniority must be rehired first should have similar effects.

The job security laws have also made it more difficult, or more expensive, to fire workers for shirking or showing gross negligence in their work. The rules on layoffs due to "lack of work" are less problematic for the employer, since he himself determines what constitutes lack of work. The rules requiring consultation between management and employees on many issues also appear to work reasonably well; many firms regard this kind of mutual involvement as an advantage.

Contracting out is also regulated by the government; unions have the right to veto an employer's wish to contract out work, except in the vaguely defined situation when the required competence is lacking within the firm. These rules can no doubt increase the short-term job security experienced by those already in the firm (insiders). The flip side of that, again, is that the insiders may be able to raise their wages, while keeping the unemployed (outsiders) from getting work. The rules can also hamper work specialization and hence efficiency. Problems may also arise when the negotiating parties, in collective bargaining, agree to a list of approved contractors; such a list could restrain competition in goods markets.

Much of the job security legislation seems adapted to a static economy with homogeneous labor and a Tayloristic work organization (that is, routine, assembly-line type work). It seems less appropriate for today's dynamic—even turbulent—world with increasingly heterogeneous labor and increased demands on firms' ability to adjust.

The modern theory of the firm sees the firm as a bundle of contracts, with a web of relations to other firms, which make it difficult to define the boundaries between the firm and the market; contracting out is often located in this vague boundary area. Government regulation that complicates contracting out, therefore, limits the firm's ability to adjust to new conditions.

Limitations on the firm's right to contract out are often defended by a desire to block "nonserious" subcontractors, specifically those hiring "illegal labor" (paying nonunion wages or evading taxes). Unions are apparently thought to have information about which firms rely on such labor. However, fighting the black labor market is a police function that should not—according to the principles that the commission adheres to—be entrusted to a special-interest organization. If one were to abolish the right of unions to veto contracting out, one could instead devote increased government resources to fighting economic crimes—which we propose for other reasons later on.

The right to use various conflict measures in labor disputes is very generous in Sweden. One example is the right to strike in support of employees in other firms. Another example is the right of public employees to strike, a right that extends to public authorities. The right of public-employee unions to select key employees for a strike gives public employees in Sweden a particularly powerful weapon, one that is forbidden in most other countries. A further example is the right to block out firms that employ nonunion labor, even when these firms are not involved in any labor dispute.

It is also remarkable how lightly both legislation and the courts have treated certain contract violations in the labor market, especially in the case of wildcat strikes. Penalties have recently been raised, but they are still very small compared to the penalties for other types of contract violations.

Conclusions

It seems clear that some labor market regulations create a conflict between short-term job security for the individual and the need for a well-functioning labor market and flexible firms. It is likely that the negative effects for society as a whole have increased over time, as the need for flexibility in the economy has increased. If current legislation represented a reasonable trade-off between distribution and efficiency when it was first introduced, there should be good reasons to change it now to allow for more flexibility and growth.

Job security legislation also implies a conflict between the security of those who have jobs and have had them for a long time, on the one hand, and those who are seeking work, on the other. A high wage level and legislated job security for insiders come partly at the expense of the rights of outsiders. They particularly hurt weak groups in the labor market, mainly youths and unskilled workers, including some immigrant groups. Their productivity is often not high enough to justify union wages, including employer contributions, when they first enter the labor market. They are then forced into a vicious circle: if they never get a foothold in the labor market, they will never gain the experience that could motivate the higher wage (Ståhl 1993). This is a very serious problem for many youths and immigrants. It is also a growing problem with the drastically increased immigration in recent years.

We refrain from detailed proposals on labor legislation, because a special government committee is currently examining many of these issues. In our view, however, it is not sufficient to modify the rules regulating hiring and firing of workers, as we suggested in chapter 2. It is also necessary to undertake other reforms, in particular, liberalizing the seniority rules and abolishing restrictions on the right to contract out. These latter reforms are motivated by long-run efficiency—as well as equity—reasons.

It is possible that liberalizing seniority rules, as an isolated measure, might lead to more early retirements, as firms do not bear the cost of early retirement. This merely reinforces an argument we will make later: that the rules for early retirement should be coordinated with those governing sickness and work injury. Firms should also be made to bear a considerable share of the cost of these insurance schemes. Such a reform is urgent, because there are signs that the rate of early retirement is increasing rapidly.

Regulatory reform in the labor market will obviously have redistribution effects. It is difficult to quantify these, however. If the rules are changed in the direction we propose, insiders stand to lose in the short term, while outsiders stand to gain through improved opportunities to become employed. Ultimately such redistribution effects must be weighed against the long-term gain in efficiency that will accrue to large population groups.

Proposals

The Labor Market

28. Liberalize or abolish the present rules governing the dismissal and reemployment of labor. If the rules are modified rather than abolished, each firm could be given a certain quota within which the rules do not apply.

29. Firms should be responsible for a substantial share of the costs of early retirement pensions, in order to reduce the temptation to place the burden of shedding labor on the taxpayers.

30. Abolish the trade union's right to veto contracts by tender.

31. Abolish the right to blockade enterprises with unorganized labor that are not involved in a conflict, unless the employees request such a measure.

32. Breaches of contract in the labor market should result in sanctions, as severe as elsewhere.

Financial Markets after the Financial Crisis

In chapter 2 we discussed different methods for quickly guaranteeing or restoring the capital base of banks, that is, recapitalizing the banks, which would allow credit expansion and a smaller gap between banks' lending and borrowing rates.

It is also desirable to avoid future banking crises. The most important lessons taught by the 1980s is perhaps (1) that monetary and fiscal policy should not once more be allowed to overheat the economy; (2) that regulatory reforms in financial markets should be carried out with great caution; and (3) that individuals and institutions need to acquire more knowledge and experience in working in a deregulated environment.

It is essential to deal with today's crisis in the financial sector in a way that is consistent with long-term efficiency, as a number of complications may follow in the wake of the financial crisis:

• Banks might again be tempted to take excessive risks if they believe that the taxpayers will foot the bill; thus today's handling of the crisis may create new problems of "moral hazard." However, unpleasant memories of the recent past probably prevent this from happening again in the near future. The immediate problem is more likely the opposite: the banks may have become overly cautious in their lending decisions.

• It is inevitable that competitive conditions among banks become distorted as a result of selective government rescue actions for certain banks. But it is important that these distortions are minimized, which was a guiding principle for our proposals in chapter 2.

• A well-functioning and competitive financial market requires many players and a multitude of financial instruments. Therefore it is essential that government policy facilitates the emergence of new owners and new financial institutions. The Swedish banking sector is strongly cartelized, and this allows it to maintain large gaps between lending and borrowing rates.

• It is important to quickly get away not only from government ownership of banks, but also from comprehensive government guarantees. Such guarantees are not consistent with a competitive system, as new entrants are likely to be discriminated against as long as the guarantees are in place.

One way out of the broad guarantees offered today may be for the government in the future to limit such guarantees to the payment system as such rather than giving them to all financial institutions. In this context it is worth considering limiting government insurance to so-called narrow banks, which only hold low-risk assets (Urwitz and Viotti 1993). Such banks can offer the general public various types of deposit accounts, including checking accounts, and thereby provide a functioning payment system. In return for the guarantees, these banks should hold only government bonds on their asset side. Banks that wish to engage in private lending should have to raise the necessary funds from sources that are not insured by the government. There is no reason why a narrow bank cannot be a part of a financial conglomerate. To avoid the government guarantee affecting other parts of the conglomerate, it is necessary that the operations of the narrow bank can be effectively audited and separated from the rest of the company.

Pluralism and competition are needed not only in the banking sector, but also in the bond and money markets. An important step in this direction would be to split up the enormous concentration created by the large government social security fund (the AP fund). This fund, which holds approximately 35% of all bonds in Sweden, should be subdivided into many independent institutions, each with its own professional board. Normal competition is not possible with such a dominant player, because other players in the market have to guess at all times how the major player will behave.

The foreign exchange market, too, lacks the pluralism and number of actors necessary for a well-functioning market. Ever since the krona started floating, the margin between buying and selling rates has been wide. When the Riksbank ceased "being the market," foreign exchange traders seem to have suffered from a kind of "learned helplessness." New market makers are needed in the foreign exchange market to balance the three major banks.

There is also a need to provide the private sector with risk capital. The banks may have become overly averse to risk taking after their recent experience. More private shareholders and more large shareholders who are willing to assume long-term responsibility as active owners are needed.

Capitalism cannot function without capitalists—despite apparent hopes to that effect among some Swedish social reformers. Private wealth accumulation is impossible as long as private saving is discriminated against, as it has been in Sweden during several decades, especially prior to the 1991 tax reform. From this viewpoint, the recent increase in saving is encouraging, though the increase was so abrupt that the economy could not adjust to it in the midst of a deep recession. The Swedish saving rate has simply approached that of other developed countries.

It is also important to stimulate the emergence of a larger number of institutions that not only hold shares, but are also willing to play an active ownership role. The government has recently contributed in this regard by dissolving the large so-called wage-earners funds (controlled by government-appointed individuals) and by channelling some of these funds to a number of separate venture capital companies. But more is needed for a well-functioning risk capital market. For reasons that will be made clear, we propose that the social insurance system in Sweden be reorganized to allow for increased private insurance. That could greatly increase the market for risk capital, especially shareholding, in Sweden. The goal should be a capital market with a large number of actors and many diverse financial instruments.

PROPOSALS

> *The Financial Market*
>
> 33. Major changes in the regulatory framework of the credit and capital markets should be carried out with greater caution than during the 1980s.
>
> 34. Divide the General Pension Funds into independent units, to improve the functioning of the bond market.
>
> 35. Consider guaranteeing the payment system without guaranteeing bank credit. A possible method is to introduce so-called narrow banks, whose deposits are guaranteed, and whose assets consists solely of government bonds; they would still be fully equipped to handle all types of accounts, including checking accounts.
>
> 36. Stimulate increased diversity in financial markets, not only by selling (parts of) the banks taken over by the government to new, Swedish or foreign, owners (point 12), but also by avoiding situations where private shareholders are treated less favorably than institutional owners.
>
> 37. Create more leeway for private income insurance to broaden the stock market.

The Public Sector

The Crisis of the Welfare State

The crisis of the welfare state is a crisis of efficiency and credibility. Public-sector monopoly in the production of public services leads to unnecessarily high costs. Tax-financed provision of services makes it difficult to know whether these are provided in the amount and quality desired by individual consumers. Moreover, expenditure programs—whether they involve services or transfer payments—and associated tax finance create incentive problems in the private sector.

Many citizens have also begun to doubt that the ambitious goals of the welfare state can be achieved in the future. This doubt is nourished by the present large public-sector deficits and the threat-

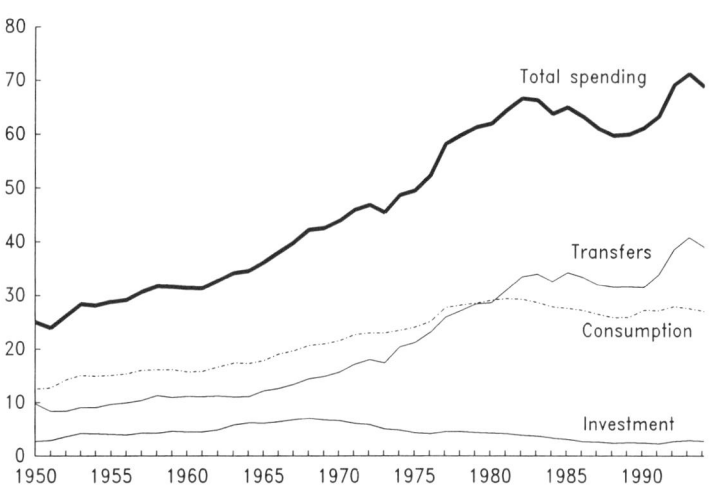

Figure 3.4
Public-sector expenditures 1950–1993, relative to GDP (percent)

ening financial crisis in local governments; the latter will probably necessitate reductions in the provision of many publicly provided services, including child care, health care, and various other social services.

Behind these problems lies an apparent difficulty for the political process during recent decades to set limits on the scope and generosity of the welfare state. Figure 3.4 shows the growth of public expenditure. Public spending has grown from approximately 25% of GDP in the early 1950s to the present level of more than 70% of GDP, which is the highest in the OECD area. (As earlier pointed out, it should be observed that some benefits that are taxed in Sweden are untaxed in other countries. In terms of *net* government expenditures, Sweden is therefore somewhat less extreme than what these gross figures would suggest.) Both transfer payments and public consumption have contributed to the expansion. The number of public employees has increased from fewer than 500,000 in 1960 to about 1,600,000 in 1993.

The generous systems of public support make it tempting for individuals to exploit these instead of trying to improve their standard of living through productive effort. High marginal tax rates add to this temptation, because they make it more difficult for individuals to raise their income and consumption level by work in the open labor market.

A main task for Swedish economic policy must be to deal with these problems through structural reform. Many observers became aware of these problems during the economic crisis in the early 1980s, when the public-sector deficits reached crisis proportions, the rate of economic growth was low, and unemployment was high. As the economy turned around after large devaluations, assisted by an international boom, employment increased and the deficit fell, and the awareness of the need for structural reforms seemingly faded. Today we have to solve the same set of problems in a much more difficult situation, where the growth impulse from the private sector is weaker and the public-sector deficit is higher.

Ideally, the amount of public-sector spending should be determined by a calculation of the costs and benefits of public expenditure. Against the value of increased public-sector spending one should then set not only the *direct* costs of the necessary tax payments; one should add the *indirect* economic cost due to distorting effects of taxes on the behavior of consumers and producers. As a realistic example, let us assume that one krona of increased tax revenue causes a further indirect distortionary cost of .5 krona. This implies that an additional public expenditure should be undertaken only if it generates benefits at least 1.5 times as large as the tax payments required to finance it.

However, this kind of calculation is rarely made in the political process. Therefore we need a set of constitutional rules that require that public expenditure decisions be based on a more realistic assessment of benefits and costs. The reforms of the budget process that we propose in chapter 5 (and to some extent in chapter 2) aim precisely at this. Without rules that require that the gains to society are set clearly against all the costs, the list of desirable public activities can be made arbitrarily long.

It is of course impossible to evaluate the activities of the welfare state without taking a position on the appropriate division of responsibilities between the individual and the state. As emphasized in chapter 1, we envisage a society in which each individual takes more responsibility than she does today in Sweden for her allocation of consumption over time, for the economic security of herself and her family, and for her use of health care and other social services.

In the following we discuss different aspects of the welfare state: the tax system, social insurance, and the production of social services. We conclude by providing concrete examples of how one could actually carry out the budget savings necessary to stabilize the public debt.

Continued Tax Reform

A common view, which we share, is that the Swedish tax system, in particular during the last two decades, has distorted economic incentives and led to a waste of resources. The 1991 tax reform marks a significant improvement of the system. The previous patchwork of distortionary taxes has been replaced by a unified and broad-based tax system with moderate marginal rates of income tax. The tax reform was a substantial achievement of the political process, in that long-term considerations of the general interest triumphed over the short-run demands by special-interest groups. We consider it of utmost importance to preserve the gains made by the 1991 reform.

We also believe that it is important to avoid further tax increases and to agree on a program for further gradual tax reductions in the long run. Otherwise, those who were led by the reform to expect a more stable environment, with reasonable returns to education, work, and saving, might be disappointed in their expectations for a long time ahead. The government may badly need some increased revenue in the short run to reduce the current large deficits. If so, we recommend that it raise revenue by increasing the actuarial premia in the social security system, as well as by actually collecting decided taxes more efficiently.

The 1991 tax reform lessened the distortionary impact of the tax system, but with public expenditure of 60%–70% of GDP, the tax wedges are still substantial for most households. High-income earners with a marginal tax rate of 50% have a total marginal tax wedge of approximately 70%, while the total tax wedge for the majority of income earners is about 60%. In this calculation we have taken account not only of the income tax, but also the value-added tax, the (pure tax element of the) payroll tax, and the reduction of income-related contributions (rent subsidies, child support, etc.) when income increases.

At the present level of public expenditure there is not much that one can do to reduce the tax wedges. However, a few remaining weaknesses in the tax system can be corrected without changing the overall tax level. One such weakness is the nominal taxation of capital gains and capital income, which means that the real tax burden varies with the rate of inflation. It is difficult to justify a tax system in which inflation determines the real marginal tax rate. While the real marginal tax on capital income is 30% in the absence of inflation, it may well come close to 100% with 10% inflation (depending on how sensitive nominal rates of interest are to the rate of inflation). A switch to "real taxation," where higher inflation does not automatically lead to higher taxation in real terms, would be a definite advantage. This would also fit well with the system of indexed bonds that we proposed in chapter 2. "Real taxation" would obviously imply that the tax level as a share of GDP would no longer increase with inflation. But this is just the other side of the requirement that the tax burden of individuals should be independent of inflation.

The double taxation of corporate dividends is another weakness. The corporate income tax as a whole gives few reasons for complaint; it is at a modest level compared to that of other countries. But the double taxation of dividends distorts the cost of equity capital. It has different consequences for large and small firms, as large firms can more easily raise equity capital abroad. Because many other countries now have single taxation of dividends, it becomes more profitable for foreigners than for Swedes to own shares in Swedish firms.

Consequently, for large corporations the problem of double taxation is not that capital accumulation in Sweden is hampered by high costs of capital; the problem is rather that a large part of Sweden's corporations may come to be owned by foreigners just because of our tax legislation. It is difficult to see any reason why we should encourage foreigners to buy up Swedish corporations by way of discriminatory taxes; thus there is a case for abolishing the double taxation of dividends. If one should want to stimulate foreign investment in Sweden, there are other methods that do not discriminate against Swedish shareholders. For small or medium-sized firms with limited access to international equity markets, double taxation will lead to a higher cost of capital than would single taxation, as well as to a higher cost of capital than for large firms. This adds to the case for abolishing the double taxation of dividends.

In principle there are two ways to solve this problem. One may either abolish the corporate income tax or remove the taxation of dividends in the personal income tax. There are strong reasons to choose the latter alternative, because the corporate income tax may be the only available instrument for taxing foreign incomes from share ownership in Swedish firms.

Such a reform would be costly in terms of tax revenue; the revenue loss might be of an order of magnitude of 5 billion kronor (0.4% of GDP). It would also lead to a redistribution of income in favor of shareholders. Both these effects could be counteracted by refraining from the planned reduction in the corporate income tax from 30% to 25%.

The taxation of small businesses has long been a serious problem, but in recent years much has been done to solve it, though more could certainly be done. For instance, in addition to the double taxation problem, the inheritance tax remains a problem, as it makes it difficult to pass the ownership of a business on to the next generation.

It is important that taxes are visible. Stores are required by law to display their prices; it is equally reasonable to require that taxpayers receive correct information about the taxes they pay. In the absence of such information it is not possible for them to make rational calculations. This implies not only that the value-added tax should be accounted for on all sales receipts; it means also that employers' income statements to their employees should include information about payroll taxes. It is furthermore important that local taxes be made as visible as possible, especially when the current freeze on local tax rates is abolished.

The government should also make an increased effort to ensure that taxes due are in fact paid. Each year tens of billions of kronor illegally avoid taxation. At least some of this amount could be collected by combining more resources with better coordination between the police, the public prosecutor, and the tax authorities (National Council for Crime Prevention 1991). The return on additional resources in this area appears to be very high.

PROPOSALS

Taxation

38. Adhere to the principles of the 1991 tax reform; do not increase marginal tax rates; avoid introducing new asymmetries into the tax system.

39. Index capital taxation, so that real tax rates become independent of the inflation rate.

40. Eliminate double taxation of corporate profits by repealing the tax on dividends to shareholders. Compensate for the loss of tax revenues by not reducing the corporate tax rate from 30% to 25%.

41. By using tax reform to make shareholding as advantageous for individuals as for institutions (point 36), current discrimination in the supply of equity capital to small enterprises could be curtailed.

42. Taxes should be made as visible as possible; they should also be called taxes and not fees; the gross wage, including payroll taxes, should be reported along with the wage payment.

43. Intensify measures against economic crime, so that more of the taxes decided upon by the Parliament are actually paid.

Social Security Reforms

Social security is the collective term for a number of public income insurance schemes. Figure 3.5 shows what is involved and how the various components of social security have developed over time. Altogether the gross expenditure on social insurance (exclusive of

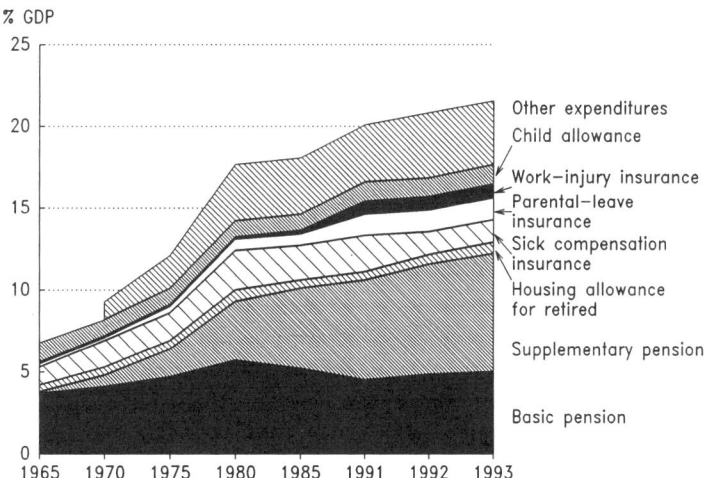

Source: Riksförsäkringsverket.

Figure 3.5
Social insurance payments, relative to GDP (percent)

unemployment insurance) has increased from less than 7% of GDP in 1965 to more than 20% at the present time. The diagram shows that one can trace most of the increase to the ATP system (the income-related pension scheme) and "other expenditure," which includes dental care and medication. Individuals' adjustment to changes in rules explains much of the expenditure development. More liberal rules (introduced in 1977) governing work-injury insurance contributed to increased expenditure. Stricter rules for sickness compensation, on the other hand, contributed to decreased expenditure in 1991 and 1992. The social insurance system aims at creating income safety and at redistributing income over an individual's lifetime. The academic literature has focused on two justifications for such a system to be mandatory:

• *The free-rider argument.* In the absence of mandatory social insurance, some individuals would choose not to save or not to insure themselves; they count on others, in particular the taxpayers, to assist them should the need arise.

• *The paternalistic argument.* Without a mandatory system, some individuals might underestimate their need for saving and insurance.

In health and life insurance, one must also take into account:

• *The adverse selection argument.* High-risk individuals may find it difficult to buy insurance on a voluntary basis, if their high-risk status is known by the insurance companies. If it is not known, their high risk may instead raise insurance costs for their fellow citizens, some of whom will then choose not to obtain insurance.

In discussing the future of social security, it is important to keep the distinction between these arguments in mind.

Problems
It is now generally recognized that social insurance systems are also associated with serious problems:

• Because tax finance predominates, the social security system adds to the tax wedges.

• Difficulties in raising the necessary tax finance contributes to the public-sector deficits in certain periods.

• With existing pay-as-you-go systems, demographic changes as well as variations in GDP growth cause instability in the distribution of income between various groups in society, for example, between retired people and employees. This is one of the weaknesses of the present ATP system. In particular, a period of declining GDP, as in 1991–93, results in a substantial redistribution of relative income in favor of the retired.

- Some individuals, not originally intended to be beneficiaries of the system, have adjusted their behavior so as to become just that (the problem of moral hazard). The general view of what constitutes sickness (including the view of the administrators of the system), is influenced by the system of benefits, particularly if the symptoms of sickness are diffuse.
- Some people are tempted to abuse benefits. The authorities are forced to apply close controls to stop the abuse, if the legitimacy of the system is not to be undermined.
- Within certain systems—particularly work-injury insurance and early retirement pensions—the criteria for benefits have not been sufficiently restrictive.

Sweden is far from the only country having serious problems with its social insurance and other transfer systems (see Scherman 1993; Söderström 1993; and Korpi and Palme 1993). But because our systems have, for a long time, been relatively generous, the problems here have acquired larger dimensions than in most other European countries.

Repair Work Under Way
It would seem that the repair work on the social security system that has recently been initiated will solve some of these problems. Increased co-insurance, or deductibles, which have recently been introduced in some systems, are important for all kinds of insurance to lessen problems of moral hazard and abuse. Within the health insurance system wage earners now carry some risk themselves in the form of one unpaid day of absence (deductible) and a lower level of compensation (co-insurance) than before. Employers bear some of the costs by having to pay sickness wages during the first fourteen days of absence. For nonpermanent injuries from work, the previous 100% replacement ratio will be reduced through coordination of work-injury insurance with health insurance; moreover, the burden of proof of work injury will be moved back to the person filing a

claim for compensation. There are also current proposals for somewhat higher wage earners' contribution to work-injury insurance and for less advantageous conditions for part-time pensions. These are further examples of current and suggested steps in the direction of a more efficient social security system.

Long-Run System Design
When discussing reforms of social security, it is useful to begin by considering long-run reforms. In our opinion, the argument for mandatory insurance is weaker the higher an individual's income. In a rich society it is reasonable to make stronger demands than in a poor society on the individual's ability to insure his income himself, beyond the level provided by the state. Thus the free-rider motive becomes less relevant when the level of individual income increases, both in absolute terms and relative to others.

If one wishes to move toward a society with more individual responsibility, there are good reasons to limit compensation in the mandatory systems to a form of basic assistance. This may be a fixed amount, the same for everybody, or it may be income dependent up to a certain level. The very idea of basic assistance must imply a ceiling on the mandatory benefit level, which is low enough for large groups to find it attractive to acquire additional insurance by themselves. The individual need for income insurance above the basic assistance level could then, to a considerable extent, be left to voluntary insurance, individual or collective.

There are three alternatives for the long-run design of a mandatory basic assistance system:

Alternative 1: Basic assistance that is independent of income.

Alternative 2: Basic assistance that increases with income.

Alternative 3: Basic assistance that decreases with income.

Alternative 1 is more favorable than the present system for low income earners, because the finance of the system is likely to be income-dependent with fees (taxes) that are either proportional or progressive.

Within alternative 2, one can imagine different degrees of compensation for the loss of income, with a purely actuarial system having the closest dependence of benefits on earlier payments; in this case the expected value of the benefits is equal to the expected value of the individual's payments. For the concept of basic assistance to be meaningful, under such a system the ceiling for benefits and fees must not be so high that many or most people do not see any need for further income insurance.

Under alternative 3, the benefits would fall rather than rise with increasing incomes. One could imagine either a set of fixed rules governing the relation between incomes and benefits (as in various versions of the negative income tax), or discretionary assessment of every individual's need for support (as in social assistance schemes). The latter case would mark the transition from "universal" to "selective" social policy. Universal, or generalized, social policy had been a hallmark of the Swedish welfare system. Selective policies, however, may seem to be particularly attractive from the point of view of low-income groups. But a well-known and serious problem with such systems is that individuals and households with low incomes would face very high marginal tax rates; this is frequently referred to as poverty traps. We therefore caution against constructions of this type, except in the case of social assistance that will remain the lowest of the social safety nets.

The frequent occurrence of poverty traps is, to some extent, due to different systems having been designed independently of each other, without regard for the combined marginal effect. A general public pension, provided in equal amounts to all, can be seen as a way to hold down the number of people applying for social assistance. Such basic assistance evidently implies somewhat higher public expenditure than selective social assistance, but it involves lower administrative costs and less government control over individual lives.

Mandatory basic assistance should in our opinion be founded on four basic principles: One, the system should not seriously harm the economy by creating distorted incentives. Two, the system should be *economically robust* in the long run. Benefits should be sensitive to developments in the economy, so that variations in the growth of population and GDP do not lead to unreasonable shifts in the distribution of income between the beneficiaries and the working population. Three, the system should be *politically robust*; it should be easy to understand and it should command broad political support. This presupposes that it is generally regarded as reasonable and fair. Four, the system should be protected from the vagaries of day-to-day politics. Benefits should be difficult to change through political intervention, motivated by the needs of stabilization policy or by fluctuations in redistributional ambitions. Citizens must be able to plan their lives on the basis of a relatively stable environment.

The fourth principle argues for removing social insurance from the government budget. Such a reform would increase the possibility of long-run stable contracts between individuals and the insuring institution. A related argument is that such a removal would diminish the risk of "overexpansion." According to many observers (see Scherman 1993), the development of the Swedish system up to now can only be explained by its central role in the political process.

An important question is whether the basic assistance scheme, if the financing is removed from the government budget, should even be managed within the public sector. One argument for having the system publicly managed is to keep down the administrative costs; there are some obvious economies of scale both in the collection of fees and in the payment of benefits.

If instead the management of the basic assistance system is left to the private sector, given that participation is mandatory for all citizens, the role of the government will be to regulate and control the insurance institutions that operate the system. The most important argument in favor of this solution is that it will reap some benefits of competition, and freedom of choice for consumers, even though it might result in higher costs. There is evidently a trade-off between the amount of regulation on the one hand and the degree of competition and freedom of choice on the other.

Removing social security from the government budget and ensuring that the system is independent is yet another application of our general idea that there ought to be clear divisions of responsibility in society. The political system ought to delegate certain tasks to institutions that are protected from short-run political interference. There is an obvious parallel here to our proposal that the central bank have a position of considerable independence.

If this removal is carried out, it is important that the system be self-financed, whether it be funded or not. But one should not replace a system of state control by a system of corporatist control—that is, joint control by employer and labor organizations—as has been proposed for health insurance. This again follows from our view that it is desirable to reduce the confusion of roles between private organizations and the state. It is important that individual workers and firms are able to decide on their insurance coverage independently of the organizations in the labor market. Moreover, powerful labor-market organizations should not, in our opinion, also become powerful in the capital market—which is just what they would be with large funded systems of the corporatist type. If the government gives up its monopoly, it is reasonable that individuals should have the right to choose their own insurance company.

The ceiling in the mandatory systems should not be set so high as to undermine the whole idea of a basic assistance. At present the ceiling is 7.5 times the so-called basic amount. (Currently only about 10% of income earners reach this ceiling. The basic amount is an administratively decided sum that is raised each year to keep pace with inflation. It is used in various parts of the social insurance system and is currently about 33,000 SEK, about U.S. $4,000.)

We do not take a position on the choice between the case where the basic assistance is a fixed amount for all and the case where it increases with income. In reality, one would often expect a combination of the two; the benefits must then not only have a ceiling, but also a floor. This floor cannot be lower than the social welfare norm.

If one follows the principle of providing insurance against income loss, we believe that the compensation level should be at 70%–80% of previous income. Moreover, the system ought to be actuarially fair, so that the expected value of benefits is equal to the expected value of fees. This principle is easiest to achieve for health insurance and old-age pensions. (It is an open question whether, and to what extent, fees should be differentiated between groups of individuals according to their risk.)

Concerning unemployment insurance, we have already proposed that higher fees be paid by individuals and individual firms. (Today the government pays more than 90% of the cost.) One suggestion is to let workers, firms, and the government each pay one-third of the total fees, as they are all, in some sense, responsible for unemployment. Here too, we recommend a mandatory system, but with the basic insurance held with an insurer of the individual's choice. The insurers would then have strong incentives to keep down the cost of unemployment, for example, by organizing and financing training for the unemployed, which maximizes the probability of getting a new job (see Calmfors 1993). But insurers should not be allowed to refuse insurance to particular individuals in the insured group.

As regards health and work-injury insurance, we propose that they be integrated into a single system with a uniform compensation level. Both health insurance and work-injury insurance should incorporate an element of co-insurance, both for the employee and the employer. The premia should therefore be differentiated between firms according to their observed frequency of work injuries; the intention here is to avoid subsidizing sectors and firms with particularly large risks of work accidents. Work-injury insurance should be designed as a mandatory insurance for well specified injuries and not for diffuse symptoms.

In this extended health insurance system we would include what was previously called "sickness pension," that is, the present early retirement pension. To qualify for this, a satisfactory medical certificate should be considered absolutely necessary. Early retirement "for labor market reasons," which is in principle disallowed under the existing rules, should also be prevented in practice, which requires stricter application of the rules. Firms should pay part of the cost of early retirement of employees.

In a similar vein, we have not taken a position on the choice between fixed and income-related basic assistance. We do not have a firm view on whether the ceiling should be constant or increase with the level of real income in society. If the present ceiling (of 7.5 times the "basic amount" of social security) remains constant in terms of purchasing power, it will eventually, with growing real incomes, become a basic assistance with the same amount for almost everybody. The more weight one gives to the free-rider argument for social security—and hence to the idea of basic assistance—and the less to the paternalistic argument, the less reason there is to increase the ceiling in response to real income growth.

Voluntary individual and group insurance on top of the mandatory system leads to complications. The reason is that abuse at high levels of total compensation not only hurts the voluntary supplementary systems, but also increases the costs in the mandatory systems. The simplest way to avoid this is to deduct private insurance payments, in excess of a certain level, from the benefits under the mandatory insurance. This corresponds to the manner in which private insurance companies handle the problem of "overinsurance" (see Wadensjö 1993; and Scherman 1993).

In some cases individuals can, at their own discretion, move between different kinds of insurance systems to obtain as favorable conditions as possible, for example, between unemployment insurance, work-injury insurance, health insurance, and compensation for looking after sick children. To avoid such "benefit arbitrage" the various systems should be as uniform as possible. The principle is the same as in the 1991 tax reform, where the intention was to strive for uniformity of rules to prevent tax arbitrage.

We would expect that insurance systems outside the public sector will more often be funded than government-operated systems. One reason is that a nongovernment system cannot rely on the power of taxation in the case of future strains on the system. There is no doubt some advantage for society as a whole with funded systems. One advantage that is often advanced is that a funded system would lead to higher saving than nonfunded schemes (even if actuarial). The reason is the limited ability of individuals to borrow against their funded pension insurance. In the case of funded systems, it is important also to consider the consequences for the functioning of the capital market.

Our proposal of letting the insured themselves choose their insurance institution is in line with our previous recommendation of promoting a capital market with a plurality of agents.

Those transfer systems that are not insurance systems in a strict sense should be removed from the social insurance sector. One example is the so-called parental leave insurance, which, although it provides compensation according to the principle of income loss, is not insurance in the sense of covering an insurable risk. Regular dental care is also not an insurable risk; however, there is a need for an insurance to cover excessive costs. Both parental leave and (normal) dental care insurance should be reclassified as allowances; together with other purely tax-financed transfer systems they should remain within the government budget.

Several reforms have recently been passed to make conditions in different parts of social security more uniform. Some of the arbitrage possibilities between the various parts of the system have thereby been eliminated, but figure 3.6 shows how complicated, and asymmetric, the social insurance and transfer system still is.

Figure 3.7 illustrates the type of system that we propose, with a floor, a ceiling, and (possibly) an income-dependent part in between. As a special case there would be no mandatory income-dependent part at all. The mandatory system would in that case only contain a fixed amount: the floor and the ceiling in figure 3.7 would coincide.

Chapter 3

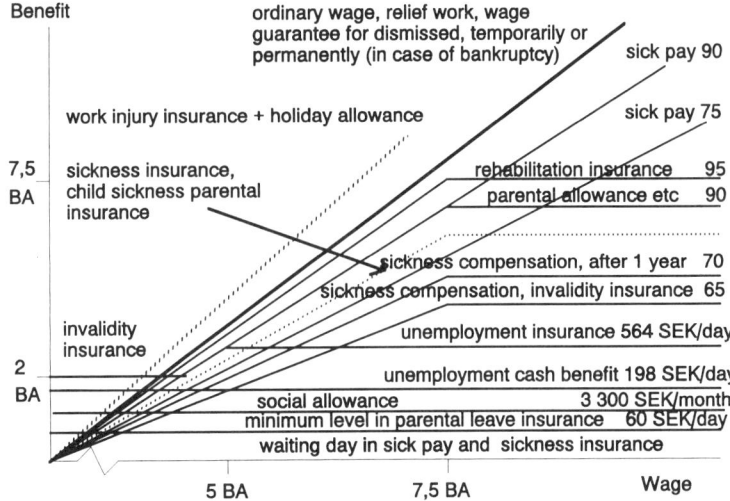

Note: BA= basic amount (see text for explanation).
Source: Own calculation with assistance from Riksförsäkringsverket.

Figure 3.6
Existing social insurance (July 1993)

If the floor, ceiling, and income-dependent part were to differ in different parts of the system, the picture of the social insurance system as a whole will naturally be more complex than shown in the diagram.

Transitional Problems
The next question is how to phase in such a new model in a situation where we already have a comprehensive social security system. It is, first of all, important that the systems are subjected to reform before they are removed from the government budget and (possibly) from the public sector. Moreover, the implementation of new rules should be gradual, so that individuals have time to adjust their plans. Before removal from the public sector the size of co-insurance (deductible) should also be increased. At benefit levels of 70%–80% of previous income, the co-insurance should perhaps be sufficiently large to avoid serious incentive problems, including moral hazard.

Some reforms have already been implemented or planned within unemployment insurance, health payment, and compensation for nonpermanent work injury. These reforms appear rational: they com-

Efficiency 113

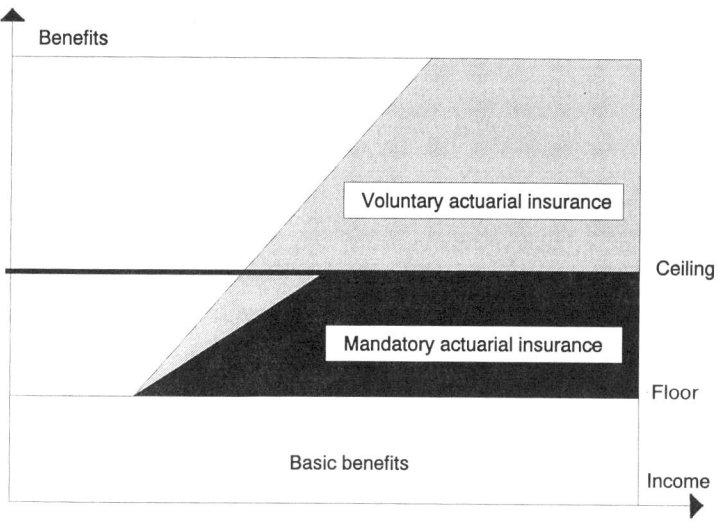

Source: Own calculation with assistance from Riksförsäkringsverket.

Figure 3.7
Stylized future social insurance

bine a reduction of the benefit levels with an increase in the number of days of unpaid absence.

The subsidized part-time pension ought to be abolished fairly soon, since it is relatively new and has not had much time to influence people's saving habits. The sickness pension (early retirement) should, according to our proposal, be fully integrated into the health insurance system, with strict demands on medical evidence. There is certainly a demand for flexibility of retirement age, but this should be taken care of by a flexible pension age with actuarially determined benefits.

With old-age pensions it is important to proceed cautiously, because pensions are very long-term contracts between the individual and the government. It should, however, be possible to gradually change the so-called 30–15 rule—full pension after 30 years and benefits based on the best 15 years of earnings—to a more actuarial 40–40 rule.

Successive reforms of this kind within the existing system could mark the beginning of the more radical transformation that we propose. However, certain groups, particularly among women, may get into difficulties, and some remedial action may be necessary. One such remedy would be to give a married person (and other long-term cohabitant) a legal claim on the pension rights of their spouse. Another would be to make child care generate pension rights during more years than is presently the case.

The motive for the reforms that we have proposed is, of course, to achieve a better functioning insurance system. But the increased co-insurance (deductible) naturally also means budgetary savings for the public sector. However, the savings will not be as large as could perhaps be expected, given the magnitude of these schemes. First, the benefits are taxed. Second, with reduced benefits more people will wind up at income levels where they qualify for other types of benefits. Net savings will therefore be substantially less than gross savings. As a rough illustration, we estimate that a further reduction of the compensation level in all income insurance schemes (exclusive of unemployment insurance and pensions) to 70% would imply a reduction of public expenditure of a modest 5 billion kronor, about half a percent of GDP. Much larger public-sector savings would be obtained if unemployment fell by a few percentage points. To achieve substantial savings requires a more drastic reduction of benefits, which is only possible if one abandons the income-related compensation principle, to a considerable degree. (The maximum savings, in the extreme case when an unchanged social welfare assistance level would be the only safety net are calculated later on.)

Complications
Reforms of social security typically involve not only redistributions over the individual's life time but also among individuals, primarily of annual incomes. They may also involve redistributions of income between generations. Going toward more actuarial systems will, of course, also affect income distribution. Many might, however, consider actuarial systems more fair than the present system with its many arbitrary redistributions between individuals with identical lifetime incomes.

We are, of course, aware of the political difficulties of adopting our proposals, not least because of their distributional consequences. It is safe to count on resistance from many interest groups. But reforms can be made more attractive if—like the 1991 tax reform—they are made comprehensive, so that different interest groups balance each other. By choosing a comprehensive strategy, rather than a succession of partial reforms, it should be possible to convince individual voters that they all stand to gain in the long run; after all, both benefits and fees apply to all citizens. All of us will—with a certain probability—become sick, unemployed, and old. For each one of us, therefore, a reform that covers the entire social security system has both positive and negative aspects. Because reform along the lines we suggest improve the efficiency of the economy, large groups of the population—probably the overwhelming majority—could come out as long-run winners.

Proposals

Social Security

44. Separate the social insurance system from the government budget, possibly also from the public sector, but only after the system has been reformed.

45. We recommend a compulsory basic social insurance system that combines a fixed amount, equal for all, and an income-dependent amount. The proportions between these two components may vary among the types of social security.

46. Make the income-dependent component of the social insurance system actuarial, at least for health insurance and the pension systems. As regards unemployment insurance, a solution where employers, employees, and the government share the costs equally seems reasonable.

47. Differentiate insurance fees for injuries in the workplace to reflect the frequency of injuries.

48. Set the ceiling on mandatory insurance payments and fees low enough such that large groups of citizens find it desirable to acquire voluntary income protection. This can be expected to give rise to a substantial increase in private saving.

49. Legislate a ceiling on the sum of mandatory and voluntary insurance, to preclude subsidization of "overinsurance" and abuse.

50. Equalize, as far as possible, the benefit levels in all social security systems between which individuals are likely to move.

51. Make sure that insurance suppliers do not cause others, for instance taxpayers, to incur substantial costs, by ridding themselves of costly policyholders.

52. Merge the insurance against illness and workplace injuries into a single system, with the financial burden shared between households and firms.

53. Do not transform the present publicly administered system into a system managed by the parties in the labor market, that is, into a corporative system.

54. In funded systems, the assets of policyholders should be kept separate from both the public sector and the finances of firms. A government inspection agency should also be set up.

55. In reforming the social insurance system, it should be kept in mind that old-age and early retirement pensions imply long-term contracts that cannot be changed suddenly.

56. Transform those components of the social insurance system that do not provide proper risk insurance (such as childbirth and child care benefits) into a pure benefit system, and retain them in the government budget.

Public Consumption

Efficiency Problems in Public Services

Public consumption accounts at present for approximately 28% of GDP and for one-third of total employment. Most public consumption consists of social services (child care, education, health care, care of the elderly). These social services are provided at the local government level, where they are produced by monopolies and financed by taxes. Even when there is no law against competition from private producers, it is difficult (often impossible) in practice to compete with heavily subsidized public-sector activities.

The arguments for public provision of services are often distributional: everyone should have equal access to schools, hospitals, or old-age institutions of a certain minimum quality. This means that in the Swedish welfare state, people have typically had few opportunities to choose among different alternatives or qualities. The principle of equal access has often had to give way to another principle, namely, that everyone should consume an identical quantity and quality.

The problems of public-sector production are well known:

- Public-sector production under monopoly often leads to high costs of production.
- Requiring a uniform standard of service often leads to low satisfaction of diverse individual needs.
- Subsidized prices sometimes imply overconsumption, sometimes excess demand and queues.
- Rationing often means that the highly educated receive priority of service.

Solutions to these problems are neither simple nor uncontroversial. Efforts to reform the system have been initiated both by the central government and by local governments. The point of departure for the reforms has recently been to accept more pluralism and freedom of choice, as well as competition on more equal terms from private producers. But reforms are still tentative and not based on a shared view of what is, or ought to be, the responsibility of the public sector and what can be left to individual decisions.

High Costs of Production
Within the private sector it is well documented that competition acts as a spur to efficiency. Still, when it comes to Swedish public-sector production, the burden of proof has come to rest on those who maintain this position. However, numerous studies show that lack of competition leads to important efficiency problems in the public sector (Productivity Delegation 1991).

A number of studies carried out under the auspices of ESO, the Expert Group on Public Finance (an independent agency under the ministry of finance), indicate that productivity in some parts of the public sector on average fell by 2%–3% annually during the 1960s and 1970s, that is, by about 25% during a decade when the public sector expanded drastically. More resources were required every year to produce a given amount of services at a given quality level—with the qualification that it is difficult to take proper account of quality changes.

Studies of cost differences between similar activities in the Nordic countries show that the costs in Sweden were sometimes close to twice as high as in the neighboring countries. Only some of the cost gap can be explained by measurable factors like, for example, more personnel and more floor space per child in child care institutions.

In primary schools Sweden has the highest cost per pupil in the OECD area, while at the same time pupils show rather mediocre achievements. An important cause of increasing costs has been a dramatic growth in the number of administrators. Another has been an increased density of teachers, partly caused by the expansion of teaching immigrant children their native language (see Fägerlind 1993; and Flam et al. 1993).

An analysis of differences in efficiency should preferably be based on comparisons of the same kind of production, carried out in the public or the private sector, and under conditions of monopoly or competition respectively. Such studies are difficult in Sweden, as there rarely exist private alternatives; this may in itself be an argument for allowing more pluralism. An exception is dental care, where studies have shown that private dental care has substantially lower costs than public care. One reason for this is that private care uses less office space and fewer nurses.

International evidence indicates that efficiency in service production does not primarily depend on whether production is private or public, but on whether it takes place under conditions of competition on equal terms between many independent producers (Bishop and Kay 1988; Borcherding et al. 1982). Thus the main argument for allowing private and cooperative alternatives is to allow as much competition as possible, including the prospective and actual competition from new entry. It is difficult to see why free entry should not be allowed in areas where public monopolies are the dominant source of supply. Specific motives for government involvement can be met in other ways, for example, by public inspection and control, public-sector financing, and quality requirements in connection with governmental procurement.

Large efficiency gains thus seem possible by stepping up competition. Studies show that these gains may lie in the 10%–50% range. They are probably larger in education and health care than in technical services, which are already exposed to some competition. But, by now, efforts to improve efficiency in the public sector have gone on for several years. In certain areas, such as health care, the potential for further cost decreases has therefore probably narrowed. Such a cost reduction of 25% in local government production of education and health care services may not be unrealistic and would represent savings of 35–40 billion kronor, corresponding to 2%–3% of GDP. It is clear that an improvement of this magnitude cannot be achieved in the short run.

Above all, it will take some time before a competitive supply emerges. In the meantime, one may achieve considerable cost reductions within the public sector by increasing local cost accountability and introducing result-related rewards. Danish experience show that one can get quite far by using such methods (Schaumann 1993). In Sweden, health care is an area where new methods are currently tried out with some success. In particular, attempts have been made to separate the roles of the county administrations as producers of health care and as sources of finance, to introduce profit centers and internal pricing schemes within hospitals, and to expose certain activities to competition, either from private or from other public producers.

An important but neglected question is how to distribute the gains from increased productivity (Flam et al. 1993). To maintain incentives to further productivity improvement, producers must be allowed to keep part of the gains. Moreover, a competitive system can only function if one accepts the consequences of competition. This implies that successful units must be allowed to expand, while the less successful ones are forced to contract or even to close down. Unfortunately, politicians seem to find it simpler to reduce production in all units than to close down the least efficient units.

Lack of Consumer Sovereignty

Efficiency is not only a question of producing certain goods and services in the right way; it is also a question of producing the right goods. In private markets this is achieved by each individual consumer choosing freely according to his tastes and needs, with supply adjusting accordingly. In the public sector, supply is politically determined and mostly standardized. This is not a necessary consequence of tax financing. In principle, tax finance can be reconciled with freedom of choice and consumer sovereignty for specific services. As an example, government subsidies can be paid to consumers in the form of vouchers, which can be used to pay for certain types of services. A voucher system allows both competition and pluralism in production, as well as freedom of choice for consumers. A practical example of this in Sweden is the financing of transportation services for the elderly; elderly people who are disabled and cannot use public transport can get vouchers for taxi rides. During the last few years many local governments have started experimenting with similar systems in schools, day care centers, and health care.

Arguments are often heard against freedom of choice. They usually point to the risk of social segregation. It is said that people with good education and high incomes will ensure that they get high-quality health services and that their children get a good education, while others may not. There may be a risk of this kind, but the effect could also go the other way. Today there is considerable segregation because only high-income earners can afford to pay twice for their services—first via their tax bill and then through private unsubsidized alternatives. There is also substantial segregation along income lines between different residential areas. Free choice of schools for all may help break this segregation.

Welfare losses from limited freedom of choice are difficult to measure and have not been studied much; still, some observations can be made. First, it is impossible to satisfy different preferences by a uniform supply. Individuals are different and they demand different things, not only in their private consumption (which is generally accepted), but also in social services. There is no reason to believe that diversity and freedom of choice are less important for social care and education than for other goods and services. "Good quality" means different things to different people. If every kindergarten, school, and old-age home attempts to be all things to all people, it will either become very expensive, or many people will become dissatisfied.

Second, the quality content of care and education services is particularly difficult to specify and control through a bureaucratic system. Typically, quality cannot be measured objectively; it depends on the personal qualifications and characteristics of people like teachers and nurses, as well as the personal values and experiences of the consumers.

Third, the absence of prices tends to create excess demand, because the consumer need not weigh benefits against costs and choose accordingly. An example of what may happen when choice is allowed is the case of a kindergarten that was able to cut its costs by as much as 38% simply by dividing the children into different groups on the basis of their daily length of stay, and adjusting the fees accordingly (Ministry of Social Affairs 1993). The level and quality of service could thus be improved significantly for a given cost of public services by allowing free consumer choice. Alternatively, costs could be cut with an unchanged level and quality of service.

When individuals and families are allowed to choose and are forced to pay for themselves, they will be more selective. If the resources available to producers are linked to consumers' choices, producers have an incentive to produce the right thing in the right way. The potential cost reductions or welfare gains are difficult to estimate, but it should be kept in mind that the gain from increased freedom of choice should be added to the conventionally measured productivity gain. If social segregation should turn out to be a problem, the policy should be supplemented with selective assistance to disadvantaged groups. It is unreasonable to prevent freedom of choice for almost all children, and their parents, because the authorities have not developed methods to assist the most needy.

Different Solutions in Different Areas
Local government consumption consists of very different activities. The best methods to achieve higher efficiency and more freedom of choice will naturally differ across these activities. Competition through contracting out is a straightforward method—and already in frequent use—for technical services. It is also relatively easy to achieve both competition and freedom of choice in areas like child care, schools, and old-age care. These areas are characterized by small-scale production, and the quality of service is relatively easy to assess by the consumer.

Real freedom of choice presupposes a differentiated supply without far-reaching and extensive political control. Today the discussion about freedom of choice in the schools concerns schools offering, for example, music or sports specialization. But it should also be possible for parents (and their children) to choose schools with more hours of instruction, more homework, and more emphasis on some subject than prescribed by state minimum requirements. Public supervision is needed to ensure that the minimum requirements are met.

Health care is probably the most complex area. It is characterized by asymmetric information between health personnel and patients, as well as by lack of cost consciousness, which arises because a third party (the insurer) pays for the treatment. Moreover, especially within hospitals, production is highly specialized, and efficient internal pricing is difficult to achieve. Certain types of outpatient care are also highly price elastic. The general experience in the health care area is that each model—private or public—has its advantages and disadvantages, and that no country seems to be satisfied with its own system (Arvidsson and Jönsson 1991; Culyer et al. 1992). The most reasonable approach is to proceed by allowing local, small-scale experiments, and this is what has started to happen in Sweden. [These questions are currently being studied by a special government commission on health care.]

Poor Redistributional Accuracy
Public consumption is often motivated by equity arguments. But tax-financed consumption is not necessarily an accurate instrument to reach income-distribution goals. Public consumption, like regulation, offers excellent possibilities of hidden income transfers, which explains why this is also an area of great special interest group activity. It is well known that certain public services are utilized more by the highly educated and their children than by others.

Above all, the present subsidies to child care outside the home can hardly be justified from an equity point of view. The subsidies to local-government day care centers arbitrarily transfer income in favor of the 40% of families with small children that use the centers. Subsidies are much smaller to those 20%–30% of families that rely on other kinds of publicly subsidized day care (such as care in other peoples' homes). Finally, the 30% of families that do not use any child care outside the home do not get any subsidies at all. From an egalitarian perspective it would have been easier to justify cash transfers or vouchers in the same amount to all families. Another possibility would have been tax deductions for the costs of child care.

Conclusions
Important initiatives have recently been taken to improve public-sector efficiency. The current but temporary freeze on local government taxes has forced local authorities to seek less expensive solutions. The transition to general instead of earmarked central government grants has made it possible for local governments to try out solutions better adapted to local conditions. Changes in the rules governing assistance directly to consumers have enabled more competition on equal terms between private, public, and cooperative producers. Competition and freedom of choice have increasingly

become guidelines in local government reform. These reform efforts should, in our view, continue.

But an efficiency drive in local government may create serious transitional problems. Perhaps the most serious one is that certain services may temporarily disappear; it may take time before private and cooperative producers are able to take over from phased-out public producers. There are a number of reasons for this, such as lack of suitable building space, finance, or management skills. Local authorities may help ease the transition, for instance, by offering training courses for future entrepreneurs in the service sector.

Explicit payments for services delivered by the public sector can be a first step toward a more deregulated structure of production. During the transition period local governments can then learn to handle the problems that arise when responsibility for production and finance become separated: how to design contracts, how to carry out evaluations. At the same time, those in charge of the public production units can prepare for the new conditions and some of them may themselves take steps to become independent entrepreneurs. This kind of development is already occurring in some municipalities and this may diminish the risk that certain service production disappears in the future.

One problem with compensation for services delivered, in the absence of budget constraints, is that it may lead to an increase in total expenditure even though unit cost goes down. Some form of cost control, through regulation of fees or a ceiling on total expenditure, may therefore be required.

Local consumption is today regulated by the central government through minimum standard requirements, grants to local governments, and restrictions on local tax rates. The question is how far this limitation of local autonomy should be taken. The relationship between central and local government is discussed in some detail in chapter 5. Here we will only briefly discuss some aspects of these complicated questions.

Today's system of tax-equalization grants to local governments should be changed. This system acts as a powerful brake on local incentives to increase the tax base in their own communities. With today's rule, an increase in the tax base is almost completely neutralized by reductions in central government grants.

It is also essential that the state limits its regulation of local service supply to the necessary minimum. The social rights of citizens that local authorities are required to meet (entitlements), should be limited to basic services available to and demanded by all. Schools provide an example of such a service. Child care does not, because many do not use child care institutions outside of the home.

Experimentation and pluralism are essential ingredients in reform. We do not yet know what the new structure will or should look like. Central government guidelines or nationally uniform systems may produce large and nationwide mistakes, instead of small and local ones. Detailed centralized regulation also limits our knowledge about feasible alternatives. New and potentially costly reforms should therefore be tried out on a small scale before they are adopted more broadly.

Let us summarize our views. All public production that is not an exercise of government authority should be exposed to competition. The proposals for competition in public procurement, recently put forward by the government, should be extended to the social service sector. Moreover, consumers should be allowed to express their demands directly to producers, for example, through vouchers. In this way consumers get a direct influence on the supply of services, and there is no need for interpreters such as politicians and public-sector administrators.

Barriers to entry should be removed. The obstacles to new and efficient forms of production in local communities are partly the same as the barriers to entry more generally (ESO 1992b). Limitations on competition in today's local government sector should provide justification for complaint to the Competition Board (*Konkurrensverket*).

A number of institutional changes could contribute to higher efficiency and better control of local government activities. A first step would be to require uniform and more operational principles of accounting in all municipalities; among other things, this would make it easier to compare performance across municipalities.

Another important step is to improve municipal auditing. It is necessary to establish a local government counterpart of the National Audit Board (*Riksrevisionsverket*) with power to introduce sanctions against violation of rules.

Finally, local referenda on proposals regarding expenditures or taxes can be expected to inject new life into local democracy and to provide for more rational local government decisions.

Proposals

The Public Sector

57. The central government should not interfere with production of services at the municipal level more than is absolutely necessary.

58. Social rights or "entitlements," as defined by the central government, to be provided by the municipalities, should be confined to generally recognized, basic services.

59. Reform the national system for redistribution of income among municipalities to increase the incentives for each municipality to enlarge its own tax base.

60. Reforms of public-sector activities should be based on small-scale experiments at the local level.

61. All provision of public services, aside from the exercise of government authority, should eventually be subjected to competition; complaints about restrictions on competition should be made to the Competition Board (*Konkurrensverket*). Barriers to entry should be removed and the playing field should be leveled.

62. Require an efficient system for auditing and evaluating local government activities, and create a counterpart to the National Audit Bureau for the municipalities. Require that the accounting practices of the municipalities be uniform and operational to allow a comparison of costs and achievements.

63. Natural monopolies should not be privatized without first examining the possibilities of regulating them (this holds in particular for infrastructure).

64. Consider the introduction of a mandatory referendum in connection with tax increases in municipalities.

Toward a Balanced Government Budget

In chapter 2 we discussed the need for strengthening the government budget to gain control of the public debt development. We will now illustrate in a concrete way how this can be achieved. Some of the most important assumptions behind the calculations in chapter 2 are:

- The real interest rate is 5%.
- The consolidated public debt amounts to 11% of GDP in 1993.

- Public consumption grows at the same rate as GDP.
- Transfers grow by 2% per year in real terms.
- Public-sector revenues grow at the same rate as GDP.

We make calculations both for a pessimistic (Alt. P) low-growth, high-unemployment alternative, and for an optimistic (Alt. O) high-growth, low-unemployment alternative.

In Alt. P, GDP decreases by 1.5% in 1993, increases by 1.5% in 1994 and by 2% during 1995–98. Total unemployment (the sum of open unemployment and labor market programs) falls only slightly from 12% in 1994 to 10% in 1998.

In Alt. O the growth rate is assumed to be 3% rather than 2% annually from 1995, and the unemployment rate is assumed to fall successively to 5% in 1998.

Under these assumptions, the budget balance must be improved by approximately 130 billion SEK in the pessimistic case and 100 billion SEK in optimistic case, to stabilize the consolidated public debt at between 40% and 50% of GDP toward the end of the decade. Although we have not used the concept of "structural" budget deficit, we arrive at an estimate of necessary budget savings that is of the same order of magnitude as several recent estimates of the structural budget deficit. To some extent the amount depends on the time path of the consolidation of the public-sector deficit. In our proposal, 10 billion SEK are saved in 1994 and another 30 billion per year from 1995 through 1997 (Alt. O), or through 1998 (Alt. P). In table 3.3, only the accumulated balance of savings in the fourth or fifth year is given. The exact time path is less important, as long as the time path for budget improvements have the same general shape.

Certain large budget items are crucial. In the budget proposal of 1993, transfers to banks amount to approximately 2% of GDP; they are assumed to be eliminated over two years. The value of the assets that the government receives in exchange later on is difficult to estimate but will, of course, affect the government debt position. Another uncertain factor is possible EC membership. We will return to this question at the end of the section.

Basic Considerations
As we have already emphasized, one should distinguish carefully between expenditures that stem from long-term contracts between the government and various beneficiaries, and those that stem from

short-term contracts. Old-age pensions and student loans for higher education are long-term contracts, whereas most others are short-term, in the sense that the individual is able to compensate a reduction in benefits by increasing his savings or by acquiring various types of insurances.

On the other hand, it is difficult to justify that any particular group should be totally exempt from benefit reductions in a situation where overall conditions are totally different from those that existed when the systems were constructed. In such a situation, it seems natural to start by reducing those benefits that have been added most recently, such as the system of partial pension or the possibility of earlier retirement. But the ability of the beneficiary to actually bear reductions must also be taken into account.

In our opinion, expenditure cuts should not be made by common percentage reductions across the board. Priority must be given to the core activities of public-sector activities, whereas more peripheral activities can be left to private or cooperative initiatives. Both in the case of consumption and transfers, priorities should be set and choices made on the basis of general principles of the role of the state in society.

The examples of expenditure cuts that are given below only serve to illustrate, in a concrete way, the implications of the required budget savings. None of them should be considered as our own most preferred proposals. Moreover, if a certain expenditure is not among the examples, that does not mean that it cannot, or should not, be reduced. In the existing fiscal dilemma, all expenditures must be open to reconsideration.

Effects of Expenditure Cuts

When reducing public-sector expenditures, consumption as well as transfers, it is necessary to distinguish gross and net effects on the budget. Given that most transfers are taxed, the tax base shrinks when transfers are cut. In addition, different systems are interdependent. The minimum level specified by the social welfare level limits the budget saving when various benefits are reduced. By consequence, it is a fairly complicated matter to compute the actual net effect of lowering a certain income transfer. It is necessary to know the number of beneficiaries, their income levels, their family situation, etc. Our estimates are based on calculations made for the commission within the ministry of finance. The models used in the calculations do not include effects from induced changes in behavior.

Closing the Budget Gap: Rough Estimates
The commission is not committed to any particular distribution of the expenditure reductions. We have rather seen as our task to present a number of alternatives. The amounts are approximate, and the different alternatives should be considered as rough estimates rather than as full-fledged calculations. In the calculations, we assume that expenditure cuts already decided upon, or presented in the budget proposal for the fiscal year 1993–94, will actually be implemented. By contrast, general announcements of ambitions to cut certain expenditure categories for the future have not been included.

Proposed or Already Decided Expenditure Cuts
According to the 1993 budget proposal, the budget saving from previously decided expenditure cuts amounts to 10 billion SEK (Govt. Bill 1992/93). Moreover, the rescheduling of public investments will reduce expenditures in 1997, relative to 1993, by approximately 5–10 billion SEK, provided this will in fact be a rescheduling and not an expansion. The decision to dismantle interest subsidies to housing investments will cut expenditures by 4–5 billion SEK each year, which yields a total reduction of 15–20 billion SEK at the end of the period. So far, the government has decided to reduce total expenditure in 1997 by 30–40 billion SEK, compared to 1993.

Public Consumption
In the reference calculations of chapter 2, public consumption is assumed to grow at the same pace as GDP. This conforms with the trend observed since the beginning of the 1980s. If public consumption is kept constant in real terms—an ambition declared by the government in its budget proposal—the deficit would fall relative to GDP, which would contribute to stabilizing the debt. Compared to our reference alternative, this can be expressed as an expenditure cut by 9.5% of total public consumption in 1998 in the low-growth alternative (1.5% in 1994 and 2% each year through 1998) and 10.5% in 1997 in the high-growth alternative (analogously calculated).

The costs of public consumption at the national level are expected to reach 114 billion SEK in 1993. Keeping this expenditure level constant in real terms will place it about 10 billion SEK below the reference trajectory in 1998. At the local level, the requirement of constant real consumption yields a reduction by about 25 billion SEK in 1998 relative to the reference trajectory, starting from the 1993 level of 280 billion SEK. In order that central government expenditures be reduced accordingly, it is necessary to cut central government transfers to the municipalities by the same amount; the present figure of those transfers is about 80 billion SEK.

It must be stressed that the problem of expenditure reduction is not solved simply by declaring that public consumption should remain at its 1993 level. To implement this goal, it is necessary to take concrete measures at the local level. If such measures are not forthcoming, expenditure cuts will have to be made, or else taxes have to be raised.

Social Insurance

The main components of the social insurance are the sickness compensation and parental insurances, the insurance against work injuries, the pension system, and special allowances (for example, child allowances). In Sweden health insurance comprises daily allowances and certain health care benefits (subsidies to medical examination, drugs, etc.). Health care itself is almost entirely financed by county-council taxes. Some expenditure cuts have already been made by reducing the replacement ratios. The pension system includes the basic pension and also additional benefits, that is, the general supplementary pension (ATP), and the part-time pension.

Table 3.1 shows the maximum potential for gross and net expenditure reductions in these systems. We estimate the possible savings in the extreme case, when all social transfers are limited to a fixed amount—equal for all—corresponding to the 1993 level of social welfare assistance. According to this estimate, the total net saving from such a reduction across the board amounts to 134 billion SEK, that is, half the gross amount. Clearly the potential budget savings become considerably larger in this draconian case than in the case we considered before, when replacement ratios were lowered to 70%. Note that the figures related to each particular system cannot be added, because of the interdependencies.

Table 3.2 illustrates a number of combined expenditure reductions in the income transfer system, at different levels and with different profiles. Alternative 1 saves 9.6 billion SEK net by a reduction in particular of the family support, whereas alternative 2 achieves about

Table 3.1
Total savings potential in certain income transfer systems, 1993 (billion SEK)

Transfer	Gross exp.	Tax share	Income-tested all.	Minimum standard	Net exp.
Taxed transfers					
Health insurance	32.0	10.9	4.0	1.7	15.4
Parental allowance	18.8	5.7	4.2	1.0	7.9
Unemployment insurance	14.0	4.8	3.6	−0.1	5.7
Pensions	165.7	45.0	25.6	32.1	63.0
(of which ATP)	99.2	28.3	44.1	−0.3	27.1
Nontaxed transfers					
Child allowances	18.5	—	—	4.2	14.3
Housing allowances	16.6	—	—	9.4	7.2
Total	265.6	66.0	—	65.4	134.2

Note: The figures relating to unemployment insurance have been normalized at 5% unemployment.
Source: Ministry of Finance.

the same level of reduction by cutting income insurance, with only a marginal contribution from the pension system. To reach the larger expenditure reductions of alternatives 3 (20.2 billion) and 4 (29.6 billion), it is necessary to combine and extend the cuts in the previous alternatives.

Among the remaining components of the social insurance system, costs in dental care insurance are about 4 billion SEK in 1993. One possibility is to reduce it to an insurance against high costs. An analogous solution could be chosen for the drug cost insurance. The total saving potential from these two systems is estimated at about 5 billion SEK.

Other Transfers
Transfers are made also to firms, organizations, adult education, the press, political parties, certain cultural institutions, etc. If one takes the view that members of organizations and users of certain public services should carry a larger part of the financial burden, savings can be made also here. Only a few examples are given; other subsidies may also be eligible for reconsideration.

National government support to private organizations amounted to 7.5 billion SEK in 1989/90 (SAFAD 1991). Moreover, public support

Table 3.2
Examples of savings in the income transfer systems (billion SEK)

Measures	Savings
Alt. 1: Reduced family support	
Parental allowance reduced to 80%, ceiling lowered to four basic amounts, two waiting days when children are ill	4.4
Two waiting days in health assurance	0.6
Child allowance for the two first children income-tested; no extra allowance for three or more children	7.9
Tax revenue lost	−1.8
Income-tested allowances	−0.4
Minimum standard	−1.1
Total net saving	*9.6*
Alt. 2: General reductions	
Replacement ratio in health insurance, parental allowance, unemployment insurance reduced to 70%; two waiting days	13.5
No extra child allowance for three or more children	1.3
General supplementary pension (ATP) reduced from 60% to 58%	3.3
Tax revenue lost	−5.9
Income-tested allowances	−0.7
Minimum standard	−1.0
Total net saving	*10.5*
Alt. 3: Combined measures	
Replacement level in health insurance, parental allowance and unemployment insurance reduced to 70%; ceiling reduced to four basic amounts; two waiting days	18.5
No extra parental allowance for three or more children; all parental allowances income-tested in connection with housing allowances	8.3
General pensions reduced by 3%	4.8
Tax revenue lost	−9.3
Income-tested allowances	−0.9
Minimum standard	−1.2
Total net saving	*20.2*
Alt. 4: Combined measures, sharpened	
Replacement ratio reduced to 70%; ceiling reduced to four basic amounts; two waiting days	18.5
Child allowances dismantled	18.5
General pensions reduced by 5%	8.3
Tax revenues lost	−10.5
Income-tested allowances	−0.7
Minimum standard	−4.5
Total net saving	*29.6*

Source: Ministry of Finance.

for sports activities amounts to 8 billions, most of which is a subsidy to sports facilities at the municipal level.

Public expenditures on cultural activities at the national level is 4 billion SEK. This comprises, among other things, support to the press (0.5 billion). Most of the press support is, however, indirect in the form of a reduced value-added tax rate on advertising, corresponding to a tax expenditure of 2 billion SEK.

Increased Revenues
Our calculations are based on the assumption that budget balance should be achieved mainly by reducing expenditures, and that the average tax rate should not increase. That taxes decided by parliament are actually collected is, however, of central importance to the legitimacy of the tax system. Tax evasion hurts not only the government but also law-abiding firms. The total tax revenue lost through different forms of economic crime is, for obvious reasons, difficult to estimate. The additional tax revenue that can be collected by increasing the auditing and surveillance capacity of the tax authorities has, however, been estimated at 10 billion SEK (Magnusson 1993).

We have argued that a large part of the burden related to measures against unemployment should be borne directly by firms and employees. Strengthening the Unemployment Benefit Fund (financing unemployment benefits) is thus in line with the long-term interest in this respect. If the burden is to be borne equally by government, employers, and employees, the fees paid by the latter two must be raised considerably. The total expenses from the fund in 1993/94 is projected at 42 billion SEK. An equal partitioning would imply raising the employers' fee by 2.2% of the total wage bill, and that of the employees by about 3,200 SEK per year and full-time employee. Adjusting the fees to correspond to an open unemployment rate of around 4%, would yield 20 billion SEK in public-sector revenues.

Closing the Budget Gap—Three Alternatives
Table 3.3 summarizes three different alternatives for stabilizing the public debt at a given level. The first two alternatives refer to the "optimistic" high-growth, low-unemployment case; the last to the "pessimistic" low-growth, high-unemployment case. The gap to be closed is 130 billion SEK in the pessimistic case (in 1998) and 100 billion in the optimistic case (in 1997). The first two alternatives differ

Table 3.3
Eliminating the budget deficit: three alternatives. The optimistic alternatives assume stabilization of the public debt by 1997, the pessimistic alternative by 1998.

	Optimistic alternatives		Pessimistic alternative
Decisions already made or announced	40	30	40
Public consumption	40	0	35
Transfers	0	40	35
• insurances, allowances	—	(30)	(25)
• dental care, drugs	—	(5)	(5)
• organizations	—	(5)	(5)
Increased revenues	20	30	20
Total	100	100	130

mainly in their distribution of cuts in transfers and public consumption. In the pessimstic case, it is necessary to cut both.

EC Membership
These calculations do not include budget costs for future EC membership. According to the directives given to the commission, the long-term goal of the government is to lead Sweden into the Community. We do not know when Sweden will join, if membership becomes a reality. Further, the budget expense associated with membership is difficult to estimate. The membership fee is subject to negotiation. A certain return flow to Sweden from the EC funds can be expected, but the tax revenue from this flow is very uncertain. Certain subsidies from the Community assume a matching grant from the Swedish government, which increases government expenditures.

According to preliminary information received by the commission, the net cost associated with membership would be in the range of 10–20 billion SEK per year. Because certain Swedish tax rates, like that on alcoholic beverages, would have to be cut, there would be a direct loss of tax revenues in the 5–10 billion range. EC membership would thus require the closing of an additional gap of 10–20 billion, and additional tax increases of 5–10 billion to compensate for the losses. (Of course, the tax base may also increase by membership.) Transitory rules may affect expenses during the first years.

Chapter 3

Effects on Employment
The required savings in public consumption were formulated in terms of a constant expenditure level in real terms. The effect on public-sector employment depends on the development of real wages. At unchanged real wages, employment in the public sector may be maintained. If real wages increase, employment must decrease accordingly. To the extent that productivity goes up, at given real wages, the quality or quantity of services may increase.

Conclusions
Expenditure cuts of the order of magnitude that we have discussed will be felt by almost everybody in one way or another. A precondition for budget cuts of this size to be politically feasible is that they be perceived as fair. The distribution of the burden may, of course, be affected by the composition of the budget cuts. We will return to income distributions and equity-related problems in chapter 6.

It is important that the measures taken be consistent with the goals for the public sector in the medium and long term. If expenditure cuts of the indicated size are not considered possible, only two alternatives remain. Either the elimination of the budget deficit must be deferred, implying an even larger public debt, or else taxes and fees must be raised even more.

As should be obvious from the previous discussion, the present situation requires exceptionally strong discipline concerning both expenditures and revenues. Recent proposals for new expenditures or tax reductions—making publicly provided child care a "civil right," along with expanded benefits to the handicapped, export subsidies to agricultural products, etc.—appear very difficult to justify. In line with our proposals in chapter 5, anyone who advocates such changes should be obliged to specify which other expenditures should be reduced or which taxes increased.

PROPOSALS

Balance in Public-Sector Finances

65. The public-sector debt should be stabilized primarily through expenditure cuts.

66. Public expenditure cuts should not be distributed evenly, but be based on explicit priorities.

Efficiency

67. Under favorable conditions (with respect to the growth rate and unemployment), keeping public-sector consumption fixed in real terms, and raising revenues by SEK 20 billion (fees to the Unemployment Benefit Fund and more efficient tax collection), are sufficient to stabilize the public debt by 1998, given expenditure reductions already decided upon. If, instead, public-sector consumption should expand in proportion to GDP, transfers have to be cut by SEK 40 billion beyond what has already been decided upon. If revenues are not increased, both public (sector) consumption and transfers have to be cut. If GDP growth turns out to be one percentage point weaker per year than assumed in these calculations, and the unemployment rate five percentage points higher, another SEK 30 billion in expenditure cuts or tax increases will be necessary.

68. If such expenditure cuts are not accomplished, the public debt cannot be stabilized before the turn of the century without substantial tax increases.

69. Any proposal for increased expenditure should be matched by cuts in other areas.

4 Growth

Productivity growth in Sweden declined drastically in the beginning of the 1970s. But, as shown in previous chapters, institutions and decisionmakers did not adjust to the new conditions; rather, they seemed to presume that a permanent high rate of productivity growth was something of a natural law; nominal wages and public expenditures continued to grow as if nothing had happened.

A low growth rate is, however, also a problem in itself. A small change in the annual growth rate that persists over a long period has huge consequences for the standard of living. Between 1870 and 1970, GDP per hour of work in Sweden increased by more than a factor of 17—one of the largest increases recorded for this period (Maddison 1982). In Australia the corresponding factor was only about 4. In 1930, Argentina, Australia, Great Britain, Czechoslovakia, and Uruguay all belonged to the group of the very richest countries. At present none of them belong to this group. Slow economic growth may cause a country to slide far down the world income ladder during the course of half a century.

It may take a long time before changes in the official GDP statistics are experienced as a real problem in everyday life. This is because the standard of living, both for a single household and for a country, depends not only on the flow of income during a single year. Like the household, the country has at its disposal a large stock of various capital goods accumulated during earlier years; this stock continues to yield services that are not being accounted for in the GDP figures or in household income statistics. Important examples are the households' stocks of durable consumer goods, like cars, boats, and furniture, as well as city environments and public infrastructure. Visitors to Stockholm of the 1990s therefore find it difficult to detect the ongoing relative decline. In the same way, however, visitors to Buenos Aires of the 1950s and London of the 1970s found it difficult to detect the ongoing decline that is so apparent today.

The concept of standard of living, as well as that of economic growth, can be given a narrow or a wide interpretation. A narrow interpretation focuses on what is contained in traditional national accounts, that is, gross domestic product or gross national income. A wider interpretation includes other factors important for welfare, such as the physical and mental health of the population and the general cultural climate in society. Whereas the conventional interpretation allows a useful quantitative description, it is more difficult to define and measure the wider concept of welfare and economic growth.

This chapter discusses the preconditions for productivity growth and how they can be influenced. In the main, we limit ourselves to growth of GDP. However, in the last section of the chapter we broaden the perspective. We discuss the important issue of the distribution of income between generations and how this is influenced by the conventional public debt, the pension debt, and what may be called "the environment debt."

Points of Departure

In chapter 1 we emphasized that productivity growth in Sweden since 1970 has been slow in comparison to previous decades and to the OECD average. This of course also explains the lagging behind of relative real wages in Sweden (see Jakobsson and Jagrén 1993).

But as suggested in chapter 2, the problem is more serious than indicated by the productivity statistics. For Swedish industry to preserve its international competitiveness and its market shares, it has been necessary for its relative unit labor costs to fall. In the short run, lower relative unit labor costs make it possible for a country to increase its market shares. In the long run, however, the relationship is less simple. During the 1980s, countries like Denmark, Japan, and Germany succeeded in combining gradually higher relative unit labor costs with increased market shares. Sweden, by contrast, has experienced both decreasing relative unit labor costs and declining market shares (again see Jakobsson and Jagrén 1993). This shows very clearly that the causes of today's crisis must be sought at a deeper level. Sweden's falling market shares, which have continued despite gradual downward adjustments of unit labor costs, suggest that the country has either remained stuck in sectors with declining relative prices in world markets, or has lost its former lead in product quality. In the economic development literature such falling terms of trade is usually seen as a characteristic feature of developing countries, with pronounced inability to reallocate resources.

Large Swedish corporations have increased their investments abroad much more rapidly than in Sweden. Such increase in direct foreign investment is not unique to Sweden. In most other OECD countries, foreign direct investment grew more rapidly than both domestic investment and world trade. However, Sweden's share of total foreign investment has increased more than proportionately, as Swedish direct investment within the OECD area more than tripled during the past decade. Foreign direct investment in Sweden, by contrast, has been somewhat less than would be expected from the size of the economy. However, the main reason for the imbalance between outward and inward investment is the large outgoing flow (Isaksson 1993). To some extent, research and development activities of Swedish corporations have also moved out of the country.

Whereas corporations in Sweden have lost competitiveness, the same is not true for Swedish corporations. What they have lost in Sweden, they have gained in their foreign subsidiaries. Swedish firms have done better than Sweden. This suggests that the problems of competitiveness and efficiency have domestic causes.

It is well known that the devaluations in the early 1980s only led to a modest shift of resources to the traded goods sector. Moreover, the modest shift was concentrated to Sweden's traditional export industries. The balance between exports and imports of "knowledge-intensive" products actually deteriorated during the 1980s (Ohlsson 1992).

One often hears that manufacturing industry in Sweden has become "too small." The present share of manufacturing in total employment is only one-fifth, while services count for approximately 70%. However, a large service sector is common to all industrial countries and does not necessarily give cause for concern. The problem is rather that Sweden lacks a well-functioning and competitive service sector. The Swedish service sector is very much oriented toward the domestic market, and production often takes place under monopoly conditions, especially in the public sector. International integration will, however, force the service industry to adapt to increased competition.

In chapter 3 we discussed requirements for efficient resource use, that is, for a high level of productivity. We emphasized the importance of well-functioning markets, appropriate economic incentives, flexibility, and free entry. Growth of productivity is, of course, necessary for the standard of living to increase. Conventional and modern growth theory show that this demands a continuous accumulation of physical capital through investment in buildings and machinery, of human capital through education and training, and of productive knowledge through technological change. Empirical studies of single countries, using methods of growth accounting, as well as comparative studies of several countries, confirm that these factors are crucial for productivity growth. We organize our analysis below according to this classification before returning to the broader question of how the general social environment shapes the process of accumulation.

Physical Capital

Private Investment

During the last two decades investment as a share of GDP has been lower in Sweden than in the OECD. The gap has been a couple of percentage points, reaching a maximum during the 1978–85 period. During the latter half of the 1980s, Sweden again approached the OECD average. At the same time employment in Sweden expanded, while it continued to fall in other European OECD countries. During the last twenty years the capital-labor ratio grew less rapidly than before and less rapidly than in the OECD. This explains some of the slow labor productivity growth in Sweden. Another consequence is that the labor force works with a capital stock that on average is becoming older.

In the manufacturing sector, gross investment has, however, kept pace with investment in important trading partners during the 1970s and 1980s (see Jakobsson and Jagrén 1993). But since the number of hours worked has grown relatively fast, the capital stock per hour worked has grown somewhat more slowly. It is often asserted that too much investment in Sweden has gone into buildings at the expense of machinery. This assertion finds no statistical support, however; machine investment relative to GDP has generally kept pace with that of the other OECD countries. The share of machine investment in total investment increased from a little over 70% in the 1970s to a little over 80% in the 1980s. These results support the general view that the decline in Sweden's rate of productivity growth cannot mainly be ascribed to insufficient private investment, at least not in manufacturing.

In an open economy the primary determinants of physical investment are the relative rates of return on domestic and foreign capital assets. As we pointed out in chapter 2, the domestic rate of return is largely determined by the relation between labor costs, the exchange rate, and the cost of capital. Macroeconomic stabilization policy, which influences these variables, therefore becomes crucial for investment. In chapter 3 we also stressed the role of domestic private saving for investment in small and medium-sized firms, given that these firms have limited access to international capital markets.

Productivity growth, of course, not only hinges on the volume of investment, but also on its allocation among industries and firms. Because the previous tax system discouraged dividend payments, profits were plowed back into the industries where they arose, even when the return was modest and the growth prospects poor. Recent reforms of the Swedish tax code have eliminated most of these distortions (OECD 1993). However, previous distortions are still embodied in the existing capital stock and may therefore continue to exert a negative influence on the rate of productivity growth.

Infrastructure

Private physical investment depends mainly on the general economic environment, including economic incentives, which makes much of the general analyses in this report relevant. Public-sector decisions play a more direct role for that part of physical investment that goes into infrastructure like transportation, energy, and telecommunications. Such systems either have characteristics of public goods or display significant economies of scale and often very low variable costs, which makes it difficult to generate private investment in these sectors. Alternatively, private ownership may lead to underutilized capacity. The public sector has therefore been heavily involved in both investment and production. Thus we devote specific attention to this type of physical investment.

Because producers, subcontractors, and users do not themselves bear much of the cost of public-sector investment, they often form interest groups to push for investment beyond the level that can be justified from a social point of view. It is important that the general interest is enabled to make its voice heard above those of local, regional, and sectorial interest groups. The nature of infrastructure is thus such that in private hands it tends to become too small. If in government hands, it may overexpand in fields with strong pressure groups, whereas it may underexpand in fields with weak pressure groups.

In recent years, there has been considerable debate in Sweden about infrastructure investment, both as an engine of growth and as an instrument of stabilization policy. The transport sector, especially road investments, has been emphasized as particularly important in both of these respects. It is therefore necessary to examine whether investments in transport have some unique characteristics that are not taken into account in public decisions about infrastructure investment.

Roads and railways played important roles in the early stages of industrialization, but now they are much less powerful sources of growth. The network of roads in Sweden hardly grows any longer, and new investments are mostly designed to improve quality. It does not generate much new traffic, nor is this the intention. Outside of the densely populated areas the most important gains are time savings (42% of total gains), lower risks of accidents (26%), and less wear and tear of vehicles (12%), (Jansson 1993a). Within urban areas, the essential effects lie in rerouting traffic and in reducing noise and accidents.

A study of the Road Authority's own investment plan has estimated the order of magnitude for the efficiency gains (see Carlén 1993). The total future time savings for goods transportation resulting from an investment program of 50 billion kronor is estimated at 11.4 billion kronor. Annual transportation costs in industry will be reduced by 600–700 million kronor out of a total of approximately 40 billion. On average for private industry, transportation accounts for 4% of total costs. Consequently, even such a comprehensive program reduces total costs in private industry by only 0.06%.

Transport costs depend not only on infrastructure, but also on the pricing policies of transportation firms. In international comparison, truck transports in Sweden are expensive. Cartels within the trucking industry explain some of the high costs. This suggests that the opening up of the Swedish market to foreign transportation firms may be a much more efficient method of reducing transportation costs in industry than a massive program of road investment (see Flam et al. 1993).

No comparable economic analysis exist for the railway sector. Railways require large and stable flows of goods and people. These conditions are rarely met in a sparsely populated country like Sweden. The development of new or better connections becomes expensive, because a large part of the existing network depends on subsidies even for current operations. This is true even if a high value is attributed to environmental benefits (Jansson 1993b). Extending the railway network to shorten travel time to the continent will have little effect if corresponding investments are not made by the northern EC countries.

The Swedish telecommunications network has high quality compared to other countries. It is easy to get through, and prices, both for households and firms, are among the lowest within the OECD area. Swedish conditions are comparable to those of the Netherlands and the other Nordic countries. The Nordic countries have adapted new techniques like mobile telephone systems at the highest rate in the world. However, modernizing the network to include data communication and other advanced services is a time-consuming process; a new nationwide network will not be complete before the turn of the century.

A very large part of the public infrastructure is in the domain of the local government sector. It includes water supply and sewage, local streets and roads, energy, and public buildings. Few would claim that such systems play a key role in the growth process; nevertheless, the capital stock involved is very large. According to the Association of Local Governments (1991), insufficient maintenance is a problem only for municipal streets and roads, and raising annual maintenance expenditure by 1 billion kronor will be sufficient to solve this problem. There are no indications of comparable problems in the area of water supply and sewage. Energy is a sector that is harder to judge. Investments in this field will depend on the rate of depreciation, as well as on changes in demand, environmental and security requirements, and energy prices.

Public buildings make up a large share of local government budgets, and there will be a large need for reinvestment sooner or later. The main problem today, however, is that the buildings are utilized at such a low rate. In fact, large gains can be made by selling off some of the stock and by utilizing the remaining stock more efficiently.

A survey among industrialists concerning the general investment climate in Sweden confirms the picture of a well-functioning infrastructure (NUTEK 1992; IVA 1993). This is particularly striking for a poll taken internationally; here Sweden comes sixth among the twenty-two industrialized countries that were included. The result is least impressive for the railways, where only 56% expressed satisfaction.

In summary, it seems hard to justify the idea that additional infrastructure is a crucial factor for economic growth in Sweden. This is not to say that particular bottlenecks may not be significant, but such problems should be subjected to conventional economic analysis in each individual case. Moreover, infrastructure investment has in fact already increased substantially in the early 1990s after a marked decline in the 1970s and 1980s.

Potential long-run effects on productivity growth may be found—if anywhere—in new types of infrastructure, where there is considerable uncertainty about the development possibilities. Investment in such areas also do not typically have the support of the powerful interest groups associated with today's and yesterday's systems of infrastructure.

One such area is information technology. Many consider this area to be strategic for the general development of society, including the production system. Information technology may be particularly important for the expanding service industry. In the short run, there is little reason to expect investment in this area to generate large employment effects; the latter are primarily indirect and connected with new services or production processes. Sweden's geographical position and low population density, as well as the country's long industrial traditions in telecommunications, make it natural to look for projects with a long-run potential in this field.

It is not the commission's task to identify individual projects. We will nevertheless mention a concrete proposal that is currently being discussed. Networks for advanced communications application have recently been developed in the United States, Japan, and the EC. The programs cover research, pilot application, and technological diffusion within information technology. A Swedish counterpart is now being discussed in collaboration between R & D organizations and potential users in the private and public sectors. The technology in this field makes it possible to organize various social activities independent of their distance in time and space. Applications include education and information transmission, design and problem solving in industry, as well as rescue activities and artistic production.

Such a system is a good example of public-good type infrastructure. Financing should be on a risk-sharing basis to ensure the active involvement of all concerned. The project under discussion has a total budget of 500–600 million kronor over a six-year period, which is no more than the cost of 20 kilometers of highway. The dynamic effects of the information technology project is likely to be considerably larger.

Decision-making for Infrastructure Projects

Studies of decision processes for infrastructure in Sweden, primarily for road investments, have shown that actual decisions bear little relationship to the priorities that come out of social cost-benefit calculations (Jansson and Nilsson 1989; RRV 1990). Local, regional, and other interest groups distort decisions so that the taxpayers' money generates considerably less than its potential social benefit. It is important to ensure that efficient decision procedures are respected, by giving appropriate incentives to the actual users of public funds. Such incentives could be created along the following lines. When parliament decides on the budget for the Road Authority, it also implicitly defines the lowest acceptable rate of return for investment projects. If the Authority deviates from the list of priorities and carries out projects with a lower rate of return, the total budget ought to be reduced, so that the same average rate of return as before can be maintained.

A further step is to use uniform cost-benefit criteria to rank projects not only within a single sector, but also between different sectors. This may yield even higher social gains.

It is also important to maintain high standards for information regarding large infrastructure investments. Assertions of significant dynamic effects play an important role in the debates about large projects, but they are often not specified, and probably exaggerated. Projects within information technology probably offer the best chances of such dynamic effects, and we have already presented one concrete illustration.

PROPOSALS

> *Infrastructure*
>
> 70. The situation in the labor market justifies speeding up infrastructure investments. Over a longer time period, however, there are no compelling reasons to raise the investment level above what has already been decided. The commission has found no indications of serious deficiencies in the traditional infrastructure (roads, railroads, harbors, etc.).
>
> 71. It is important to ensure that new types of infrastructure are developed, particularly in the area of information technology.
>
> 72. By creating better incentives for the decision process concerning infrastructure investments, these can be made more sensitive to the results from cost-benefit analyses.

Human Capital

We have seen that physical capital accumulation can only explain slower growth in Sweden to a limited extent. Therefore, we instead turn to human capital accumulation. Human capital measures individual knowledge and skill accumulated both through work experience and educational effort. The costs of accumulation consist of the direct expenditure on education, but most important, of the earnings foregone during the time spent on education. The benefits to the individual take the form of increased earnings, a more rewarding work situation, and a higher social status. It is mainly the pecuniary benefits and costs that can be analyzed with some degree of precision. This limitation should be borne in mind when building policies on the foundation of the analysis.

The private return on investment in human capital is commonly referred to as the educational premium. It measures—in percentage terms—how much investment in education increases the wage. Looking across income groups it is, of course, misleading to compare annual incomes, because these neither reflect individuals' past costs of acquiring their present income-earning capacity, nor the time profile of their earnings. Lifetime income is therefore the appropriate concept.

Accumulation of human capital is important for economic growth in several different ways. Human capital can be seen as a separate factor of production, which together with labor, capital, and intermediate goods is used in the production of goods and services. It can capture a quality dimension of labor input, which allows more meaningful measures than straight hours of work. Moreover, it is a source of innovation, which plays a crucial role in the process of economic growth. A country with a large stock of human capital will find it easier to import and adapt technology from other countries. These aspect have all been emphasized in recent theoretical research on economic growth. (See Barro and Sala-i-Martin 1993, for a textbook treatment.)

Recent empirical research gives support to the hypothesis that human capital is an important factor in economic growth; this comes out, for example, from analysis of growth data for a large number of countries (Barro 1991; Mankiw et al. 1992). It also becomes possible to explain why many poor countries have had low rates of growth, in spite of the fact that a low (physical) capital-labor ratio ought to yield a higher rate of return on capital than in the richer countries. The labor force simply does not have sufficient knowledge to exploit modern technology. Sweden experienced similar difficulties with the introduction of steam power at the pre-industrial stage of economic development.

If individuals deciding about investment in human capital had full information and took full account of all social consequences, there would be no reason for public policy concern. But the picture is more complicated. Knowledge is a good whose value can only be fully appreciated once it has been acquired. It is also dubious to assume that very young persons are fully able to take decisions with consequences for the rest of their lives. This is probably the chief reason for compulsory education.

Moreover, education benefits not only the individual student, as a number of external effects can be identified. Such effects arise, for example, for close collaborators in the workplace; if the level of education of an individual's co-workers goes up by 10%, her own productivity may, according to some studies, increase by 3%–4% (Lucas 1990). In certain cases these effects can, however, be captured by the wage-setting process within the firm.

Investments in human capital also create externalities between firms in an industry, as well as between industries. The reason is, of course, that labor, which embodies human capital acquired in school or at the workplace, is mobile between firms in a market economy.

Education has one further diffuse, but nevertheless important, external effect. The skills that one learns are utilized not only in the labor market. Education increases the individual's political and cultural resources. A high level of education facilitates political discourse and is a precondition of a well-functioning democracy. Investment in education, in other words, is important also for the cultural and political life of a country.

The Standard of Education in Sweden

How does Swedish human capital come out in an international comparison? As regards the duration and coverage of education, Sweden does not distinguish itself among the ten to twelve most developed countries, its main competitors in world markets. In an international perspective, a relatively small share of a cohort of Swedish youths goes into higher education after high school. Furthermore, much of higher education in Sweden is nonacademic. A very small share of each cohort goes on to graduate studies. As noted by Sohlman (1992), the picture remains the same even if one includes adult education provided by local government or by private firms.

Sweden is thus, at most, an average country among developed nations when we consider the coverage and duration of education in the population. Sweden is not an average country, however, when it comes to educational costs. On the contrary, Sweden's expenditure on education relative to GDP is among the highest in the world. This is illustrated by table 4.1.

More detailed comparisons of costs, for instance between elementary schools in the Nordic countries, confirm the impression of an expensive school system in Sweden. The cost gap relative to the Nordic countries is narrower in education than in child care, however.

With respect to educational achievement, Sweden is not above the average for the other developed countries. According to the best available studies on school achievements—within the so-called IEA program—students' knowledge is most satisfactory in oral skills and English, while they appear poorer and more unequally distributed in mathematics, writing skills, and foreign languages other than English (see Fägerlind 1993). The frequency of university-level graduations has declined during the 1980s. Those modest achievements are confirmed by the polls taken of industrialists (IVA 1993). Business

Table 4.1
Public sector spending on education in the OECD (percent of GDP)

Country	1980	1986	Country	1980	1986
Australia	5.4	5.3	Ireland	6.4	5.8
Austria	5.4	5.3	Italy	4.4	—
Belgium	5.8	5.4	Japan	5.7	5.0
Canada	6.8	6.7	Netherlands	7.7	6.6
Denmark	6.6	7.1	New Zealand	5.7	4.9
Finland	5.2	5.3	Norway	6.9	6.6
France	5.1	5.6	**Sweden**	**9.0**	**7.3**
Germany (FRG)	5.0	4.3	U.K.	—	5.0
Greece	2.3	2.7	USA	4.8	4.8

Source: OECD 1990.

managers with an international outlook are most dissatisfied with the knowledge of high school graduates.

Five percent of the employees in Swedish manufacturing corporations in 1987 had a university education. This is considerably less than in, for instance, Japan, the United Kingdom, and the US. The German number is lower because technical education programs of short duration are not included in the statistics. The lack of a broad range of educational programs is especially important for the competitiveness of the low and intermediate technology manufacturing industry. But industry appears to have difficulties with absorbing and using highly educated labor. Only a few branches of industry—pharmaceuticals, computers, telecommunications products, and a few others—have a reasonably high share of employees with university or research training. Swedish data for these industries reveal a statistically significant relationship between productivity growth and the number of employees with university education, just as theory predicts; for the remaining industries there are no clear effects (Central Bureau of Statistics 1991). However, the knowledge-intensive sector is still too small for its growth to have substantial effects on industrial employment as a whole. This fits with our earlier observation that Swedish industry is not particularly technology intensive.

Incentives for Education

Comparative studies of countries at different stages of economic development show that the educational premium, on the whole, is higher in the less developed countries. (A broad survey of incentives for education is contained in Henrekson 1993.) In the industrialized countries the premium averaged 12% during the 1960s and 1970s, both for high school and university education (Psacharopoulos 1985). In the same study, the rate of return on education in Sweden varies between 7.5% for civil engineers and 13% for medical doctors. A Swedish study (Björklund 1986) gives an average figure of 7.8% for 1968, declining successively to 3.5% in 1981. Even lower figures have been calculated for individuals born after 1950. New estimates for 1991 (Edin and Holmlund 1992, 1993) indicate that the premium may have gone up during the last few years. This is largely due to the tax reform and to the new system of financial support for students. But it will take a long time before these changes show up in the composition of the active work force.

The conclusion from these studies is that the rate of return on education has long been below the average of similar countries. The low dispersion of after-tax earnings, connected both with the structure and ambitions of Swedish wage bargaining, as well as the pre-1991 tax system, probably explains most of the low returns. However, the variations between different types of education have been considerable.

The quality of the educational system may also have deteriorated. If so, the human capital embodied in individuals is overestimated if measured often by years of education. There are indeed indications that such a deterioration has occurred (Fägerlind 1993). Low expected returns may have lowered student motivation or, alternatively, the rapid expansion of the school and university system may have lowered the quality of the faculty.

Job-related adult education is also of great importance for developing society's stock of knowledge. In Sweden both the private and public sectors every year spend large amounts on personnel education. The estimated expenditures on personnel and adult education for the late 1980s amount to about half the expenditures on formal education. But, as with formal education, there is some doubt whether incentives are appropriate.

The question of incentives has chiefly to do with the individual's earnings profile over time. Given lifetime earnings, the high initial wages typical in Sweden yield a flat earnings profile. Lower initial wages allow more scope for rewarding those who continue to improve their qualifications. With such rewards, the employee also acquires an interest in the long-run productivity of his workplace. A disadvantage, though, may be a loss of flexibility because the ties to a single firm become very strong. However, according to Mincer and Higuchi (1988), the Japanese industries with the steepest earnings profile also have the highest rate of productivity growth and the lowest rate of labor turnover. Compared to the United States during the period 1960–1980, the Japanese earnings profile was three times as steep, labor productivity increased four times as fast, and the labor turnover was one-third of that of the United States.

The wage profile in Sweden has become considerably flatter during the last two decades; work experience has thereby become less important for earnings. The relative wage of young workers has increased very sharply. According to Edin and Holmlund (1992), wages in the age group 18–19 increased from 55% of those of the group 35–44 in 1968 to 80% in 1986. This development is unique to Sweden; in other countries the relative wages of young workers have fallen during recent decades (Davis 1992). For workers in manufacturing, the wage profile has become extremely flat, whereas it is steeper for clerical staff; in the former group, there is hardly any wage increase after the age of 21 (Björklund and Fritzell 1993). One method for achieving a steeper wage profile, while combining theoretical and practical education, is to return to a system of workshop schools or to adopt a trainee (apprentice) system along German lines.

One specific problem is that the public sector has a particularly flat earnings profile even for clerical workers, and this creates imbalances in relation to the private sector (Zetterberg 1989). The public sector finds it relatively easy to attract the newly educated, but difficult to keep those with more experience and qualifications.

The egalitarian, so-called solidaristic, wage policy, which has been characteristic of postwar wage formation in Sweden, has not only attempted to enforce the principle of "equal pay for equal work." Another objective, articulated since the 1950s by labor union economists (Landsorganisationer 1951), has been to encourage rapid structural change through an upward pressure on wages. Though such policy contributes to squeeze out low-productivity firms and sectors, it obviously creates difficulties both for investment in physical capital and for investment in human capital and technology. Implicitly it also assumes that technical progress proceeds at a predetermined rate, independent of incentives, and that it shows up in the form of a continuous modernization of the capital stock. But as argued above, productivity growth to a large extent depends on physical and human capital formation and on the interplay between them. The solidaristic wage policy, therefore, damages the incentives that are important for the process of modernization.

A flat and inflexible earnings profile was probably less important for the modernization process at the time when most firms were organized according to principles that left workers with little scope for individual action. But as personal improvement, as well as high flexibility, become increasingly important, the disadvantages of a flat earnings profile become more serious.

Possibilities for Reform

The central task of education policy, in a broad sense, is to support the individual's interest in his own development at all stages of his working life. This is not a policy where immediate results can be expected; education policy must have a long-run perspective because of the long gestation periods of education. But a continued advancement of knowledge is necessary if Sweden is to defend and improve its international position.

The public debate about the contents of the school curriculum has been pursued under the implicit assumption that the total number of teaching hours is given. This is striking in view of the fact the Swedish school system has very few hours of teaching per year in international comparison. The amount of homework also appears to be modest. It has increased somewhat during the 1980s, but from an extremely low level. These two factors—the annual hours of teaching and the amount of homework—are the most significant ones in international comparisons of knowledge among students. They therefore ought to occupy a more central position in discussions about the design of the school system than questions like the student-teacher ratio, size of schools, and other factors that do not have any statistically established consequences for knowledge among students (see Fägerlind 1991, 1993).

It has not been possible for the commission to estimate in detail the consequences of raising the number of teaching hours. Growing cohorts in the future, of course, increases the demand for teachers at an unchanged student-teacher ratio. But as this ratio is low in Sweden, both in an international and a historical perspective, a higher student-teacher ratio should still be possible. One could also increase the number of school days per year, which could certainly provide a reason for raising teachers' salaries.

The grading system is currently being reformed. The discussion about this issue has been rather technical and has focused on the construction of the grading scales. But it is more important to consider how learning is affected by grades as a selection mechanism. For grades to perform well in this respect, something more than a fine-graded scale is required. It is also important that students with an interest and a talent in a certain subject are stimulated to develop it. Grades in relevant subjects should therefore be assigned appropriate weights in the admission process to higher education. Returning to the previous system in which mathematics and natural science got higher weights in the admission to engineering education, medical schools, etc., would be a step in the right direction. One of the technical universities has already decided to reintroduce this system.

Budget allocation for higher education is about to change. Reforms will make each university's budget depend, to some extent, on the achievements of the individual institution. This is clearly an improvement. Great care will, however, be necessary in designing the budgetary allocation rules, so as not to create the wrong incentives.

Individual departments are of course the basic units of the universities. The rules must be designed to strengthen the departments to sustain quality of research and teaching. Academic departments need to have a critical mass, in particular at the graduate level. The typical Swedish university department has only one or a few professors. The disadvantage of this system is that resources for research are spread too thin among too many departments in the country.

The authorities have recently announced that they want to increase the number of Ph.D.'s during the 1990s. This ambition is laudable, considering that the number of Ph.D.'s is relatively low in Sweden, particularly in comparison to the United States and Japan. But it is essential both for undergraduate and graduate education that the expansion does not outrun the supply of qualified teachers.

A central aim at all levels of higher education must be to increase the percentage of students who actually complete their education. Another aim should be to reverse the trend toward increasingly longer completion times. Much will be achieved if the new budget allocation system can contribute to solving this problem (possibly combined with the proposal by Bröms (1992) for a new system of student finance).

We have already stressed the need for lifelong education. Adding to and renewing one's knowledge ought to be a natural part of each person's professional life. In particular, we would like to emphasize the importance of this for the teaching profession. Adult education within both private firms and public institutions plays an important role. It does not appear particularly sensible to reduce the scope of the adult education provided by local government, as has recently been suggested; reallocation of resources and increased efficiency in the system is certainly called for, however. Larger savings can be obtained by cutting public-sector subsidies to study circles, where the case for public support is much less clear; these activities are frequently more in the nature of consumption (or leisure activities) than productive investment.

Studies of the role of human capital in economic development indicate that individual incentives to acquire knowledge should be strengthened. This raises the issue of income differentials, and hence the distribution of income. As we have already argued, this is a question of the distribution both over the life cycle of a given individual and among different professions and groups of citizens. Economic incentives that redistribute income over the individual's lifetime are relatively unproblematic from the point of view of redistribution policy, because they simply involve lower initial wages in exchange for higher future rewards to labor market experience and education.

One complication is that policymakers cannot directly influence pre-tax earnings profiles, except in the public sector. However, there is a lot to be done. The earnings profiles in the public sector are even flatter than in the private sector. Going toward more decentralized wage formation in the public sector will lessen the central government's direct influence, but the market forces of decentralization and deregulation should themselves lead in the right direction.

Individuals may be encouraged to acquire education in either of two ways. One way is to lower the costs of education through increased access and higher subsidies; another is to let differences in levels of education be more strongly reflected in wages. Both probably have a role to play. Easy access and low costs of education are crucial for a broad social recruitment and thereby for the distribution of knowledge and income. But exclusive emphasis on subsidies does not strengthen incentives to continued education beyond basic professional training. Moreover, subsidies encourage the consumption element in education, rather than the harder, productivity-enhancing training.

Our discussion of human capital should certainly not be interpreted as an argument for general and unconditional wage increases for those with a university education. Wage increases do not automatically generate new human capital; in the worst case they only lead to higher costs. The public sector has a high share of employees with an academic education, but it is not distinguished by particularly high productivity growth. Naturally, an efficiency-enhancing wage structure must take account of a number of factors other than the length of education—for example, if the education is relevant for a particular task, and if a particular profession is attractive for reasons other than the wage level. Improved wage incentives should of course be based on a positive association between earnings and employee effort.

It is essential to clarify how higher rewards for education affect the distribution of income in society. Partly it is a question of redistribution of income over the life cycle, which should not be a big problem—one is not twenty years old all one's life. But a higher educational premium also redistributes income among social groups. Measures that increase access to education and labor market mobility can, however, mean that education will contribute to increased equality. Young people from families with no tradition of academic education seem to be more sensitive than others to the economic return on education (Nilsson 1991). The expansion of education during the 1960s and 1970s is probably the single most important political reform in the postwar period, contributing to a more equal distribution of pre-tax income, as well as to increased social mobility.

Recent research on the interplay between income distribution and economic growth suggests that an equal distribution of income and wealth before taxes and transfers may actually have a positive effect on economic growth (Persson and Tabellini 1994). There will then be less need for redistribution via taxes and transfers, and the wide tax wedges that are detrimental to growth can be avoided. A generally high level of education of the whole population will tend to generate just such an even distribution of pre-tax incomes.

Of course, a well-educated labor force is not sufficient to ensure a high rate of economic growth. It is also essential that firms are flexible enough to use the available skills; they must be able to hire new workers when new skills are required. Modernization often requires young and newly educated employees. Regulations, particularly in the labor market, should therefore not be allowed to prevent firms from renewing the skills of their work force. This is particularly important for a small country at the outskirts of Europe, as the production of standard durable consumer goods tends to move to countries with larger home markets. Sweden's future opportunities lie in providing an attractive environment for firms, which are increasingly dependent on flexibility, an innovative climate, a supply of highly differentiated goods and services, and a high degree of adaptation to customers' needs. This certainly requires a well-educated labor force.

PROPOSALS

Investments in Education

73. Wage differentials motivated by skill differentials provide an important incentive for productive investments in human capital.

74. Skilled manual workers should be better rewarded in the wage-setting process.

75. There are good reasons for subsidizing education, but the educational system should not be dimensioned in such a way that subsidies are capitalized by a small group that manages to receive education in fields where admission is restricted.

76. Raise the requirements in core school subjects such as Swedish, foreign languages, and mathematics—that is, abilities that are important regardless of the field a student chooses for specialization in the future.

77. Reduce costs in the educational system by reverting to previously lower teacher-student ratios.

78. Increase the number of school days and hours per year, so that traditional core subjects (such as mathematics, languages, and natural sciences) can be expanded without encroaching upon the humanities, aesthetics, and/or physical education. Increase the amount of required homework.

79. If more resources are required for the educational system to carry out its programs, they may be taken from other types of subsidies to children, such as the day care system or child allowances; such a

reform would then amount to a redistribution over time of the total support to children.

80. Increase the competence of teachers by continuous retraining. Use a steeper wage profile as an incentive.

81. Weight school marks for different subjects when students are selected for higher education.

82. Reintroduce the old system of "workshop schools" into private enterprises, for instance in the form of apprentice systems with a combination of theoretical education in school and practical training in the workplace.

Technology

International comparative studies indicate that research and development are important for productivity growth. At 2.9% of GDP, the total expenditure on R & D is relatively high in Sweden. However, private-sector R & D activity is concentrated to a few large transnational corporations, and therefore reflects an economy with a significantly larger production base than the Swedish economy alone. If one adjusts for this, the figure comes down to 2.2%, which is less impressive in an international comparison. Moreover, R & D expenditure has recently stagnated in most branches of industry; between 1985 and 1991 expenditures in real terms went up only in the pharmaceutical and telecommunication industries.

The public sector finances about 40% of all R & D in Sweden. Government-supported research is concentrated to the university system, which absorbs roughly 85% of total government expenditure on civilian R & D. Government financing of private R & D is completely dominated by defense contracts. From the point of view of industrial development this is not favorable, given that exports from this sector are surrounded by regulations—for good reasons.

Only about 1% of public R & D expenditure goes to small and medium-size enterprises, which is unfortunate. These firms get their new technology mainly through their role as suppliers of intermediary goods and services to larger firms.

In recent years some observers have worried that Sweden is losing strategic research-related parts of its large corporations to foreign countries. It is a fact that Swedish transnational corporations have moved some of their R & D activities abroad, though most corporations have retained the overwhelming part of all their R & D activity in Sweden; only a few have moved it all abroad. The increase in their foreign-based R & D is mainly due to acquisitions of foreign enterprises that contain R & D units.

Knowledge as a Public Good

To justify government action in the R & D area, it is useful to classify knowledge into three categories: general scientific knowledge, basic technologies, and firm-specific knowledge. The conditions for the production of knowledge vary across these three categories. Knowledge produced by scientific research is a typical public good in that it can easily be used by others than those who have generated it; it is therefore widely regarded as a government responsibility. The standards of quality in this type of research are set by the scientific community itself, and incentives are related to scientific priority and career possibilities within the scientific community.

By contrast, the knowledge produced by firm-specific R & D can often be appropriated by those who built it, for example, through patenting. The quality criteria here are related to commercial success, and the incentives are the profits of firms and the incomes and other benefits of the employees.

There is, however, also evidence of substantial external effects at the industry level, and even at the national level. Benefits of investments in research and development are to a large extent reaped by other firms in the same or related industries. Estimates of this effect are on the order of 20%–100% with a mean value of approximately 50% (Nadiri 1991). Diffusion of knowledge also seems to take place between different industries, especially within a given geographical area. Knowledge therefore has some of the characteristics of a public good, the benefits of which accrue to many economic agents.

Incentives in the intermediary category of basic technology runs the largest risk of being insufficient. The individual researcher interested in scientific priority may find the academic level too trivial; whereas the individual firm interested in profits may find it too difficult to appropriate the prospective (social) returns. This is a problem, as basic technologies may be quite important for technological development and economic growth for the economy as a whole. It is probably in this area that the Swedish R & D system has its greatest weaknesses. Much of the resources from government support have gone to basic research and to university training at various levels. Moreover, the university-based R & D system is not particularly well adapted to the needs of small and medium-sized enterprises, in which much of the long-run growth potential probably can be found. Large corporations are often able to translate their problems into scientific language, whereas smaller enterprises typically lack this ability entirely.

To promote a more efficient production of basic technology, one should make a coordinated effort to develop the necessary skills and to improve technological networks. This should contribute to the development and spread of new knowledge among various institutions and firms. However, one should also be aware of a number of risks in such a process. One significant risk is that producer interests collect public research money for projects that would have been carried out in any case, or that have low returns. On the other hand, it cannot be left to public agencies to assess which areas of technology will be of commercial interest to Swedish firms. Another well-known problem is how to close down programs whose mission has been completed, or which have failed.

Government financial involvement should be as general as possible and based on clear criteria that allow for subsequent evaluation. Because Sweden is a small country, the evaluations should be done at least partly by foreign experts, like the evaluations of different scientific fields that are today carried out at the initiative of the various research councils.

It is difficult to recommend a general model for public involvement in the financing of R & D spending. On the contrary, one can make strong arguments for adopting different strategies for different fields of technology. Germany and Japan have tried a number of models in practice (see Andersson et al. 1993). One possibility is to create flexible research institutes with a very small permanent staff, which hire the majority of the researchers on temporary contracts. Another possibility is to create R & D programs that are limited in time. The main purpose of all such efforts is to improve communications between research institutions and industry, so as to ensure both quality and relevance. It is also essential that universities preserve their integrity and are not reduced to being consultants, or induced to give up initiating scientific research.

It should be possible to overcome some weaknesses of governmental R & D efforts revealed in international studies. Even though the effect of R & D on growth is substantial, government support often seems inefficient and in some cases completely without noticeable effects (Lichtenberg 1992). A possible explanation is that public involvement tends to be selective—"picking winners"—and without success. Such an approach almost by necessity tends to be directed toward existing firms and technologies. The main purpose of public policy should instead be to promote technological development that is important for many firms and products, especially for new or emerging firms. This argues for general and broad-based support. We therefore caution against highly selective industrial and technological policies.

PROPOSALS

Technological Development and Diffusion

83. Government support to R & D activities should be general, not selective.

84. The main responsibility of the government in regard to technical development and competence should continue to be education and research.

85. To reduce the risk that generic technologies are undersupplied with resources, the government should support technological development in such areas.

86. To the extent that research institutes are created for R & D purposes, they should have a small permanent staff supplemented by temporarily contracted researchers.

The Growth Environment

In the introduction to this chapter we argued that it is the general economic, social, and political environment of households and firms that is decisive for productivity growth. Chapters 2 and 3 discussed precisely how to create a favorable environment for firms and individuals, emphasizing macroeconomic stability, well-functioning markets, and good incentives. These general conditions have somewhat different implications for different types of firms. In a growth context it is especially interesting to focus on three types of firms: large multinational enterprises, firms with new and risky projects concerning both processes and products (risk enterprises) and fast-growing firms (growth enterprises).

The Multinational Enterprises

Multinational firms transfer both physical and human capital, as well as technology, between countries. Relative to its size, Sweden has remarkably many and large multinational corporations. They account for about half of manufacturing employment in Sweden, almost 60% of exports and 90% of expenditures on R & D in manufacturing. Altogether, they have now more employees abroad than in Sweden.

Their foreign operations have allowed these firms to grow much larger than would otherwise have been possible. This in turn has made it possible for them to spend much more on R & D, which has benefited their domestic operations. Moreover, the main part (more than 80%) of their R & D has so far been located in Sweden, which most likely has had positive effects for Swedish R & D more generally.

One explanation for the imbalance between foreign investment in Sweden and Swedish investment abroad is probably that the Swedish market is small and distant from the main European markets. From an early stage, the small domestic market has pushed Swedish firms into international markets, with both sales and production. At the same time the small domestic market may have kept down foreign firms' interest in investments in Sweden. During the second half of the 1980s unusually high foreign investment by Swedish firms was motivated partly by a desire to position themselves to face EC integration and partly by capacity limitations and labor shortages in the overheated Swedish market. This is a reminder of how important it is to create favorable conditions in Sweden for enterprises with an international orientation.

Swedish multinationals have recently had faster productivity growth abroad than in their Swedish plants. In the mid-1960s, the productivity level in their European subsidiaries was 25%–30% lower than in the Swedish plants. At the end of the 1980s it was almost at the same level, and in some countries considerably higher (Swedenborg 1991; Andersson 1993). This has made it more difficult for some of the Swedish parent companies to compete with their own foreign subsidiaries, without a relative fall in domestic wage costs.

Internationally mobile corporations choosing between investment and production in Sweden and abroad make acute the question of

Sweden's competitiveness. If Sweden wants a stronger and faster growing industrial sector, the country has to offer an attractive business environment, that is, favorable conditions for innovation, research and education, a good infrastructure, competitive labor costs, and generally good incentives.

It should be emphasized that certain recent changes in Swedish legislation have improved the conditions for foreign investment in Sweden. In its evaluation, the OECD (1993) notes several important changes in Swedish legislation regulating foreign ownership. During 1990 and 1991 restrictions on foreign ownership in banking and financial services were abolished. In 1992 the business acquisitions act was repealed, and a number of simplifications were introduced in the rules governing the establishment of new firms. Limitations on foreigners' right to acquire shares in Swedish corporations were abolished on January 1, 1991. The legislation regarding foreign direct investment has thereby been liberalized to an even larger extent than previously recommended by the OECD.

Spokespeople from Swedish industry and especially from foreign industry have emphasized the advantages of EC membership. A common view is that the Swedish market alone is too small to justify new entry. To some degree, this view may be based on lack of information; foreign investors seem not to be fully aware of the nature of the Swedish free-trade agreement with the EC and of the European Economic Area Agreement.

Risk and Growth Enterprises

The problems of particularly risky enterprises deserve special attention. Such firms develop and utilize innovations, the returns on which are more uncertain than the return for average investments. Ohlsson (1992) maintains that the shortage of risk capital is a severe limitation on the operations of such firms in Sweden. If so, there may be a need for special financial market institutions that intermediate between project entrepreneurs and investors who are willing to take large risks. To provide risk capital requires a special ability to judge both people and projects, and considerable time may be involved in the development of projects. In chapter 3 we discussed in general terms the difficulties and possibilities associated with the mobilization of risk capital. Private risk capital corporations, for example, those recently created in connection with the winding up of the so-called wage-earners' funds, could play a constructive role in this area.

Successful risk enterprises often develop into growth enterprises, that is, into firms that grow at especially high rates. These, too, face particular problems. Growth enterprises can be found in most industries and regions, and they differ widely in terms of size.

Entrepreneurs in such firms turn out to be different from average business managers in some important respects. A growth enterprise normally starts either as a subsidiary of a larger company, or by some enterprising individual breaking loose from such a company. It is characteristic of growth enterprises that they tend to rely heavily on external subcontractors, while maintaining control of product development, design, and marketing. Those entrepreneurs who insist on controlling all aspects of the production process have often set rather strict limits to the growth of their firms.

It would probably be a mistake to use the experience of growth enterprises to draw general conclusions about successful policies for sustainable growth in private enterprises. However, it is obvious that competence and attitudes are at least as important as external conditions.

Growth enterprises themselves consider the major external obstacles to growth (Ahrens et al. 1992) to be the corporate income tax system, the lack of adaptation to the EC system, the limited supply of risk capital, and the limited access to skilled labor. This contrasts with slowly expanding or contracting firms, which tend to emphasize labor market legislation, taxation, regulations, and monopoly. Regulations, such as labor market laws, therefore seem mainly to interfere with enterprises that are not growing rapidly. This is natural, since slow-growing or contracting enterprises have a stronger need for labor turnover to survive and possibly also to prepare for future expansion.

The study of growth enterprises therefore yields a somewhat different perspective on the appropriate public policy for growth. Of course, successful long-run growth for the economy as a whole presupposes that both "risk and growth firms" and "ordinary firms" have favorable working conditions.

The Social Climate

Economic growth also depends on a favorable and stable social climate. This factor is indisputable, as available empirical studies suggest (Alesina et al. 1992). Stable relationships between major interest groups in society make it easier both for individuals and collective bodies to take long-term decisions. A society characterized by mutual suspicion, lack of legitimacy, and destructive social conflict cannot form the basis for positive economic development. Our suggestions for improving the performance of the Swedish economy are based on such concerns.

PROPOSALS

General Economic Environment of Firms

87. The government can stimulate economic growth in much the same way as it can stimulate the efficiency of the economy: by improving the general economic, social, and political environment of firms and households, rather than interfering with the conditions and decisions of particular sectors or enterprises.

88. Due to the uncertainty regarding the importance of different factors for economic growth, the government should try to influence a broad spectrum of factors that are likely to have favorable effects.

A Wider Concept of Economic Growth

Public Debt, Pension Debt, and Capital Assets

The major problem of public debt occurs when the debt grows without limit. In chapter 2 we therefore proposed a program of debt stabilization (for the consolidated public sector) at slightly above 40% of GNP in 1998, alternatively 50% one year later. How problematic is such a stabilized public debt?

Higher public debt means that present generations exploit public policy to redistribute income to themselves from future generations. From a democratic point of view this is awkward, as future generations cannot vote today. This conflict may be expressed in terms of our recurrent distinction between special and general interests. Here the current generation represents the special interest, whereas all generations together represent the general interest. What, then, are the disadvantages for the future generations that inherit a large public debt?

The most obvious disadvantage is that a higher public debt may "crowd out" part of the private capital stock, either in the form of less domestic capital formation or less claims on foreign debtors. Future real incomes before tax thereby become lower than otherwise.

Another disadvantage arises, because the generations who have pushed the state into debt will be holding claims on the state. These claims are either direct, in the form of government bonds, or indirect, in the form of claims on private funds—pension funds or life-insurance companies—which in turn hold government bonds. Because the taxes needed to pay the interest on the public debt largely will be paid by future generations, their taxes will be higher—unless they manage to escape these interest payments by passing them as a new bill on to the next generation, like a chain letter. The net annual transfer from the future young to the current generation will equal the amount of the public debt times the real rate of interest after tax.

A further burden on future generations is that the taxes required to service the public debt create incentive problems in the form of tax wedges, which diminish economic efficiency or require a lower level of public expenditure than otherwise, or both.

The public debt is not the only liability transferred to future generations. The pension liabilities in a pay-as-you-go system of the Swedish type is another kind of debt that is passed on. Future payments of public pensions (after tax) are paid for by the taxes or pension fees by subsequent generations. The parallel to the public debt is obvious. Future interest payments on the public debt are also, as we have seen, paid for by taxes on future generations. The payments are received by the retired generations both directly or indirectly, in the latter case largely in the form of private pension payments from financial institutions that hold government bonds in their portfolios. The next generation can again, when its turn comes, pass both the pension debt and the public debt on to the following generation according to the chain-letter principle. The problem is that the chain may be broken through default on both the pension debt or the government debt. One generation may then find itself as the game's true loser, possessing a claim that the next generation fails to honor.

What is the order of magnitude of these redistributions? At the end of the 1980s the net financial debt of the public sector was approximately zero. Assume that the debt level is stabilized slightly above 40% of GDP. With a 3% real after-tax rate of interest (5% real rate, 2% inflation, and a 30% capital income tax), this means that future generations have to redistribute 1.2% of GDP to bond holders for generations to come. This can be compared to existing pension liabilities. With the present pension rules, and assuming 2% GDP growth, the pension payments require taxes on earnings amounting to 23% of GDP before tax, roughly 12% after tax. The pension debt is thus about ten times as large as the public-sector debt.

Our numerical example shows that a lowering of the net pension payments by one-tenth—which for an average retired pensioner corresponds to his gross compensation level being reduced from 65% to 55%—would neutralize the reduction of future generations' incomes implied by raising the public debt from 0 to 40% of GNP. Considerations of this type follow naturally from the public-sector budget cuts that we formulated in chapter 2 and discussed in more detail in chapter 3.

However, our generation not only leaves debts. We also leave assets in the form of real capital, claims on foreigners, human capital, and technology. Obviously, the next generation pays something for these assets; part of its wealth comes from its own savings, and it pays for its human capital through income foregone during its years of study. But it also receives some of its assets for free, in part through bequests and gifts from its parents, in part through inheriting public-sector infrastructure. It is important to remember that the return on the next generation's labor would only be a fraction of its actual value, if that generation had been forced to start from scratch, that is, without physical capital or knowledge. Through investments in physical capital and technology our generation has created the possibility for high real wages in the future. The worthless capital stock of former socialist countries in Eastern Europe today provides a striking reminder of how important it is for the standard of living to inherit a productive stock of physical capital and technology.

During the last thirty years, our generation has roughly doubled these stocks, as GDP has increased by a factor of two. We have thus increased the resources of future generations by many times more than the public and pension debts that we leave behind. These resources are embodied in the total stock of capital and its associated technology.

Transfers between generations can be studied in much more precise terms than has been possible in this report. In the United States, studies have already been published on a fairly complete set of accounts regarding intergenerational transfers (generational accounting; see *Economic Report of the President* 1993). We recommend that this type of accounting be introduced in Sweden to increase the general public's understanding of actual intergenerational redistribution. But we have already said enough to suggest that our generation should not have too bad a conscience, if we succeed in stabilizing the public debt along the lines indicated, and if we refrain from further increases in the pension debt. This can be done mainly by reforming the pension system in the direction of a more actuarial system, particularly by relying more on funded systems, so that each generation pays a larger share of its own pension.

Growth and the Environment: Conflicting Goals?

We also owe a debt to the environment. In the public debate, the environmental effects of economic growth are typically related to the emissions of toxic or acid substances into air and water. However, such substances are no longer the dominant threat to the Swedish environment. Studies of environmental protection during recent decades show that emissions from such sources have fallen to rather low levels. Moreover, the improvements have come about at modest costs. This is partly the result of a policy whereby restrictions have been tightened gradually and in line with the successive modernization of the real capital stock. Frequently, new technology is both more efficient and better adapted to the environment. The most serious problems now are connected with diffuse sources of emissions, like consumer goods, vehicles, and contamination of agricultural soil. These are not related to the growth process in the same direct way as the emission of smoke and acids.

A main reason for these new tendencies is the increasing importance of knowledge, which has altered the nature of economic growth. Every dollar of GDP in the developed industrial countries requires successively less inputs of material like steel and energy, whereas the input of knowledge increases. The connection between the output and the external environment accordingly becomes weaker; here the curve describing the relation between output and emissions is falling. The developing countries are instead on the rising part of the curve, where the conflict between economic growth and the environment is more acute. At the same time it should be clear that the larger per capita production in the industrialized countries still makes the per capita effect on the global environment much higher in the developed than in the developing countries.

The scope of this report does not allow a comprehensive analysis of environmental issues. We restrict ourselves to a few points. The most efficient method of resolving conflicts between economic growth and environmental concerns is to use environmental fees. These are usually more compatible with the principles of a market economy than quantitative regulation. The most serious current environmental problem is probably that of the climate. If Sweden—either unilaterally or within the framework of an international agreement—were to undertake substantial reductions of carbon dioxide emission, this would have powerful effects on energy supply and transportation in Sweden. This would be particularly true if nuclear power was to be dismantled within the next decades.

The concept of sustainable economic growth has come to occupy a central position in the global development debate. Although this criterion has few direct implications for economic decisionmaking, it is valuable in providing a vision for the discussion of policy. This vision emphasizes how important it is to pay attention to the long-run consequences of current decisions.

In recent years, much work has been done to extend the methods of national accounting to also include natural resources; to some extent, this development has responded to the criticism that traditional concepts were unduly narrow. There are, of course, difficult problems both with definitions and practical implementation. An example of a preliminary attempt in this direction is Jernelöv's (1992) estimate, the so-called environmental debt, measuring costs of restoring or compensating for accumulated environmental deterioration. His result is that this debt presently amounts to 260 billion kronor and that it grows by an annual amount of 6–7 billion kronor. As in other areas of income and wealth accounting, the stocks are notoriously more difficult to evaluate than the flows. Moreover, many items are missing, and some of those which have been included may be questionable. An emission of carbon dioxide is included by 2.5 billion kronor per year in spite of growing Swedish forests absorbing more carbon dioxide than we emit. The work on green national accounts is still in its infancy, but it is both important and promising.

The main objective of an extended system of accounts is not to evaluate all resources in monetary terms. It is rather to obtain some idea about the order of magnitude of policy effects in various fields, so that possible conflicts between policy goals can be identified. A multidimensional concept of resources is important to prevent a negative development in one area being hidden by a positive development in some other.

We have stressed the importance of long-run sustainability in all areas of policy, not only in the resource and environment field. No area is necessarily more important than others; there is therefore a case for seeing long-run sustainability as a more general restriction on current policy. As argued in previous chapters, Swedish economic policy has long been deficient in this respect.

PROPOSALS

Bequests

89. To ascertain whether one generation passes on a burden to future generations, we suggest that a system of generational accounting be developed; it should to the greatest possible extent comprise all assets and debts transferred between generations.

90. To protect the natural environment from damaging effects of firms' and households' activities, we recommend—in line with mainstream economics—that the government use taxes and subsidies rather than regulations. An important example is environmental charges.

91. We recommend the development of "green national accounting" in the government budget proposal, supplementing (but not replacing) traditional national accounting.

5   Democracy

It is impossible to understand the economic crisis in Sweden unless one also understands the deficiencies of the political system. A weak institutional framework for macroeconomic policymaking has contributed to the inflationary tendencies, the recurring cost crises, and ultimately the current high unemployment level. Abrupt changes in the tax system and in the regulations of financial matters help explain the financial crisis. The political proclivity of choosing standard solutions explains why service production in the public sector is largely monopolized. The power of special interest groups over the political process explains why government regulations hamper competition and efficiency in many markets. Political decisions designed to enhance income safety and to equalize the income distribution—by themselves salutary ambitions—have contributed to low savings and the slow accumulation of human capital during the last two decades.

An important factor behind deficiencies of the political system is that special interests exert a strong influence over political decisions. Moreover, short-term tactical considerations often overshadow long-term efficiency aspects. The actual decision-making process in the political system differs considerably from what is required for the state to protect the long-run general interest. It is therefore important to reform various political institutions and mechanisms in Sweden. Even though it is economic necessity that has convinced us about the need for political reforms, the reforms we propose are also designed to revitalize Swedish democracy.

Political reform has of course to be based on certain principles, which in turn depend on value judgments. Our recommendations are guided by the general principles laid down in chapter 1: active citizenship, pluralism, and a clear separation of responsibilities.

Democracy: Ideal and Real

Citizenship

A well-functioning democratic system must be based on active citizenship. The core of citizenship is self-determination, which can be exercised by individuals as well as by groups. A democratic society does not presume that individuals interact as isolated atoms; instead democracy presumes organization and common rules. In a historical perspective, one may therefore see democracy as a gigantic experiment, an effort to combine freedom and order, according to rules designed by the citizens themselves.

Citizenship is a combination of duties and rights. One fundamental duty is tolerance: to respect the self-determination of other citizens. Many rights are, of course, laid down in laws. A possible discrepancy between formal and real rights always exists, however. To exercise his rights, the individual citizen needs certain resources. Even though material resources, such as personal income and wealth, are more evenly distributed in Sweden than in other countries, there are nevertheless large differences between individuals as well as between social classes. Today the most serious threat to a reasonably even distribution of resources, and also to the idea of active citizenship, is the rapid rise in unemployment.

Principles of Democracy

To implement genuine democracy requires translating some general prerequisites into specific social institutions. The minimal criteria of democracy are valid regardless of time and place. Popular sovereignty cannot be realized without general and equal suffrage, free and fair elections, freedom of association, freedom of speech, and freedom of the press. But when it comes to the next steps, beyond these minimal criteria, there are innumerable opinions on how to design rules and institutions. The general theory of democracy has no answer to questions such as what election system is the best, how often referendums should be held, what is the appropriate role of the central bank, or what is the appropriate distribution of power between central and local levels. Different countries have chosen different solutions. Moreover, the practical institutions of democracy may have to be modified in a changing society.

Comparative political science has developed a series of concepts and theories to analyze variations in democratic governance. One fundamental distinction is between monistic democracy and pluralist democracy (Dahl 1984). The monistic conception of democracy assumes that all political power emanates from a single center and, of course, that this center is democratically controlled. Efficient democracy then translates into the high ability of the state to control other institutions in society.

For a pluralist view of democracy it is not sufficient that state power is efficient and democratic. Democracy also depends on how the rest of society is organized. Monistic democracy does not require more than a state and a people consisting of isolated individuals. Pluralist democracy also requires the coexistence of a multitude of independent institutions, such as voluntary associations, churches, firms, universities, and mass media. Our proposals concerning pluralism both in the market system and in the public sector are clearly in line with this idea. An organized civic society is the prerequisite for pluralist democracy, and hence for an open, dynamic, and free society.

The Swedish conception of democracy is now moving from a rather monistic view toward a more pluralist view. The present problems of governance in Sweden may, therefore, partly be seen as an experiment with new forms and institutions, as well as an attempt to instill more pluralism into the big welfare state. Examples are the attempts to find alternatives to traditional market regulations, social security systems, and the organization of care for the young, sick, and elderly.

Pluralism

A pluralist society is based on a mixture of different organizational principles. No method for social coordination is "the best" in the sense that it fits all problems and all situations. Every institution has its drawbacks and limitations. The market is a superior method for organizing efficient production in conformity with consumer preferences, in particular if there is competition. Yet there are many demands that the market cannot satisfy. Legislation based on majority rule is necessary to maintain common rules for the entire society. Yet legislation cannot replace voluntary involvement by individual citizens in all fields. An independent judiciary is necessary to interpret legal norms, enforce voluntary contracts, and protect individual rights and freedoms. Yet there are many social coordination problems the courts cannot solve. Universities maintain the autonomy of the scientific republic and launch new ideas. Yet many social problems lack a scientific solution. Local self-government allows citizens to decide common matters. Yet externalities that extend over the borders of local communities, and the importance of enforcing the law in a uniform manner, limit the merits of local autonomy. The family is one of the basic units of society. Yet the modernization of society and the increased labor market participation of women are changing the role of the traditional family. Voluntary associations reflect the spontaneous organization of civil society. Yet strong special interest organizations can obstruct the general interest.

The basic problem of social organization is not to choose a single institution over others, but to find a combination that allows each institution to develop its own inherent qualities while simultaneously limiting its shortcomings and undesirable side-effects.

Clear Responsibility

The various institutions of society must have distinct tasks and appropriate incentives. A pluralist society must therefore be founded on a clear division of responsibilities. This division is expressed by clear distinctions between different spheres of society.

The realization of this principle assumes that society consists of a multitude of individual and collective actors, each accountable within its own domain. Rules and institutions draw the lines between different actors, lay out the responsibilities, and devise methods for resolving conflicts. In this way the constitutional ideal of separation of powers is extended to the entire society. Pluralism also demands that strong interests be counterbalanced by opposite interests.

Accountability means that an agent has a clearly defined task and that he experiences rewards and punishments as the result of his own actions. In real life, however, accountability does not always coincide with power and legitimacy. Power is based on freedom to act and resources allowing an ability to influence. An agent is legitimate if other actors grant it trust and consider it to have the right to take certain actions. There are, however, several possible cases of mismatch between accountability, power, and legitimacy.

Accountability without power and without legitimacy means that someone may be punished for failures without being able to influence the outcome or being obeyed. Power and accountability without legitimacy can be efficient, but is not based on consent and therefore often breaks down, perhaps even in violent forms. The ideal is, of course, that accountability, power, and legitimacy coincide to allow for efficient exercise of responsibility. The exercise of accountability must be based on clear objectives and efficient methods of scrutiny and control. In a pluralist system, tasks and responsibilities are of course often delegated by way of contracts, which often are long term.

Institutional Changes

It is one thing to demonstrate deficiencies in institutions, quite another to suggest remedies. Many countries have found that reforms of their political institutions have led to unintended outcomes. This is not, however, an argument for abstaining from making any effort to improve the political system; it is more of a reminder that the intended effects are not always realized. Non-action—preserving the status quo—is, however, also an act.

The perfect constitution is an utopia. Democratic systems are, however, inherently self-correcting. Successful democracy can learn from mistakes and adapt to changing conditions. History gives many examples of successful constitutional reforms in which countries have been able to improve their system of government.

Distinct Institutions

The actual working of contemporary Swedish politics differs greatly from the general principles of the Swedish constitution. An important reason is that roles have become ambiguous and accountability unclear. In our opinion, the reestablishment of clear responsibilities would improve the political system.

The Swedish state has over the years taken on an even greater number of tasks, which it has found increasingly difficult to manage. We believe that the state should concentrate on a limited number of fundamental tasks for the common interest of society, such as granting basic rights and freedom of citizens, economic safety, a reasonably even distribution of income and wealth, and providing collective goods and basic infrastructure, as well as assuring macroeconomic stability.

A weakening of the executive has caused problems for Swedish parliamentarianism. The government should therefore be strengthened and the control functions of parliament simultaneously extended. In many cases, public administration plays an ambiguous role. The responsibilities of government ministries and agencies should be defined more precisely. The borderlines between the executive and various administrative agencies should be clarified, and the latter should focus more on their specific objectives and results.

Central government regulation has drastically impeded local self-government. The municipalities should, in our view, be given more independence but also more responsibility.

Organized popular movements have, over the years, become increasingly integrated into the public sector with the emergence of different types of corporatist institutions. It is important that the voluntary organizations regain their independent role in civil society. As the public debate has been more and more dominated by mass media, it is important to strengthen the independence and competence of mass media.

The State

Strengthened Parliamentarianism

There are, in principle, two different ways to organize the relationship between the central branches of the state. Separation of powers means that the different branches are mutually independent. Power is in this case divided between the legislative and the executive. Parliamentarianism means instead that the executive is the focus of power. The cabinet remains in office as long as it is tolerated by parliament. Thus the most important role of parliament is to set the general political direction by forming the cabinet, scrutinizing its activities, and exercising accountability.

The political system in Sweden has—as in most other European countries—developed from separation of powers to parliamentarianism. The old constitution from 1809 was based on the doctrine of separation of powers, typical of its time. The new constitution from 1974 underscores instead that the Swedish democracy is founded on a parliamentary polity. Yet elements of the idea of the separation of powers remain (Tarschys 1984). The ongoing debate on the role of the Riksdag indicates that there still is tension between the principles of separation of power and parliamentarianism. The present political system has not fully drawn the consequences of the principles of parliamentarianism.

A parliamentary polity means that the legislature is the major representative of the people, and that the cabinet rules the country. The Swedish system worked fairly well in the years when the cabinet could rely on stable support in the Riksdag. As this support gradually has eroded, the cabinet has also found it increasingly difficult to exercise its constitutional tasks.

The weakness of Swedish parliamentarianism was clearly shown in the government crisis of February 1990. When the Riksdag discussed the Social Democratic government bill on a general wage freeze, Prime Minister Ingvar Carlsson announced that the government would resign if the bill was defeated. A majority of the Riksdag voted against the bill and the government consequently resigned. However, the parties that voted against the bill, the nonsocialist parties and the Left (the former Communist) Party, were not able to form a new government. The Social Democrats then stayed in office with the same prime minister.

The government crises in 1990 demonstrates that even though the government has the responsibility to rule the country, it often lacks the power to do so. Bringing the political system closer to the fundamental principles of parliamentarianism therefore requires strengthening the position of the cabinet. The constitutions of other European countries provide examples of various methods whereby one may improve the parliamentary system in this respect.

The German constitution of 1949 was influenced by the negative experiences of weak governments in the Weimar period. An important ingredient in the present German constitution is the constructive vote of no confidence. The Bundestag can force the government to resign only if a new chancellor can be elected by parliament. We suggest that a similar rule be added to the Swedish constitution. The Riksdag would then not be able to vote down a government unless it is able to form a new one at the same time.

The position of the government can also be strengthened by a rule similar to article 49:3 in the French constitution. According to this article, the prime minister can ask for confidence from the Assemblée Nationale on the passing of a specific bill. The law is considered adopted unless a motion of no confidence is passed. If this type of rule is combined with a constructive vote of no confidence (à la

Germany), the government can get through important legislation, such as its budget proposal, if the opposition is not able to form a new government.

The French constitution also includes a method that prevents the parliament from dealing with government bills item by item. The government can demand a package vote so that parliament only can choose between accepting or rejecting the bill in its entirety. We suggest that this rule also be added to the Swedish constitution, but that its applicability be limited to the budget and such legislative bills that are possible to pass by a simple majority. The Riksdag should retain its strong influence over the constitution, laws concerning the rules of the Riksdag, and legislation on basic rights and freedom of individuals, which should be dealt with according to the rules in operation today (a qualified majority or the necessity to pass legislation also in the following election period). At the same time, we suggest that the supervisory powers of the Riksdag over the cabinet be enhanced.

The Cabinet: Political Efficacy
In a parliamentary polity, the cabinet is the center of executive power. In addition to external constraints, such as international events and fiscal deficits inherited from previous governments, the cabinet also has important internal constraints. For instance, the internal organization of the government ministries are crucial for the workings of the parliamentary system.

Rapidly changing demands on the government's ability to act have left only a few marks on the internal organization of the ministries. Current administrative practices are greatly influenced by earlier periods in Swedish history. Even rather late in this century, a legalistic culture has prevailed in the ministries. The cabinet has traditionally been the highest tier in the administrative system, and a large number of individual cases required administrative or juridical solutions by the cabinet. When the public sector expanded rapidly from the middle of the century, the ever more encompassing welfare state gave the ministries the role of central planning organs for different sectors of society. The primary competence of the ministries is still to process administrative cases, in addition to the task of preparing new reforms.

But some of these traditional tasks are now becoming less important. Responsibility for administrative cases is increasingly delegated to independent courts, tribunals, and agencies. Moreover, the end of public-sector expansion reduces the role of the central executive offices as initiators of new expensive reforms.

The ministries instead face new demands. A major task is to help the public sector to use its limited resources more efficiently. The changing role of the state also directly affects the ministries. They will bear a crucial responsibility for monitoring developments in different areas of government policy and for furnishing the government and the Riksdag with information about the outcome of political decisions. This type of evaluation requires information systems and analytical capacity of much higher quality than what is presently available.

The ministerial organization still reflects the different sectoral interests of the welfare state. Internal methods of coordination are therefore still very important, especially in the Swedish polity where almost all government decisions have to be taken collectively by the cabinet, and not by individual ministers. The most important coordinating bodies in Sweden, as in most other parliamentary systems, are the prime minister's office and the ministry of finance. In a coalition government, special coordination units are also crucial.

Experience from the last fifteen years indicates that the internal coordination mechanisms must be improved. There is an acute need for analyses across policy areas. The traditional budgetary process makes different sectorial interests compete with each other, leaving the ministry of finance as the supreme arbiter. The role of the minister of finance has, in this context, been reduced to a veto position toward increased expenditures. Recently the government has, rather unsuccessfully, tried to "turn the veto around," that is, let the ministry of finance set the agenda. The new model would mean that the cabinet, at an early stage in the budget process, sets the general priorities and determines a fixed frame for expenditures. The responsibility for the actual implementation would then be delegated to lower tiers in the central government administration.

The budget process is quite different from this blueprint. It is not an exaggeration to state that the present budget is no more than the sum of independently decided individual items. The blueprint model would instead start with the sum, and subsequently divide it up into smaller items.

In the blueprint model, the ministries would be responsible for monitoring events and evaluating whether the objectives of the different programs are met. Even if it is outside the scope of this report to fill in the precise details, we would like to make some suggestions and indicate their consequences.

Each successive government adopts, of course, its own internal organization, but in fact the ministerial organization has historically been characterized by a considerable degree of inertia. The division into a large number of ministries reflects the sectorized nature of the public sector. To enable the government to meet its general political responsibilities, the ministries should be reorganized into more encompassing units.

Also, the number of ministers should be reduced rather than increased. If the government becomes larger, there will be need for a smaller, core cabinet. Although small ministries have advantages in terms of oversight and governability, the need for improved coordination and analytical capacity requires larger ministries. Some analytical work that is now done in independent administrative agencies could then be transferred to the ministries. The ministerial structure should also be made more flexible. Ministries that are larger in size than the present ones encourage more comprehensive views. The boundaries between ministries could also be bridged by project groups with limited terms.

The highest administrative positions in a ministry, below the minister himself, today include the undersecretary of state (*statssekretare*), and below this position, two officers, one of administration (*expeditionschef*), the other of legal affairs (*rättschef*). From the beginning all of these were nonpartisan, legal positions. During the last decades, the position of undersecretary of state has become a purely partisan appointment, which combines the roles as deputy minister and administrative leader of the ministry.

The top-level management of the ministries is in need of improvement. Each ministry should have one nonpartisan top executive— the permanent undersecretary—on a level with the partisan undersecretary. Legal training should not be a necessary qualification. Economic expertise might be at least as important. The top executives of all ministries can form a joint board, which would play the role of the administrative leadership of the government office. The present undersecretary of state then becomes a distinct partisan position. In Denmark each ministry, below the minister himself, is led by a nonpartisan permanent undersecretary and lacks a partisan undersecretary of state. Norway has a permanent, nonpartisan as well as a partisan undersecretary of state. We recommend the Norwegian model.

Recruitment to the ministries must also be reformed. Training in law should be a necessary prerequisite only for officials with strictly legal tasks. A background in humanities and social science, in particular economics, should be emphasized. The level of academic qualifications should be raised. An operational way of achieving this is to set a target for recruiting staff with doctoral degrees.

The ministries are too much preoccupied with minor cases, many of which come from the Riksdag in the form of private member bills and questions. The government's workload is largely determined by parliament.

The Riksdag: Defender of the General Interest and Examiner of the Government

Ambiguity regarding the principle of parliamentarianism on the one hand, and separation of powers on the other, has led to a diffuse role for the Riksdag. Stronger emphasis on the principle of parliamentarianism would significantly change parliamentary practices. The canon that the Riksdag is the major representative of the people does not of course mean that all political decisions should be taken by the parliament. Rather, the parliamentary principle implies that the government rules the realm by delegation. The basic task of parliament is to hold the government accountable, by its power to overturn the government and appoint a new one. In this respect the role of the Riksdag is to set the basic political orientations and ensure that the government stays on the main course (Schück et al. 1992).

The primary role of the Riksdag is therefore to define and defend the general interest of the entire citizenry. The general interest is rarely obtained by a simple summation of special interests representing certain groups or regions. No single group or individual can monopolize the formulation of the general interest. In a democracy the general interest is formed continuously in a process where clashing arguments in public debate is an essential ingredient.

Opinions in Sweden differ about the proper role of the elected representative (Holmberg and Esaiasson 1988). Some members of the Riksdag consider it their primary task to represent their constituency. Others turn their loyalty to specific group interests, which we believe is often unfortunate for society as a whole. Every member of the

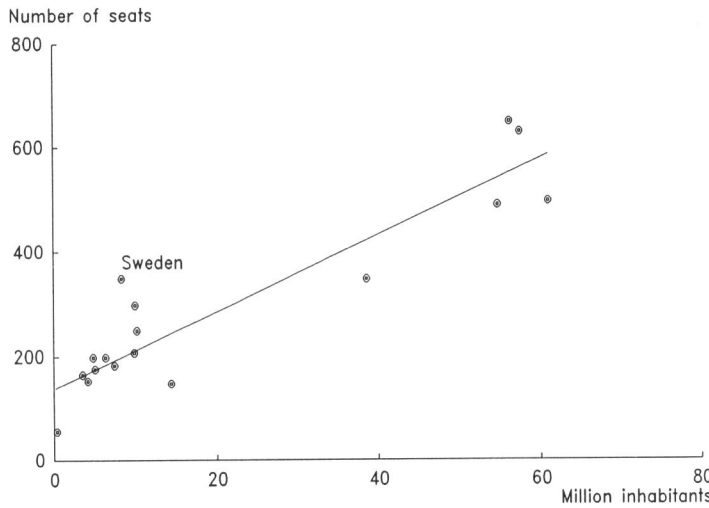

Source: Petersson 1993, adaptation of Peters 1991, table 3.3.

Figure 5.1
Size of parliaments in Europe

Riksdag should, in our view, be elected primarily to defend the interest of the nation as a whole. In the field of economic policy, this means that special interests must be constrained when they seriously threaten the long-run overall standard of living in society.

The main problem with the Riksdag today is that the public interest has difficulties asserting itself against strong special interests. Our proposals aim therefore both at strengthening the role of the Riksdag in the parliamentary polity and at making Riksdag members take greater responsibility for the general interest. If the cabinet's executive power is enhanced, the Riksdag must be given better opportunities to exercise its function as the examiner of the cabinet. We share the general view that the Riksdag, with its 349 members, is too large. There are certainly countries with larger legislatures, but the Swedish Riksdag is about double in size compared to countries with similar population (figure 5.1). A smaller Riksdag would be more efficient. It would, in theory, also be less specialized along sector lines, because each member would be forced to take responsibility for broader policy areas. We believe that the Riksdag should be reduced to about half its current size.

With elections every three years, Sweden has very short election periods. The government therefore has limited time to enforce independent, forceful, and long-term policies. We believe that the election period should be extended to four or, preferably, five years, though we do not of course believe that such a reform is the only, or even the most important, solution to the present political problems.

Some crucial conditions that determine the composition of the Riksdag are not regulated in the constitution. The power over the recruitment process lies in the hands of the political parties. Constituency organizations and local interests are very important in this process. The parties would be in a better position to raise themselves above narrow local interests if they—in addition to the constituency lists—also nominated national candidates who were more inclined to pay attention to the interests of the nation as a whole.

It is a fact, though not only in the Swedish national assembly, that recruitment to standing committees is largely determined by group membership. Farmers tend to be appointed to the Standing Committee on Agriculture and teachers to the Standing Committee on Education. One way to counteract this tendency is to introduce various formal requirements, or rather restrictions. Yet a general disqualification on the grounds of occupation or group membership would soon lead to conflicts with basic principles of nondiscrimination, as well as to practical difficulties. Personal experience from previous employment provides valuable knowledge to parliamentary work. Moreover, the influence of special interest would not be prevented, but find other roads. Both lobbying activities and opinion formation in the mass media are already common in Sweden. These tactics are especially efficacious in a country with gullible mass media. It is, however, important that the rules concerning conflicts of interest be made more restrictive.

General experience seems to indicate that special interests are particularly successful when the jurisdiction of standing committees is narrow and homogeneous and when the policy issues have concentrated benefits and dispersed costs (Hall and Grofman 1990). Thus both the competence and the incentives of the parliamentary bodies is of prime importance in this context.

The most promising way to balance strong special interests is probably to modify the tasks of the standing committees. The previous organization, based on classical state functions, was replaced in the early 1970s by a division based on sector policies. The planning philosophy of the expanding public sector also affected the internal organization of the national assembly. A natural strategy now would be to give the committees wider and more encompassing functions. The Standing Committee on Agriculture and the Standing Committee on Housing could, for example, be merged into a more general committee on industry and commerce. The Standing Committee on Finance should, as already suggested, be given a supervisory role in the budget process (Democracy Committee 1987).

Compared to other legislatures, the Riksdag gives its members considerable opportunity for private initiatives in parliament. Thousands of private member bills bear witness to all the energy that each member devotes to impressing public opinion, notably among the member's own constituency. If one decides to concentrate the Riksdag's resources on main policy choices, one must also restrict the private member initiatives. Such limitations are specially motivated for proposals leading to increased expenditures.

Today members of the Riksdag are more inclined to vote for new reforms than to evaluate previous decisions. To be an efficient examiner of the government, the Riksdag needs a qualified staff of professionals. Increased power to scrutinize and control the executive would give the Riksdag the opportunity to discover and expose both irregularities and inefficiencies. The Riksdag Auditing Office should be given more resources and it should play a more central role, more in line with the Congressional Budget Office in the United States. The Riksdag need not conduct all investigations itself. Auditing services could also be commissioned from Swedish and foreign organizations. Controls and evaluation must be conducted more efficiently and at a faster pace. The Riksdag must receive current information about the consequences of policy decisions in order for the feedback function to work properly. Discovered irregularities must lead to practical consequences, where individuals and bodies in charge are held accountable. Published reports and public hearings should be emphasized. Through systematic and effective scrutiny, the Riksdag can play a more central role in the public debate. For instance, public hearings with the governor of the central bank, along the ideas outlined in chapter 2, would certainly catch the attention of the general public.

The Budget Process

Historically, the European parliaments were formed as a way for the king to convince his reluctant subjects to pay taxes for his increasingly expensive wars and administration. The legitimacy of the Riksdag is still based on the old view that the people must consent to taxation. The 1809 constitution proclaimed that "the ancient right of the Swedish people to tax itself shall be exercised by the Riksdag alone." The present constitution states that it is the Riksdag that decides on taxes.

Today the relationship between the national assembly and the power of taxation is different. In the past the executive tried to convince the representatives to raise spending and to pay more taxes. At present it is the parliament, often influenced by strong special interest groups, that struggles to raise expenditures against the restraining efforts of the executive, especially the ministry of finance. The inability of the Riksdag to uphold the general interest against the demands of special interest groups shows that the budget process must be reformed.

Neither public sector growth nor budget problems are unique to Sweden. However, the development during the last few decades varies considerably among the OECD countries. While countries such as France, Canada, the United Kingdom, and Austria have had roughly constant or declining net public sector debts, the debt has grown almost without control in countries such as Belgium, Greece, and Italy. Statistical analysis indicates that internal factors, and not just external macro economic disturbances, explain these differences. A study of the EC countries (von Hagen 1992) indicates that the organization of the budget process clearly affects the outcome. Institutional reform may therefore be a promising way to create a better balance in the public-sector budget.

It is useful for the discussion to divide the budget process into three stages. In stage one, the budget proposal is formulated in a dialogue between the ministry of finance and the sectoral ministries. In the second stage the budget proposal is discussed and decided upon by parliament. The third stage consists of the implementation process.

The budget process involves a dilemma for politicians and civil servants. Although each individual has a general interest in a balanced and efficient economy, there are also strong special demands concerning one's own sector, region, or even private interest. This dilemma can, in principle, be solved in two different ways. One solution is to rely on general guidelines designed to maintain long-term goals. Such goals might define and implement public-sector borrowing requirements, expenditure frames, and budgets extending over several years. According to available evidence, this method is rather ineffectual. General proclamations lack the required constraining power in the actual political and administrative decisionmaking process.

A second route seems more promising. It implies that the agents are constrained by binding restrictions in each stage of the budget process. The coordinating units of the government, that is, the prime minister's office and the ministry of finance, are given a superior position. A frame for total expenditures is decided upon early in the decisionmaking process. The stage in parliament does not allow much leeway for amendments. The Riksdag is allowed to discuss specific items only after the total frame has been decided. Moreover, the budget is made transparent in the sense that all incomes and expenditures are clearly presented. The total budget frame has to be strictly adhered to also by the implementing bodies. Scrutiny and evaluation have, then, to be given a prominent role.

The actual Swedish budget process has been studied by the same methods as the one applied to the investigations of the EC countries (Molander 1992). This analysis shows that the Swedish budget process is weak in comparison with other countries included in the study. Sweden ranks, in fact, second from the bottom in terms of strictness of the budget process. It is ranked together with countries that have pursued an untenable budget policy, such as Belgium, Greece, and Italy (see figure 5.2).

Restrictions on the freedom of action, in various countries, have proven to have significant effects on the budget outcome. If we apply the results of cross-section studies to Sweden, net government borrowing in this country could be reduced by 5% of GDP and the public debt by 23% of GDP if the budget process were as strict as, for instance, in Denmark. More detailed analyses of the budget process also show that the two first stages of the budget process, in the government and the Riksdag, are the most crucial.

There is thus considerable scope for improvement. We suggest that the reforms should aim at the three stages of the budget process, and at the budget document itself. It is important that the ongoing reforms of the budget process within the central government office

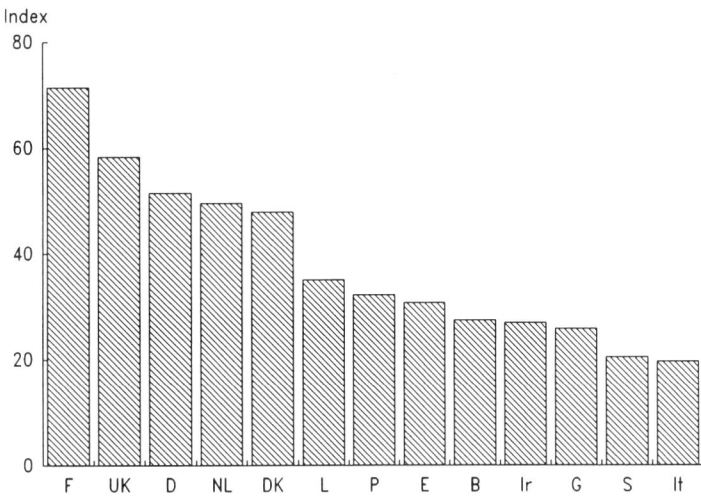

Source: Molander 1992.

Figure 5.2
The stringency of the budget process in the EC and Sweden

continue. The budget document should unequivocally declare total spending as well as its distribution between main spending areas. Early in the budget process, the cabinet has to set a total frame based on an assessment of available resources, estimated by the minister of finance. The cabinet bears of course a collective responsibility for setting these priorities. The coordinating units, the prime minister's office and the ministry of finance, are to be given a visible and superior position. It would be convenient if the fiscal year would start on January 1 rather than July 1. There are also good reasons in favor of a shorter and more condensed decisionmaking process.

Automatic rules govern a large share of the budget expenditures. Such a system might be indispensable for purely practical reasons. But in many areas, automatic indexing stimulates higher spending. This device should therefore be used with caution. Between the two extremes of automatic indexing and cash limits are several other options. Automatic rules have a drawback in that status quo of the expenditure rules is regularly taken as a point of departure in the dialogue between the individual ministries and the ministry of finance. It is preferable that expenditures are assessed more unconditionally so that the burden of proof is put on the particular ministry, not on the ministry of finance.

In the last few years a growing number of items have been taken out of the regular budget and presented in separate bills. A stricter budget process requires that this trend be stopped. The main rule ought to be that the entire budget is presented to the Riksdag in one cohesive document, such that parliament is given a total assessment of the expenditures to be voted upon. Unforeseen expenditures in one area should be charged to accounts in the same area.

The budget document must also be more transparent, so that the Riksdag can assess actual spending. If social insurance, according to our earlier suggestions, is moved outside the yearly budget process, it should be presented separately from the government budget. As long as social-security spending is part of the consolidated government budget it should, however, be presented gross rather than net so that its actual size and development are clearly visible.

Tax perks and tax expenditures are often hidden. Although explicit expenditures are regularly scrutinized in the ordinary budget process, tax exemptions are not clearly accounted for. Exemptions may therefore remain long after the original motives for them have disappeared (Mattsson 1992). After the tax reform in 1991, it is easier to document these type of exceptions. We recommend that tax perks and tax expenditures be presented and decided upon in the same way as regular expenditures.

In spite of the great importance attached to the budget process in the Riksdag, the parliamentary process has several deficiencies. The Riksdag is occupied with minor details, and it fails in its crucial task of upholding solid budget criteria. The parliamentary stage of the budget process is in dire need of reform.

The budget bill should first be referred to the Standing Committee on Finance, which would have the responsibility of assessing the overall frame and the distribution among the main spending areas. The opposition parties then have an opportunity to present their alternatives. A decision on the budget frame is made after a general debate in the Riksdag. Each standing committee then receives a fixed spending limit. Every proposal for new expenditures has to be combined with corresponding cuts. The Riksdag, finally, makes a decision on the detailed budget.

Such a strict budget process is not in any way contrary to the idea of a democratic process. Swedish MPs have a unique degree of

Democracy 189

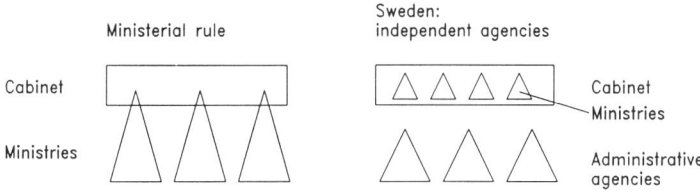

Figure 5.3
The cabinet and government agencies

freedom to launch their own proposals. In democracies such as the United Kingdom and France, private member initiatives are much more restricted. Because the constitutional changes suggested here are supposed to be decided upon by the Riksdag itself, we talk only about voluntarily imposed restrictions, designed to help the Riksdag to exercise its basic tasks in a better way.

The final decision on the budget does not mean that the task of the Riksdag is finished. On the contrary, one could say that the most important task then only begins. The Riksdag is responsible for scrutinizing and controlling the use of public funds, so that its intentions are followed. This is why it is crucially important to strengthen the Riksdag's power as supervisory body.

Independent Boards and Agencies

Sweden and, to some extent Finland, deviate from general European patterns when it comes to the organization of the central state administration (Petersson and Söderlind 1992). This organizational split between ministries and administrative boards and agencies (figure 5.3) is relatively unusual. The question is whether Sweden should adapt to European standards also in this respect, or whether there are good reasons to keep this peculiar system, the historical roots of which go back three centuries in time.

Other countries have mixed experiences with the system of encompassing ministries, which vertically integrates the executive office and the central administration. Overload and ungovernability have plagued public administration in many of the nations with this system. One remedy is to detach boards and agencies from direct cabinet control, thus approaching the traditional Swedish model.

The exact meaning of the Swedish doctrine of independent agencies is not quite clear. The Swedish constitution contains two basic rules, which point in different directions. According to one rule, all administrative boards are subordinate to the cabinet. Another rule states that neither the cabinet nor the parliament may determine how an administrative authority shall make its decision in a particular case, concerning the exercise of public authority or application of law. A widely discussed issue therefore concerns the scope of legitimate informal contacts between the ministries and the administrative agencies.

In our opinion, the traditional Swedish model should be upheld, and in fact applied more stringently. According to the constitution, the government shall rule the country. The principle of independent boards and agencies must of course not be interpreted as the freedom for civil servants to pursue their own policies against the wishes of the government. The boundary between the ministries and the administrative agencies should be drawn according to the basic distinction between the setting and implementation of objectives. Government by informal contacts involves serious risks with diffuse roles and confusion of responsibilities. Government directives have to be given by legal objectives, clear delegation, and strict criteria for the exercise of accountability.

A system with all too diffuse boundaries between ministries and administrative agencies runs the risk of sector-based special interests invading the public sector. The fundamental task of the Riksdag and the cabinet is to set general objectives by weighing different sectors against each other. The problem is that many administrative agencies are built upon and derive their legitimacy from sectoral interests. The sectoral interests are also linked by tight networks. Ministries and administrative agencies often in fact serve as embassies of special interests. One natural step would be to abolish the lay boards of the administrative agencies, which have given organized interests formal decisionmaking power in the central and regional government agencies. As explained more fully below, it is particularly important to abandon the system according to which special interest groups have representatives in these agencies; such a reform is already under way.

The role of the central boards and agencies has recently shifted as a consequence of the tendency to decentralize tasks to the regional and local levels, especially to local governments. Today the principal task of central administrative bodies is to evaluate and assess policy outcomes. One example is the dismantling of the apex in the old education hierarchy, the national board of education, and its replacement with a "leaner and meaner" agency concentrated upon evaluation and performance measures. Although the direct budgetary savings of this type of debureaucratization are only marginal, efficiency arguments speak in favor of restructuring other policymaking hierarchies in a similar way. Too many levels often hamper public administration. Individual cases are shuffled between different agencies and different levels, creating overlaps, diluted responsibility, and expensive bureaucracy.

Deregulation would also naturally reduce public-sector tasks and make for smaller administrative agencies. One can often defend central regulation with reasonably good arguments in each specific case, but the total effect may substantially impede private initiatives. It is important not to wind up in a society where nothing is permitted unless a public authority decides so. One of the basic tenets of liberal justice is just the opposite, namely, that everything which is not explicitly prohibited is permitted.

The Central Bank

The special status of the central bank as an authority subordinate to the Riksdag was originally motivated—almost two centuries ago—by a desire to protect the bank from government interference, particularly the king's abuse of power to print money. Similar incentive problems today call for a reform of the central bank law.

The position of the central bank was discussed in general terms in chapter 2. Our proposals on this issue follow the principles concerning the relationship between ministries and administrative agencies. Through delegation, an agency can be granted an independent position of execution under the condition that the institution is transparent and accountable.

The primary objective of the central bank is to protect the long-term value of money. The goal is, hence, low inflation. The right of the state to borrow from the central bank should therefore be abolished. The independence of the central bank can be secured by certain institutional reforms. We suggest that the term of office for the members of the board of governors of the Bank of Sweden be extended and that the appointments follow a rotating scheme. The governor of the Bank of Sweden should account for monetary policy in open as well as closed hearings before the committees of the Riksdag.

PROPOSALS

Central Government

92. Amend the constitution in the direction of more consistent parliamentarianism. Reinforce the position of the cabinet. Introduce a so-called constructive vote of no confidence whereby the cabinet remains in office as long as a new cabinet cannot be formed.

93. Strengthen the position of the prime minister's office and the ministry of finance. Reduce the total number of ministries.

94. Intensify the management function of the ministries. Each ministry should have a civil servant as top administrator, below the minister and alongside a politically appointed undersecretary.

95. Alter the focus in parliament from detailed issues to major policy guidelines.

96. Strengthen the parliament's resources for scrutinizing and auditing the cabinet.

97. Reduce the number of standing committees, and strengthen the position of the finance committee.

98. Neutralize the influence of interest groups in public-sector decisionmaking by sharpening the rules on conflict of interest. Assign broader areas of responsibility to the standing committees of parliament.

99. Extend the election period to four, or preferably five, years.

100. Reduce the number of seats in parliament by one half.

101. Strengthen the budget process in the cabinet office. The cabinet should stipulate budget norms early in the process, specifying both total expenditures and the expenditures of each ministry.

102. As regards the budget process in parliament, a superior and coordinating role should be assigned to the finance committee. Parliament should begin with a binding vote on total government expenditures before separate areas are considered. Proposals by members of parliament leading to increased expenditures have to be financed by cuts elsewhere.

103. The budget document should be made comprehensive and transparent. All government expenditures should in principle be decided upon during the budget process. Concealed expenditures (so-called tax expenditures) should be made visible.

104. As the direct, regulatory activities of the central administrative agencies are curtailed, their responsibility for auditing and evaluation should be strengthened.

105. The price stabilization objective of the Bank of Sweden, and its independence in relation to the cabinet and parliament (point 2), should be determined through legislation, as should its accountability to parliament.

Local Government

Local Self-Governance

It is declared already in the opening article of the Swedish constitution that local self-government is a basic tenet of Swedish democracy. Sweden has also ratified the European convention of local self-government. In our opinion, such self-government should be strengthened rather than weakened.

The major part of public-sector expansion in the 1960s and the 1970s took place in the municipalities and in the county councils. It is first and foremost these institutions that are affected by the current cutbacks in spending and restructuring of the public sector. Restructuring includes increasing competition in public-sector service production and giving individual citizens greater freedom of choice. How, then, should the public sector be reformed and at the same time local self-government be preserved and protected?

The Swedish public sector has four territorial levels, if the parishes of the state church are included. Each has the right to impose taxes. The regional level is characterized by a double command with diffuse division of responsibilities. The county council (*landstinget*) is a regional assembly appointed in general elections. The county administrative board (*länsstyrelsen*) is the primary state agency at the regional level. The governing board of the county administrative board is a strange hybrid: its members are appointed by the county council, whereas the chairperson—the county governor—is

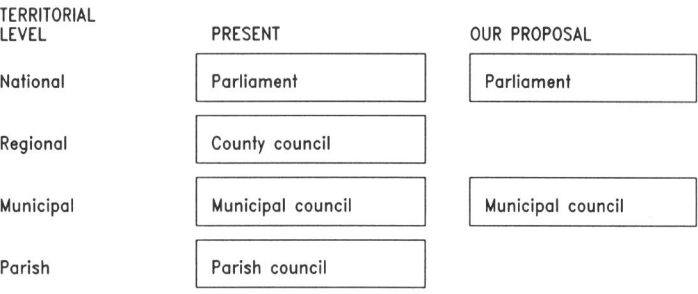

Figure 5.4
Directly elected assemblies with power of taxation

appointed by the central government. The future organization of the Swedish regions remains an open question since an official commission (Regional Commission 1992) has presented three alternative models.

According to our judgment, two regional levels within Sweden are sufficient to fulfill the demands of representative democracy (figure 5.4)—in particular as a third, European level, will most likely emerge in the future. Sweden is not large enough or heterogeneous enough to justify a development in a federal direction. Today the main task of the county council is health care. We do not find it possible to defend the present situation, which means that a sector-specific body has its own power of taxation: neither the housing sector nor the university sector has this right. For these reasons the county councils should be abolished. Regional coordination problems can be solved by contracts between municipalities or by other procedures, depending on the issue to be dealt with. The county administrative boards of the state can be reduced to small and efficient staff organizations. All members of the governing board of these county administrative boards should be appointed by the government.

Abolishing the county councils raises a problem of how to organize health care in the future. We are not prepared to suggest specific reforms in this area, but instead refer to ongoing work in a parallel commission. The organization should, according to our general principles of pluralism, be controlled by a mixture of different kinds of institutions: the state, municipalities, cooperating municipalities, foundations, private hospitals, etc. Financing may be organized by a combination of taxes and of health insurance, collective as well as individual. Proposals for the future health care system should, however, in our view be based on the assumption that the county councils are abolished.

For consistency, these general principles should also apply to the state church of Sweden—though reforms in this field has hardly anything to do with the economic crisis. The church parishes should no longer have the privilege to impose taxes, even if one decides to retain the state church system.

The idea of local self-government should, then, be applied only within the framework of the existing local governments (municipalities). Two important problems arise in translating the general idea of self-government into specific institutions. One has to do with the relationship between the state and the municipalities; the other problem concerns the internal organization of local government. Decentralization efforts in the last few years mean that the state has transferred new tasks to the municipalities and at the same time given the municipalities greater autonomy. However, the cap on municipal tax rules, decided by the Riksdag and valid through 1993, has severely restricted local self-government.

Today a strategic choice has to be made in the system of local governance. One alternative is to transform the municipalities into local state administrative agencies, financed by transfers from the state and responsible for the local implementation of national legislation and administration. The other alternative is to decentralize substantially, so that the municipalities regain their power of taxation and a wide degree of freedom in determinating their own policies. We believe that decentralization and local self-government are important principles and that the ensuing variation of policies on local levels is not only unavoidable but desirable.

In the longer run, one should thus abolish the centrally decided tax cap. Its introduction in 1991 can be seen as an extraordinary measure caused by the acute economic crisis, and as an attempt to prevent local governments from replacing the reduced state income tax by higher municipal taxes. Previously the central government had forced the municipalities to expand, but recently it decided to take the responsibility for protecting the national economy from ever higher tax rates. The drastic measures in recent years against the municipalities, such as the legislation restricting their power to set local tax rates, should be seen in this light.

Power and Responsibility

Once the municipalities regain their full power of taxation, the general principle of a clear link between power and responsibility becomes crucial. The right to freely decide on income taxes is a cornerstone in the Swedish conception of local self-government. But the power to tax has to be connected with strict rules on the exercise of accountability. The ban on tax increases should not be lifted until constitutional changes have been implemented. Otherwise there is a risk that municipalities push up the total tax pressure in Sweden without full knowledge among citizens as to who is responsible, because the central government is in charge of tax collection for all levels of government.

A fundamental prerequisite for accountability is publicity and transparency. In the present system the individual citizen is mostly unaware of the different components of this total tax bill. A separate income tax notice for municipal taxes would supply the necessary information. Another method would be to let the municipalities themselves, and not the state as in the present situation, collect the municipal taxes. Municipal accounting techniques are also crucial. The state could require that the different municipalities apply the same accounting principles.

We suggest that a referendum should be made compulsory if a municipality wants to change, or at least to raise, its tax rate. In a longer perspective, the local taxation rights can be extended to include also the choice of tax base. Local income taxes might then be combined with local property taxes and local sales taxes.

In countries with wider variation in municipal services and tax rates than in Sweden, citizens choose their residency by voting with their feet. This idea has been emphasized in theoretical work on local public finance since Tiebout (1956). Such service and tax competition may give important incentives for strict economic management, and adherence to citizens' preferences, in each municipality. (Of course, tax competition also implies a well-known externality in the form of eroded tax bases in other localities.)

Today the state tries to equalize structural and geographical differences among the municipalities by a revenue-sharing system. There may be good reasons for such a territorial egalitarianism, but central redistribution of income between municipalities may reduce the incentives to maintain the local tax base. The construction of the present system in Sweden has exactly this weakness. In due course, the revenue-sharing contribution should be tied to factors (such as the number of elderly) that are affected as little as possible by local political decisions.

Since the 1862 municipal reform act, local self-government in Sweden has been based on a combination of power and responsibility. The municipalities have been given a broadly defined area of jurisdiction. The limits have been drawn with special regard to the principles of rule of law, impartiality, and nondiscrimination. Municipal decisions can be appealed to the general administrative court system. The individual citizen's right to appeal is fundamental for a balance between individual rights and freedoms on the one hand, and local self-government on the other.

Local self-government is also threatened by parliamentary legislation on detailed rules in the form of "social rights" granted to individual citizens by the central government, but delivered by the local government (see also chapter 3). The limits of municipal competence should only be set in order to guarantee the basic requirements of individual rights and freedoms.

The internal organization of local government has recently undergone considerable reform. Previously, municipal administrative boards were frequently organized along sector lines. Other modes of organization are now replacing this structure, which was characteristic of the period of public-sector expansion. Submunicipal councils as well as buyer-seller models are recent experiments that have already given valuable experience. Their general applicability is still uncertain, however.

In our view, local self-government should be transformed in the same direction as we suggested earlier for the central level. The principles of pluralist democracy are just as appropriate for the local level. The municipal council is the local equivalent to the Riksdag. The municipal council should, according to our general principles, concentrate on long-term rules for the municipality, protect the basic rights of individual citizens, oversee the fulfilment of demands for collective goods, and interfere to correct local external effects.

Efforts to outline the perfect organizational model are futile. Neither total political control nor complete market control and privatization is desirable. Ongoing experiments will probably demonstrate that most municipalities settle for a mixture of different institutions and mechanisms. This means that municipalities will differ more.

Most important, in our view, is that different alternatives are tried and experiments allowed. Only practical experience can prove whether public agencies, corporations, cooperatives, voluntary associations, or other organizational arrangements are the best solution in each different case.

PROPOSALS

Local Governments

106. Because specific sectors of the economy should not be given the right of taxation, the county councils (responsible mainly for the health care system) should be abolished.

107. The right of taxation of the state church should, for the same general reason, be revoked.

108. The freeze on local government tax rates should eventually be phased out, as it is not compatible with the concept of local government autonomy; however, we suggest a mandatory local referendum as a prerequisite for tax increases (point 64).

Civic Society

Voluntary Associations

Special interest organizations constitute a fundamental dilemma for pluralist democracy. On the one hand, pluralism requires a multitude of independent organizations, including organized special interests. On the other hand, these organizations can become so powerful that they threaten the general interest. This dilemma is particularly critical in Sweden, where the organizations are strong and well organized. Moreover, the large public sector offers the interest organizations powerful tools in influencing and even controlling considerable segments of society.

The Swedish symbiosis between the state and interest group organizations is visible in different kinds of corporatist institutions (Heckscher 1951; Olsen 1983; Micheletti 1990; Lewin 1992; Rothstein 1992). The close cooperation between the state and various organizations has many times been judged as mutually beneficial. The state has acquired information and has been able to create legitimacy

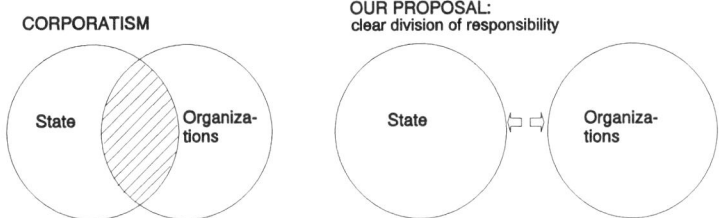

Figure 5.5
The state and the organizations

among organizations for political decisions. The organizations have, at the same time, had direct access into the political and administrative decisionmaking process. But the drawbacks of corporatist arrangements have become increasingly apparent and severe. When the state becomes more dependent on well-organized special interests, it becomes less able to defend the general interest. At the same time, the organizations have become strongly dependent on politicians and public authorities, not least financially.

The negative consequences of corporatism for the functioning of a system of voluntary associations are particularly serious from a perspective of pluralist democracy. The myth of the Swedish model is partly based on an image of vital grass-roots participation. In fact, many organizations have serious internal problems. Declining member activity and increased dependency upon subsidies have eroded the role of voluntary organizations as a channel for the voluntary involvement of individual citizens.

Proposals for reform of civic society easily become contradictory. The voluntary sector is by definition outside the control of the state. But in contemporary Sweden, the boundaries between the public sector and the voluntary associations has been blurred by innumerable contacts and dependencies. At the national level, the actual implementation of corporatism has given a few selected organizations a privileged role. It is therefore important to restore a clear division of responsibility with regard to civic society. Both central and local government have to take specific action to "liberate" civic society. It is our view that the state should stand more neutral than today in relation to various organized interests (figure 5.5). This general principle has several important consequences.

The very last decade has seen a modest reorientation toward decorporatization, which has involved primarily the central labor market organizations. The Swedish Employers' Confederation (SAF) has decided to withdraw from various corporatist bodies, for instance, the lay boards of administrative agencies. As a consequence, the state has found it less natural than earlier that unions should be represented on those boards. This decision has deprived the Swedish Trade Union Confederation (LO) of an important channel of influence. But corporatism is still alive in other sectors, not least at other levels. The organizations, in fact, often serve as substitute administrative organs for the state and the municipalities. For instance, the state still grants organizations certain privileges in labor and housing legislation, as well as in the administration of farm support. Similar interest organizations have formed in the business community, including the chambers of commerce, federation of Swedish industries, as well as various branch organizations. We believe that the state should not favor any specific voluntary organizations by subsidies or legislation.

Beside representation and influence in administrative government agencies, representatives of some organizations also exercize judicial powers as members of specific courts—the market court, the labor court, and the rents and tenancies court of appeal. According to our principle of clear division of responsibility, we believe that this type of representation should be abolished.

Contemporary trends toward internationalization and individualization pose particular challenges for the trade union movement. The Swedish model of codetermination in the field of wages and other labor market conditions is questioned in recent efforts to find a less inflation-prone and more productivity-oriented wage formation process. The European integration process also changes the situation, as European labor legislation is more individualistic and less collectivist than Swedish legislation. In Europe, legal rules and individual rights are more important than the rights of organizations and the collective agreements and negotiation procedures, which are central to the Swedish system. The role of the Swedish trade unions can therefore be expected to change.

As pointed out earlier, the competence of individual employees is becoming an increasingly important factor for efficiency and economic growth. Formal education is not the only crucial component; every job has to be based on the continuous upgrading of individual skills. This may give the unions a different role than earlier. Instead of exercising rights and powers themselves, trade unions may rather become counselors and consultants to individual members.

Restructuring of industry renders present organizational boundaries among employees obsolete. The distinction between blue collar and white collar gradually loses its importance. An amalgamation of the different trade union federations will be realized sooner or later. The state has no reason to interfere in the internal restructuring of organizations, but the state also should not take actions that freeze an archaic organizational structure.

The Swedish trade union movement has earlier proved able to combine strong protection of its members with considerations for the long-term interests of the whole nation, for instance, by advocating productivity growth and structural change. It is of crucial importance not to prevent the trade union movement from finding a new solution to its double task.

The Public Debate

An essential condition for a well-functioning pluralist system is that the power over information is dispersed. A monistic, state-controlled system means that the rulers have a monopoly over information. An open, pluralist system is based on continuous discussion, dialogue, and criticism. The Swedish constitution declares, in fact, that democracy is founded on free speech.

As always there is a considerable gap between ideal and reality. The Swedish public debate is deficient in several ways. But any attempt to suggest improvements rapidly leads to the same dilemma as the one we encountered in the case of voluntary associations and political parties. Because civic society must be safe from government control, political attempts to reform mass media may contradict this principle. But there are several ways in which political decisions may improve the general quality of public debate without favoring any particular channel or view.

Qualified public debate has to adhere to the principle of publicity, laid down in Swedish constitutional law more than two hundred years ago. All official documents are, in principle, open to the public. It is of utmost importance to safeguard this general principle. If Sweden is integrated into the European Community, it is very important to defend the principle of publicity of public-sector documents.

Mass Communication

Mass media dominate opinion formation in modern society. This means that journalists to a large extent control the public debate. The Swedish journalistic method is based on a quite specific view of the world (Power Delegation 1990). Social problems are largely portrayed through personalization and simplification. Political decisions are often described from the perspective of the individual "winner" or "loser" in special cases. As a consequence, special interests tend to be highlighted, and often favored. The mass-media logic is less well suited to the understanding of comprehensive, complex issues, and for dealing with general principles and indirect effects on the economy or society at large.

The way the mass media operate is connected to the present economic and political crisis. The crisis is of course not caused by the mass media, but the functioning of the media may partly explain why the necessary remedies have been postponed. Narrow, short-term interests have tended to overshadow the general interest in both the public debate and political decisionmaking process.

At the same time as the mass media have gained power, different interest groups have become increasingly apt in using the media for their own purposes. An important part of the daily news originates from sources and deliberate leaks from organized special interest groups. This often leaves the citizens with an incomplete and biased view of society.

The deficiencies in the mass media are certainly not an argument for state controls or regulations. On the contrary, the crucial task is to strengthen the independence of the mass media. In line with our general principles, we want to underscore the importance of knowledge and the improvement of human capital also in mass media. That many journalists are easy prey for special interests must, at least to some extent, be attributed to the journalism education offered by the state schools. In contrast to some other countries, it is unusual for journalists in Sweden to have solid academic training in fields of substance such as economics, business, or political science. We therefore suggest that the journalist training in the state education system be a graduate field of study, after a solid academic education; an undergraduate degree or corresponding competence acquired in some other way should be a requirement for acceptance to state schools of journalism.

Active Citizenship

Our proposals concerning the political system imply a redistribution of power and responsibilities. The consequences are particularly pronounced for the individual citizen. In our view of the future, the individual citizen has more power, but also greater personal responsibility. Increased education, the liberation of women, and easier access to information have led to more informed and independent citizens. There are of course still large differences in the ability of individual citizens to safeguard their own interests. Length of education is particularly important. But one should not view the social realities of citizenship only in a static perspective. A comparison with the introduction of general suffrage shows the appropriateness of a dynamic view. Demands for universal suffrage were once contested with the argument that women, poor people, and the uneducated lacked the proper insights and qualities necessary for participation in political life. The proponents of universal suffrage did not deny the knowledge gaps, but they used the arguments to their own advantage. An expanded suffrage, a process of empowerment, was asserted to stimulate knowledge and responsibility. Indeed, the segments of the population that gained suffrage quickly proved their interest and ability to improve their knowledge and willingness to participate in the political process.

Increased responsibility often also means increased willingness and competence to perform new tasks. For instance, the gap in electoral participation between citizens with high and with low education gradually decreased. Most of the voters were once men; now the election turnout is slightly higher among women. Although individualization may favor previously strong social groups in the short term, historical experience shows that knowledge and skills gradually spread throughout the whole population.

Democracy is based on combining individual and collective autonomy. Conflicts may always arise between the individual and the collective. Collective forms of organization must not replace personal responsibility and freedom. This is one reason why organizations must stand free from the state. Representatives of interest organizations must not penetrate the state, and the individual citizen must be independent in relation to the organizations.

But it is also important to point out that increased personal responsibility does not have to stand in conflict with collective organization.

Under favorable conditions, individual and collective action can be mutually reinforcing. Cooperation can enhance individual demands. Voluntary associations can be seen as a school of democracy and may strengthen individual self-confidence and power.

A pluralistic society based on democracy, market economy, and generally accepted social norms is, in our view, the only feasible route to successfully combining individual freedom with collective solidarity.

PROPOSALS

Nongovernmental Organizations

109. Interest groups should not be involved in decisionmaking in the public sector, or in the administration of justice. As a consequence, organizations should not have representatives on the boards of decisionmaking public-sector agencies.

110. The labor court, the rents and tenancies court of appeal, and the market court should be abolished, and their legal functions taken over by courts composed of legal and other expertise only.

111. Nongovernmental organizations should, to a greater extent than today, bear the costs of their own activities, thereby limiting the contributions from taxpayers.

112. The principle of public access to official records should be preserved, particularly in negotiations regarding EC membership.

113. The autonomy and competence of the mass media should be reinforced, for example, by raising the standards of journalist education.

6   Recovery

Points of Departure

The message of the commission is at once traditional and radical. It is traditional in that we stand firmly on two cornerstones of Western society: democracy and market economy. But it is radical in that we propose far-reaching changes in the Swedish economic and political system.

The economic crisis in Sweden is not only a combination of long-run deficiencies in the economic system, a very severe recession, and deep troubles in real estate and financial markets. Several of today's problems also arise from political decisions in the past and are associated with more and more obsolete institutions. It is necessary to redesign these institutions in such a way that they give politicians, authorities, and businesses greater incentives to consider the long-run consequences of their decisions. Indeed, fragmented institutional reform is already on its way in Sweden, in the private as well as in the public sector. What we do in this report is in fact to formulate a program for additional and comprehensive institutional reform, taking as our point of departure three basic principles: a clear division of responsibility, pluralism, and active citizenship.

We believe that Swedish citizens, demanding greater freedom of action today, essentially subscribe to these principles. In the society we envisage, politicians and authorities will be responsible for a narrower set of tasks, but their responsibility will increase in those areas of public life where government decisionmaking is particularly important. In today's society the fuzzy division of responsibility has led to what Erik Lundberg once labeled a mixed-up economy. In the report we combine these three principles—clear division of responsibility, pluralism, and active citizenship—in our proposals for the market sector as well as for the public sector. Market economy and political democracy are the two known methods for combining these principles.

The Market System

A market economy is a complicated and sophisticated system for coordinating millions of decentralized decisions and delegating responsibilities. Prices, wages, and profit opportunities carry information about preferences of households as well as production possibilities of firms. For the market system to work well, neither private barriers to entry nor government regulations and taxes should substantially deform prices, wages, and profit opportunities. Removing regulations and increasing competition therefore becomes important. But a market economy can, as we know, function well only if the state takes clear responsibility for important areas such as the judicial system and other public goods, external effects, infrastructure, basic economic security for the citizens, a reasonable distribution of income, and macroeconomic stability.

What the commission would like to see regarding the market system is nothing less than the restoration of those freedoms of entry, occupation, and profession that new legislation in 1846 and 1864 established in Sweden. Those liberal reforms preceded a period of unprecedented growth. But during the last century these freedoms have been more and more diluted by regulations and barriers to competition, largely due to the influence of different short-run special interests.

The Public Sector

In the same way as the market economy gives influence and responsibility to individuals in their roles as consumers and producers, political democracy gives them influence and responsibility in their roles as voters and political actors. But it is impossible to realize the idea of pluralistic democracy without a clear division of responsibility and active citizens, who act within political institutions and a set of rules that promote the long-run general interest. With such institutions and rules, public policy may be able to serve the broad general interest rather than serving narrow special interests. The welfare state is one example of how society can promote the general interest by enhancing the economic security of all citizens by various social insurance systems. But it is also an example of how distributive conflict and special interests, over time, may acquire disproportionate influence at the expense of the general interest.

This is the background of contemporary reforms of the public sector that we now observe, not only in Sweden but in many Western societies. The goal of the commission is not to dismantle the welfare state, which we regard as a triumph of western democracy. It is rather to remove those excesses and malfunctions that have become a serious handicap for the economy and thereby threaten the economic foundation of the welfare state. When it comes to transfer payments, in particular social security, our main strategy is to make the incentives more appropriate and to make the system more robust to everyday politics. When it comes to public service production, our main strategy is to allow and encourage competition and freedom of choice wherever possible.

The Necessity of a Long-Run View

Stable and long-run rules are important in both private and public life. To invest in Sweden, businesses must have a certain confidence in the stability of rules and regulations, for example, when it comes to systems governing contracts in goods and labor markets, including property rights, trade policy, and taxes. Individual citizens must know how much they need to save on their own and how much insurance they need to purchase to protect their future standard of living. They must also have a reasonable chance to assess the future returns on their own investments in knowledge and professional skills—that is, the returns to education in a wide sense.

A long-run view is also important in stabilization policy. Short-run policies often have long-run consequences both for inflation and unemployment. Policymakers in the 1970s and the 1980s avoided high unemployment by increasing employment in the public sector and by decreasing real wages through devaluations and high inflation. But these policies postponed necessary adjustment of public expenditures and of wage formation and resulted in a steep inflationary trend. When policymakers in the beginning of the 1990s no longer relied on these methods, full employment broke down in connection with the ongoing cost crisis. The earlier policies also concealed the necessity to change various institutions, including the policymaking process itself.

The Conflict between the Short Run and the Long Run

Not only do short-run measures affect long-run development. Structural long-run reform—for instance in the social insurance system and other types of government expenditures—also have short-run macroeconomic effects, at least to the extent that reform is unexpected. Therefore it is important to proceed slowly when phasing in long-run structural reform, not only to avoid destroying individual long-run planning, but also to avoid driving the economy into an even deeper recession by way of drastic cuts in public-sector spending. On the other hand, a main point in chapter 2 was that decisions about long-run reform—designed either to stabilize government finances or to strengthen the political decisionmaking process—may increase the short-run scope for expansionary stabilization policies.

But the requirement of stable rules must not become an obstacle to changes of bad rules and reforms of poorly functioning institutions. A trade-off may therefore arise between good rules and stable rules. Compromise is the only way out. The main principle must be that the rules of the game should not be changed unless large and obvious improvement are possible. It is easier to follow this principle in practice if constitutional arrangements make the rules difficult, but not impossible, to change.

How Do We Resolve the Crisis?

These general principles provide background to our concrete proposals. They may appear overly ambitious and unlikely to be acceptable in their entirety. They will obviously meet with strong resistance from many special interest groups, as well as from parts of the political system. Our justification for being so comprehensive and radical is that the current deep economic crisis has vividly revealed that the task is not simply to correct a few specific mistakes or omissions of economic policy. The crisis has roots that go back several decades and bring into question much of the existing institutional framework.

Some deficiencies in Sweden may clearly be classified as "policy mistakes," while others may more appropriately be called "system failures," even though the borderline between these two concepts is hazy. The most obvious system failures in the economic sphere are perhaps the high public spending, overly generous social security, wide marginal tax wedges, low private—including household—saving, detailed regulations and cartelization in various markets, lax anticartel legislation, and an inflation-prone system of wage formation. The weaknesses in the political system—short election periods, the organization of subcommittees in parliament, a lax budget process, strong influence of special-interest groups over the political process, etc.—may also be classified as system failures.

It is important to realize that these "system failures" are relatively new to Swedish society. They were not pronounced during the successful period of economic growth, from about 1870 to 1970. Before the mid-1960s, public-sector spending was not particularly high in Sweden (neither were tax rates), regulations in product and labor markets were not yet particularly extensive, and private saving was not particularly low.

The most obvious examples of policy mistakes in recent years are perhaps the abrupt deregulation of financial markets in the mid-1980s; the unfortunate timing of the tax reform relative to both financial deregulation and the business cycle; and the insufficiently restrictive fiscal policy pursued during the second half of the 1980s. It is also obvious that it would have been better if the cuts in public-sector spending during the early 1990s' slump had instead been made in the overheated 1980s. The abrupt increase in unemployment 1991–92 largely resulted from the unexpected discontinuation of the previous policy of accommodating domestic cost increases with devaluations and increased public-sector employment. [The preceding four paragraphs have been added to the original Swedish text.]

In discussing our proposals, let us begin by outlining our suggested reforms for correcting the political system failures.

Reformed Political Institutions

1. *The central government.* We believe that the position of the cabinet ought to be strengthened in the Swedish parliamentary system to create more concern for the long run in political decisions. We propose adopting a rule from the German constitution, namely the possibility of a constructive vote of confidence in the parliament. Such a rule implies that the incumbent government remains in office

until a new cabinet is ready to take its place. This rule may be combined with a rule in the French constitution, according to which a government proposal combined with a vote of confidence is passed if parliament does not deny the government confidence. By strengthening the prime minister's office and the treasury, it is also possible to make the cabinet more efficient and the budget process more firm. The number of ministries ought to be reduced to broaden the realm of responsibility for each ministry so that it is not captured by special interests. It is also necessary to lay down a fixed and binding frame for total expenditures and total revenues before deciding on individual budget items.

We maintain that the most important role of the parliament should be to defend the general interest and to scrutinize the work of the cabinet. The general interest could probably be strengthened if the number of parliamentary representatives were cut—possibly by half—and if the election period for the parliament were prolonged from three to maybe five years. With fewer members of parliament and fewer standing committees, each representative will be stimulated to take a broader set of responsibilities into account. One should also give the parliament more resources to make a serious and independent evaluation and auditing of the cabinet practically possible; members of parliament would then not have to rely so much on studies by organized interest groups.

Like the budget preparation in the cabinet, the budget treatment in parliament should start by fixing total expenditures and total revenues. In this process, one ought to give the standing finance committee a stronger and overriding role. After the budget treatment in the finance committee, the budget should be accepted or rejected in its entirety by parliament in one vote, in which the government may ask for a vote of confidence. On top of that, it would be desirable to limit the right of individual parliamentary members to propose budgetary amendments by requiring that new expenditures have to be matched by corresponding savings. Government agencies should be assigned clearer objectives and be held more closely accountable for how well they succeed in meeting those objectives. In particular, the central bank should be legally required to pursue a monetary policy aimed at price stability (or low inflation). It should also be given greater independence from its political principal—the parliament—in carrying out monetary policy, according to the legislated objective. However, the central bank leadership should also be held accountable for their success in meeting this task at regular and public hearings by the parliamentary committees.

2. *Local governments.* According to the commission, Sweden is not large enough, or heterogeneous enough, to motivate more than two levels of representative democracy. Nor should sectoral bodies, in our view, have their own right of taxation. The current intermediate level of representative democracy, county councils, which are in charge mainly of the hospital system, ought therefore to be abolished.

We maintain that municipal sovereignty is an important aspect of Swedish democracy. Current central government regulations of municipal tax rates should therefore gradually be lifted. Instead, it should be mandatory to hold a referendum in a municipality to change (or at least increase) its tax rate. The present central scheme of redistributive transfers among the municipalities should be reformed to give each municipality stronger incentives to improve efficiency so as to enhance its tax base.

The central government should impose less detailed regulation on local governments than today. In particular, it should be restrictive in imposing on local governments the obligation to guarantee certain "social rights" or entitlements. More effective accounting and auditing practices in local government are, however, desirable. Therefore, we propose establishing a municipal counterpart to the National Auditing Board: the Municipal Auditing Board.

3. *Organizations and society.* Even though the central government should delegate a clear responsibility for specific tasks to its own administrative agencies, it should not delegate responsibility for government authority to private organizations. Interest groups or voluntary organizations should not be represented in those government bodies that exercise regulatory or judicial tasks. For example, the practice of interest-group representatives sitting on the governing boards of government agencies ought to be abolished, a reform that is already under way. The labor market court, the housing court and the market court should also be abolished and their judicial duties performed by courts composed exclusively of lawyers and independent experts. We also argue that voluntary organizations should not be subsidized by taxpayers.

The principle of free public access to government documents should be safeguarded, particularly in connection with Sweden's negotiations about membership in the European community.

Chapter 6

Long-Run Policies

What type of economic policy is likely to bring about a more favorable long-run economic development, avoid new and serious mistakes in stabilization policy, and resolve the acute economic crisis?

When it comes to the functioning of the economic system, we concentrate on four concrete tasks: to reduce government expenditures and in this connection stabilize the public debt as a share of GDP; to construct a better functioning and sustainable social insurance system; to improve the conditions for businesses, increase competition, and bring about increased variety in the private and the public sector, as well as to stimulate the efficiency of labor and capital markets; and finally to encourage the accumulation of physical and human capital.

4. *Government expenditures.* Radical cuts of public-sector spending are necessary during a number of years to bring down the government deficit and stabilize the public debt. This is necessary if the public sector is going to be able to perform its basic tasks and decrease harmful tax wedges in the longer run.

Our proposal is to stabilize the public debt at just above 40% of GDP within five years. The principle of our proposal would not change if we had instead suggested debt stabilization within a somewhat longer horizon or at a somewhat higher level. According to our approximate analysis in chapter 2, this requires strengthening the budget with altogether about 100 billion Swedish kronor, or 60–70 billion (5% of GDP) over and above cuts decided on by January 1993 (3% of GDP). With lower growth and continued high unemployment, another 30 billion kronor (2% of GDP) in public-sector savings are necessary.

Of the 60–70 billion, we argue that 20–30 billion can be raised by higher public-sector revenues (mostly from actuarial fees in unemployment insurance) and by more efficient enforcement of the current tax law. Thus actual expenditure cuts amount to around 40 billion kronor—under favorable assumptions. We propose alternative packages of expenditure cuts. One main alternative emphasizes reduced government consumption, another diminished government transfers. An extreme case is to keep government consumption unchanged in real terms, thereby gradually reducing its share of GDP. In that case, it is not necessary to make any further cuts in public transfers beyond what has already been decided or proposed in the 1993 budget. If, however, government consumption is allowed to grow at the same pace as GDP, it is necessary to instead cut transfers with 30–40 billion kronor. To stabilize the public debt with less favorable economic growth, it will be necessary to cut both government consumption and transfers—at unchanged tax rates.

The commission stops at the point of presenting a number of alternative packages that contain different combinations of cuts in government consumption and transfers (chapter 3). We do not commit ourselves to any specific proposal, but restrict the analysis to confronting politicians with specific alternatives.

We have explicitly taken into account that spending cuts in a certain area can lead to increased expenditures in other parts of the public sector, as there are several layers of safety nets, each guaranteeing different income levels. In other words, we have measured the resulting savings in net rather than gross terms.

To successfully implement this kind of harsh stabilization program for the public debt, it is essential to abstain from new expenditure programs without accompanying cuts in existing programs. This underlines the importance of strengthening the budget process, so that proposals in the parliament to increase expenditure are not dealt with unless they contain corresponding cuts elsewhere.

5. *Social security.* In this area the reform process should continue. We specify two overriding requirements: the system should not seriously undermine the efficiency of the economy through distorted incentives or large budget deficits; the system should be robust toward rule changes initiated by temporary shifts of opinion in stabilization or redistribution policy.

The first requirement implies that each social insurance scheme should have substantial co-insurance or deductibles, for instance by limiting the replacement ratio to 70% or 80% of earlier income, maybe also by the first days of absence not being insured. (Reforms of this type have recently been started.) We have also argued that the income-dependent part of the benefits should be actuarially fair. Moreover, the ceiling for benefits that exists today should not be so high that the majority of individuals find it unnecessary to obtain voluntary supplementary insurance.

The second requirement—that the system be robust to political disturbances—is easiest to satisfy if the social insurance systems are moved from the central government budget, either to special funds that do not have the right to borrow, or else to competing insurance companies, preserving the freedom of choice for individuals. According to our principle of a clear division of responsibility between the government and organizations, we firmly warn against replacing government monopolies in social insurance with corporatist monopolies controlled by the labor market organizations.

6. *Business conditions.* A favorable general environment for private firms requires stable laws, including property rights, and functioning markets. Favorable business conditions also require a satisfactory physical infrastructure, including new types of information systems. With respect to taxes, the most important task is to protect the major principles of the 1991 tax reform, particularly the principle of "keeping half" (a ceiling of 50% for the marginal tax rate) in the income tax system, as well as to the principle of treating different types of capital assets symmetrically.

Another important challenge for policy is to restore competition in different markets. Measures initiated during recent years should be followed up by dismantling public regulations that hamper competition and by tearing down private barriers to entry. Deregulation of product markets are important, such as the housing market, the construction sector, agriculture, and transports. Labor market legislation should be made more flexible to make it easier for firms to keep those workers that are particularly important for the future of the firm, and to make it easier to choose between production in the firm and contracting. Blocking and boycotting businesses that have not entered into a collective wage agreement should be forbidden, unless employees in the blocked businesses have voted in favor of such an agreement. Increased competition and greater freedom of choice (more variety) is important also for those social services that, today, are provided by the public sector. If the government wishes to subsidize such services, vouchers given directly to households conform better with consumer sovereignty than the current system of subsidies to government agencies (production units).

Our proposals regarding business conditions aim particularly at improving conditions for small and medium-sized firms as well as for the private-service sector, which now employs more than half of the labor force.

The commission does not take an explicit position on Swedish membership in the Common Market. There are two reasons for this. First, it has not been possible in the time available to asses whether community membership would make it easier or more difficult to carry out our proposals. Second, membership of the European Community requires considerations far beyond those at the center of this report. However, our proposals are relevant whether or not membership in the community becomes a real possibility.

7. *Physical and human capital.* When it comes to physical capital, the task is primarily to improve the general business environment. Both the general public and the labor unions have to get used to higher profit margins than those that have been prevailing in Sweden during the last few decades; otherwise Sweden will not be able to compete successfully with other countries for investment and technological development.

Accumulation of human capital involves education at all levels. Primary and secondary schools should be reoriented toward more school days per year, more homework, and increased emphasis on subjects such as Swedish, foreign languages, and mathematics. Stronger incentives for education should be accepted in the form of larger pay differentials according to professional skills; a steeper wage profile over life, connected to individual skill development, is similarly desirable—not least for manual workers. It is also important to reform the application procedure for higher education, so that high school students have stronger incentives to get the most appropriate skills. It is also desirable to increase the integration between school and on-the-job training by reintroducing "built-in workshop schools" in firms; this would make it possible to integrate theoretical and practical education, possibly in the form of an apprenticeship system. An expansion of the education sector could be financed primarily by lowering the exceptionally high teacher-student ratio.

Accumulation of physical and human capital are beneficial for the development and diffusion of new technologies, as emphasized by the "embodiment theory." Government policies that stimulate investment in physical and human capital will therefore stimulate technological change. But there is also some scope for more specific policies on the part of government in the field of technology, particularly in areas that tend to fall between the natural interest of universities and firms. The government can contribute in the field of basic (generic) technologies that have their potential use in many firms and production sectors. Such technological progress can be stimulated by grants to temporary groups of researchers or to institutes. The latter should, however, not have a permanent staff, but instead rely on rotating personnel on leave from universities, firms, and government authorities.

Short-Run Policies

Three problems dominate today's acute economic crisis: the high unemployment rate, the huge public sector deficits, and the financial crisis. It is essential to come to grips with all these problems within the course of the next few years. Measures taken against unemployment and the financial crisis largely support each other. On the other hand, attempts to resolve these problems conflict with rectifying the crisis in government finances. Attempts to diminish unemployment through expansionary fiscal and monetary policies may also put at risk ambitions to avoid a new wave of inflation.

Thus there are difficult trade-offs in the present situation. Cuts in government spending to eliminate the deficit in the medium run will serve to increase the credibility of future low inflation and open up possibilities for more expansionary short-run stabilization policies. Monetary policy actions must also be combined with measures to resolve the financial crisis quickly, and in such a way that banks will be able and willing to expand their credits, and cut substantially their current interest margins.

The most serious problem today is, in our opinion, the high unemployment rate and the risk of widespread long-term unemployment. During the next couple of years, the economy tends to become a dual economy—with a rapidly expanding export sector and a stagnating domestic sector. It will take time before exports become strong enough to pull up the rest of the economy, and during this intermediary phase unemployment will continue to increase. An important task for economic policy is thus to help the expansion in the tradable sector spread to the whole economy. Only a general expansion of the national economy will cause unemployment to fall and optimistic expectations to return. All this poses major challenges not only for fiscal and monetary policies, but also for wage formation.

8. *Fiscal policy.* Despite the huge government deficit, fiscal policy can contribute to lower unemployment. The general method we suggest is to pay the citizens to work instead of paying them not to work.

The battle against unemployment should be pursued with the smallest possible effects on the budget deficits—preferably without any effects at all. This requires reallocation of the big government expenditures connected with unemployment—about 7%–8% of GDP—to cheaper activities, such as general education (high school, adult education, as well as university education) and new inexpensive forms of public works, particularly for repair and renovation. Replacement ratios in expensive government employment programs should also be lowered, for example to 80% for public works, 75% for education arranged by the Labor Market Board, and 70% for unemployment benefits. The motive behind such proposals is to increase the leverage of given government expenditures; to limit incentives to real wages increases in the labor market; and to motivate the unemployed to look for regular jobs. The last point will be particularly important in the next business upturn. We also recommend that the central government subsidize inexpensive local-government public works and programs, with salaries below those that construction workers could claim during the building boom in recent years. On top of this, infrastructure investments should be made more labor intensive by utilizing double or triple shifts.

All these proposals are intended to bring about more reductions in unemployment for given government spending. But it is also important to redirect the huge financial savings in the private sector toward real expenditures such as investments and purchases of consumer durables. These financial savings today amount to no less than 13% of GDP. What we have in mind are measures to stimulate rebuilding and maintenance programs in the private sector. Different measures are possible, but we have not had the opportunity to decide which would be the most efficient and administratively least cumbersome. It seems that deductions, or contributions, in connection with the tax system would be the simplest method. To reduce the deficits in the unemployment insurance fund and to spread the costs of unemployment between the unemployed and the employed parts of the population, we also propose raising the fees for unemployment insurance.

We propose that the legislation regulating temporary employment be modified to stimulate new hiring. One possibility is to institute a moratorium on certain aspects of labor market legislation during today's deep recession, awaiting more permanent legislation. We are aware that such a moratorium is in conflict with our general support for stable rules, but maybe the disastrous employment situation can motivate a breach of principle on this very point.

Decisions to cut government expenditure must be taken promptly. Such decisions will create some scope for more credible stabilization policies, particularly if supported by political agreements across party lines. But the cuts must not drive the economy further down in the deep downturn.

If the public-sector deficit is trimmed without increased investment and consumption in the private sector, a depressive development of the same kind as in Finland would lurk around the corner (Honkapohja et al. 1993). Planned cuts in government expenditure programs must therefore be phased in with great care, in view of the recession, or else be supplemented with temporary tax cuts, for domestic demand not to fall further. When designing a long-run stabilization program of 100 billion kronor, we have therefore abstained from budget cuts in 1993 and limited the budget cuts to 10 billion kronor during 1994. Instead, we propose budget improvements with 30 billion kronor in each of the three years 1995, 1996, and 1997. Weaker growth would require cuts of a further 30 billion in 1998.

In sum, our proposals for fiscal policy are to phase out the budget deficit successively during the course of five years, and to reallocate unemployment-related expenditures from unemployment benefits to compensation for work and education. Should private consumption continue to fall drastically, we propose a temporary cut in the value-added tax.

9. *Monetary policy.* The central bank should continue the current gradual and experimental strategy of successively decreasing short-term interest rates. This is preferable to a sudden dramatic decrease of interest rates, which could give the impression that the central bank had given up—or been forced to give up—its fight against inflation. If, as is likely, foreign interest rates continue to fall considerably, substantially lower interest rates are clearly feasible.

Confidence in the central bank's willingness and ability to check inflation in the long run gives the bank more room in the short run to stimulate the domestic economy by successively lower interest rates. If such confidence is lacking, however, expansionary policies could instead fuel expectations of much higher inflation in the future, which will result in higher expected future short-term interest rates and thereby also higher current long-run interest rates, as well as a further depreciation of the krona.

Since the huge budget deficit considerably limits the scope for expansionary fiscal policy, the greatest hope for fighting the recession today lies with monetary policy. In our view, it is risky to continue to keep high money market rates, but above all it is risky to have skyrocketing bank lending rates. In particular, such rates can push unemployment higher. If that happens, the budget deficit would increase further, which again may augment inflation expectations. Financial markets would start speculating that the government would be tempted to inflate away the growing public debt in the future. As we pointed out in chapter 2, the latter risk is both larger and more serious than the risk that gradually falling interest rates will start a new inflation wave via a depreciating krona.

Thus, it is essential that banks increase the supply of credits and that lending rates are brought down. Lower bank rates would not only stimulate investments by households and firms; the real estate crisis would also become less severe. Lower bank lending rates are particularly important for small and medium-size firms, which do not normally finance themselves either in the domestic money market or abroad.

It would be very dangerous to allow the banks to restore their equity capital through high profits due to wide interest rate margins. It is therefore imperative that the banking crisis is resolved with policies such that (1) the banks quickly exceed the capital requirement of 8%, so that an increased supply of credit is possible, (2) the incentives for the banks to restore their balance sheets by way of high interest margins are diminished, and (3) oligopolistic interest rate practices of banks are broken by entry of new actors in the market.

There are different technical solutions to these problems, such as guarantees of good or bad loans, insurance schemes, conditional credits from the government, or new equity capital. In the latter case, the first-hand alternative should be emissions of new shares in the private market. If the emission fails, the government will have to take over the bank temporarily, by picking up the newly issued shares. It should, then, quickly—within six months to one year—sell the healthy part of the bank. To put pressure on the banks to lower their interest rate margins, the government should also sell, to new Swedish or foreign owners, at least part of those banks that it has already taken over.

Some observers deplore the fact that a fixed exchange rate no longer provides an anchor for prices and wages in Sweden. But we must recognize that the anchor has let go time and again during the last two decades. The privations at the last mooring even threatened to tear up the boat.

Our recommendation is that Sweden continue its present policy with a floating exchange rate until a credible participation in a European exchange rate arrangement is a realistic possibility. This means that the krona will continue floating until Sweden is prepared to participate in a European currency union.

10. *Wage formation.* The Swedish wage-bargaining system has to change radically if the yearly increase of nominal wages is to be limited to about 4% or 5% per year. It is our assessment that this can happen in a sustainable way only if wage bargaining is limited to just one level. When it comes to large firms, this level ought to be the level of the firm. Workers in individual firms will then see more clearly than today the association between large wage increases and diminished employment. As we have noted earlier, decentralized wage formation can also contribute to a more efficient and a more flexible wage structure.

To facilitate decentralized wage bargaining, the government can abstain from attempts to pursue incomes policy; it may also decentralize wage formation in the public sector by imposing nominal cash limits on its own agencies.

Supply-stimulating measures that promote flexibility in the labor market may contribute to low nominal wage increases and thereby to a successful stabilization policy. Such measures include liberalizing the legislation that today makes it expensive to hire labor, in particular rules that limit the possibility of temporary employment.

Income Distribution

Swedish society has traditionally given high value to economic security and relatively equal living conditions for the citizens. These values have contributed to the compressed income distribution, compared to other countries. The inequality of factor incomes, for both men and women, fell substantially during the 1950s, 1960s, and 1970s. During the 1980s inequality of factor incomes has gone up somewhat, though without affecting Sweden's relative position among countries in terms of equality of income (Björklund and Fritzell 1993). In addition to very equally distributed factor incomes, Sweden's tax and transfer system contributes further to equal living standards.

The proposals in this report are designed to promote macroeconomic stability, efficiency, and growth. The reason is that it is in these areas where the Swedish economic crisis is most obvious. The crisis is not mainly a crisis for the distribution of income except for the distributional consequences of the increased unemployment. That does not mean that we can disregard the effects our proposals would have on the distribution of income and wealth. Contrary to widespread opinion, a better functioning economy does not necessarily go hand in hand more income inequality. Some of our specific proposals will certainly increase inequality in society, but others will reduce it. In evaluating the consequences for income distribution, one should therefore consider the totality of our proposals rather than looking at them one by one.

A good example is the tax reform of 1991, which in our view is one of the most constructive structural reforms in Sweden in recent years. The reform substantially reduced marginal tax rates, which by itself contributed to greater after-tax inequality for given tax bases. But the reduction of marginal tax rates was combined with broadened tax bases, partly brought about by limitations of deduction possibilities, which has made many high income earners pay higher average taxes than earlier—despite lower marginal tax rates. Even though it is too early to draw firm conclusions about the total effects, this example shows that a one-sided focus on one component in a package—in this case the reduction of the marginal tax rates—can give a distorted picture of its distribution effects.

There are other difficulties, too, when analyzing the effects on the distribution of welfare of various reforms. A particular pitfall is that studies are often limited to annual incomes. Many reforms just redistribute an individual's income across his life, with a limited effect on his total lifetime income. An obvious example is social insurance, because all citizens are stricken, albeit to a different extent, by low labor incomes during certain parts of their lives.

Another pitfall in the debate about income distribution is that effects of specific reforms are very often impossible to assess in a realistic way, even in their direction. The reason is that it is very difficult to take into account various indirect effects via the whole economic system, for example, via repercussions on employment and factor income.

A related difficulty when assessing distributional effects is that the consequences for a certain group of citizens can spread to other groups. Certain individuals might lose directly from a reform, but they may gain indirectly via higher productivity of others in the firm where they work.

A general problem in distributive politics is that wage, tax, and social insurance systems must be built on rules that only to a limited extent can distinguish between individuals on the basis of their personal traits. For any specific reform, it is therefore possible to identify certain individuals that lose out. Such individual-specific effects may indicate that the reform has weaknesses that should be corrected. But often they are unavoidable consequences of having to treat certain groups of individuals in the same way.

The distinction between short-run and long-run effects is another factor of central importance in analyzing income distribution. In a very short-run perspective, it is not difficult to think of policies that can substantially redistribute income without imposing particularly severe costs for the economy as a whole. But such policies may weaken economic incentives, and thereby harm long-run productivity growth. The result may then be that most groups—also the short-run winners—lose out. More people would agree that this would be a short-sighted and destructive type of distributive policy.

It is important to bear in mind that the concept of equality has at least two dimensions: equality of outcome and equality of opportunity. Equality of opportunity means that citizens' access to private and public services does not vary systematically with social background, social networks, sex, etc. But equality of opportunity does not imply equality of outcomes. The result for an individual certainly depends on her opportunities, but also on the choices she has made—and on random luck.

For all these reasons, it is important to look at the net effect of a suggested reform package, rather than at one reform at a time. It is also important to consider long-term and lifetime consequences, rather than annual incomes. Otherwise, any particular attempt to increase economic efficiency may be blocked, as every measure can be described as unfavorable in some dimension for a certain group of citizens. This can stop a sequence of reforms that makes all citizens, or almost all citizens, better off. In this way individual special interests can block concern for the general interest.

Stabilization policy, too, has effects on income distribution. To stimulate employment in the next upturn, we propose lower replacement ratios in both unemployment insurance and various labor market programs. In a short-run perspective, such reforms can increase income differences. But in a slightly longer perspective, lower replacement ratios may reduce unemployment by way of stronger work incentives and lower nominal wage demands, and hence indirectly contribute to smaller income differences. An important premise of our proposals in this area is, indeed, our conviction that high long-run unemployment strongly contributes to economic inequality. By recommending a macroeconomic stabilization policy that counteracts long-run unemployment, we do indeed give high priority to long-run equality in income and living standards.

Our proposals aiming at more efficient private markets also have obvious redistributive effects. Deregulation strikes against producers not previously exposed to competition; deregulation benefits consumers in the form of lower prices and a wider range of choice. Whether the net effects are positive or negative from the vantage point of equality evidently depends on particular circumstances—as well as on value judgments. Redistributions from rich producers to poor consumers are certainly easier to accept than redistributions that go the other way. The main point, however, is that regulation is rarely an efficient method—from a social point of view—to redistribute income.

When it comes to social insurance, our main proposal is that mandatory insurance should be limited to some basic protection, which guarantees all citizens a reasonable standard—either as a fixed amount, equal for everybody, or as income-dependent benefits. This means that the government should take special responsibility for the weakest groups in society. Changing the social insurance systems in the direction of more clear-cut insurance principles will, of course, be advantageous for those individuals who pay higher than actuarially fair fees in the present system. Our proposals regarding social services might also affect income distribution, even though the direction of effects varies between areas.

We have expressed sympathy for the well-known idea of increasing competition in service production by distributing service vouchers to citizens, which they can freely use as payment for social services. Through such reforms it is possible to enhance the freedom of choice also for citizens with limited economic resources.

We have stressed how important human capital is for economic growth. Any investment in human capital requires positive returns, whether this investment takes the form of formal education or the accumulation of experience and better qualifications in the workplace. To provide good returns to education, requires, of course, a certain dispersion of wages. However, an expansion of the education system and of training within firms limits the long-term inequality in earnings.

Perhaps the public will find it easier to accept and even tolerate income differences that reflect variations in competence and productive efforts, rather than smart exploitation of inflation and arbitrage opportunities in tax and social insurance systems.

It is often said that a trade-off between an efficient economy and an equal income distribution is unavoidable. This is a half-truth. The income differences that emanate from monopolies, or from privileges to certain groups, are not productivity enhancing. In these cases, increased competition can be expected to result both in less inequality and in more efficient resource allocation. It is, however, important to realize that factor income differences, reflecting rewards of differences in productive effort, are necessary ingredients in an efficient economy. It is thus easy to give examples of reforms in our report that will diminish income inequality in society, or leave it more or less unchanged, if they became practical policy.

If many efficiency-enhancing reforms are adopted at the same time, it becomes difficult to identify winners and losers not only in the long-run but also in the short-run distributive game. This strategy was exploited in connection with the 1991 tax reform. We recommend a similar strategy both in government expenditure reform and in social security reform.

Light at the End of the Tunnel?

The Swedish crisis is deep and complicated. It forces us to make many trade-offs. Trying to solve a certain problem often makes another problem worse, or creates a new one. Therefore the solutions Sweden's serious problems are bound to be painful and protracted. It is futile to look for some new, miraculous medicine. Decades of mistakes and negligence within politics and wage formation cannot be rectified during the course of a few years. Our final message is nevertheless optimistic. The crisis can be resolved, provided that we are prepared to reassess old ideas, which might have been adequate during an earlier epoch, but which today have become part of the crisis. Looking for scapegoats is useless. The crisis cannot be fully explained by the mistakes of certain individuals—in politics, the labor market, business, or the financial sector—even though such mistakes have certainly been made. Instead, individual decisionmakers have been misdirected by certain basic systems and institutions. What we need therefore is not only short-run economic measures, but also long-run reform of the economic and political system.

When it comes to long-run policies, our main message is this: deregulate markets and restore competition and freedom of choice, even though there may be some difficult transition problems. Our main message in the short run is: prevent unemployment from increasing further, and subsequently reduce it; bring down money-market and bank interest rates gradually; and prevent the financial crisis from stalling the next business upturn.

Policies along these lines enhance the chances for a recovery within the course of a few years. We can already see some promising signs in the economic situation, though the employment situation remains a formidable problem. Politicians and the general public have became much more aware of our problems, even though difficult actions remain to be taken. Deregulation of several markets—agriculture, construction, domestic air transport, and railroads—has been initiated, even though the housing market and the labor market remain strictly regulated. The deregulation process started with the financial market in the mid-1980s, even though this deregulation had an unfortunate timing relative to the tax reform and the foreign exchange deregulation; perhaps deregulation also went too fast. The new competition legislation and the treaty with the Common Market will gradually increase competition in product markets, even though Sweden's ambitions to deregulate agriculture may become stifled.

Another promising sign is that we see beginning structural reforms of government expenditure systems. Different experiments are bringing competition to the production of social services that were earlier monopolized by local governments. In the social insurance system, incentives for work and savings have been improved, and the temptation for abuse has been reduced by increased deductibles in the form of lower replacement ratios and remuneration-free days. Measures have also been taken to shrink the public sector deficit, even though the results are not yet visible because of the recession. Through the tax reform of 1991 Sweden has also a much more efficient tax system than earlier, even though it cannot become very efficient at the present level of government expenditures.

The government has thereby attacked two of the most serious incentive problems in Sweden—overgenerous social insurance and wide tax wedges. Recently, the tax burden for small and medium-size firms has also been lightened. Generally speaking, the economic, social, and political environment for business has improved considerably during the last few years. Questionnaires among managers and business leaders confirm that this is the case. At the same time, the profit squeeze and the deep recession has triggered massive productivity-enhancing measures in private business.

Our general conclusion is that the conditions are now favorable for breaking the weak productivity trend that Sweden has experienced during the last two decades, such that the economy can embark on yet another period of fast productivity growth. It is, however, important that the restructuring of the Swedish economy continue both in private markets and in the public sector.

Today it is harder to know how to handle the acute problems of stabilization policy than the long-run problems of structural change. Whatever you choose to do, something goes wrong. However, one light in today's darkness is that inflation has came down substantially. But the rapid fall in the inflation rate—that is, the drastic disinflation process—has amplified the acute economic crisis, as private agents have earlier acted on the expectations of high inflation. This is particularly true for agents in the labor market and in the real estate and financial markets.

Another promising sign is that the depreciation of the krona after the adoption of a floating exchange rate has eradicated the previous cost crisis. Firms competing in international markets are now in a better position then earlier to utilize their capacity and successively increase their employment. Gradually, experience with economic policy under a floating exchange rate will spread in the economy. Individual agents and institutions in the foreign exchange market should also gradually learn to handle unregulated capital and foreign exchange markets and a floating exchange rate.

There are also apparent ways of easing the difficult transition problems. By postponing the actual implementation (though not the decisions) of necessary government spending cuts, or combining them with temporary tax cuts, a future recovery need not be threatened. It is possible to increase the leverage of unemployment-related government expenditures and channel private financial savings to investments, repair, and maintenance. To improve the central bank's possibilities of successively bringing down short-term interest rates, one can strengthen the credibility of the central bank's long-run inflation stance by adopting a strategy of stabilizing the government finances. Institutional reforms that make the budget process stricter and give the central bank greater independence will have the same positive effect.

It is our hope that the Swedish democracy is able to change the institutions and rules of the game that have so far made it difficult to carry out a successful economic policy. We want to see our proposals about economic policy and political institutions as a contribution to the attempts of turning Sweden around.

References

Asterisk (*) denotes expert reports to the commission.

Ahrens, T., et al. 1992. *Tillväxtföretagen i Sverige*. Report to the Department of Industry, September 28.

Alesina, A., Özler, S., Roubini, N., and Swagel, P. 1992. "Political instability and economic growth." Mimeo. Cambridge, MA: Harvard University.

*Almqvist, G., et al. 1993. "Strukturomvandling för bättre tillväxt." Expert report No. 1 to the Economic Commission. SOU 1993:16. Stockholm: Allmänna Förlaget.

*Andersson, H., et al. 1993. "Teknikpolitik för tillväxt." Expert report No. 2 to the Economic Commission. SOU 1993:16. Stockholm: Allmänna Förlaget.

*Andersson, T. 1993. "Utlandsinvesteringar och policyimplikationer." Expert report No. 3 to the Economic Commission. SOU 1993:16. Stockholm: Allmänna Förlaget.

Arvidsson, G., and Jönsson, B. (eds.). 1991. *Sjukvård i andra länder—Vad kan Sverige lära?* Stockholm: SNS.

Association of Local Governments (Kommunförbundet). 1991. *Det kommunala underhållsberget*. 4 reports. Stockholm.

Aukrust, O., Holte, F., and Stoltz, G. 1967. *Instilling II fra utredningsutvalget for intektsoppgjørene 1966*. Oslo.

Barro, R. J. 1991. "Economic Growth in a Cross Section of Countries." *Quarterly Journal of Economics* 106(2): 407–443.

Barro, R. J., and Sala-i-Martin, X. 1993. *Economic Growth*. Unpublished manuscript. Cambridge, MA: Harvard University.

Bentzel, R. 1990. "Svensk ekonomisk tillväxt fram till år 2020." Expert report to Government Pension Committee. SOU 1990:78.

Bergman, L., and Hansson, B. 1992. "Vad säger måtten på produktivitetsutvecklingen?" *Yearbook of Economic Council*, Stockholm.

Bernanke, B., and Mishkin, E. 1992. "Central Bank Behavior and the Strategy of Monetary Policy, Observations from Six Industrialized Countries." In *NBER Macroeconomics Annual* 1992. Cambridge, MA: MIT Press.

Bishop, J. 1991. "Produktivitet och kunskaper från utbildning." Expert report No. 4 to Productivity Delegation. SOU 1991:82.

Bishop, M., and Kay, J. 1988. "Does Privatization Work? Lessons from the UK." London: London Business School.

Björklund, A. 1986. "A Comment on the Wage Structure and the Functioning of the Labor Market." In C-H. Siven (ed.), *Unemployment in Europe.* Timbro: Stockholm.

Björklund, A., and Fritzell, J. 1993. "Inkomstfördelningens utveckling." Expert report No. 8 to Long-Term Report 1992, Stockholm.

Bolin, O. and Swedenborg, B. (eds.). 1992. *Mat till EG-pris? Den svenska livsmedelskedjan i ett EG-perspektiv.* Stockholm: SNS.

Borcherding, T., et al. 1982. "Comparing the Efficiency of Private and Public Production: The Evidence from Five Countries." *Zeitschrift für Nationalökonomie* 1991, suppl 2.

Bosworth, B. P., and Rivlin, A. M. (eds.) 1987. *The Swedish Economy.* Washington, DC: The Brookings Institution.

Bourdet Y. (ed.). 1992. *Internationalization, Market Power and Consumer Welfare.* London: Routledge.

Bröms, J. 1992. *Målrelaterade statsstipendier.* Official report Ds 1992:123, Stockholm.

Bruun, N., et al. 1990. *Den nordiska modellen: fackföreningarna och arbetsrätten i Norden— nu och i framtiden.* Malmö: Liber.

*Calmfors, L. 1993. "De institutionella systemen på arbetsmarknaden och arbetslösheten." Expert report No. 4 to the Economic Commission. SOU 1993:16. Stockholm: Allmänna Förlaget.

Calmfors, L., and Driffill, J. 1988. "Bargaining Structure, Corporativism and Macroeconomic Performance." *Economic Policy,* No. 6.

Calmfors, L., and Herin, J. 1979. "Domestic and Foreign Price Influences: A Disaggregated Study of Sweden." In Assar Lindbeck (ed.) *Inflation and Employment in Open Economies.* Amsterdam: North-Holland.

Calmfors, L., and Nymoen, R. 1990. "Real Wage Adjustment and Employment Policies in the Nordic Countries." *Economic Policy,* No 11.

*Carlén, B. 1993. "Investeringar i vägar och järnvägar för tillväxt." Expert report No. 5 to the Economic Commission. SOU 1993:16. Stockholm: Allmänna Förlaget.

Central Bureau of Statistics (Statistiska centralbyrån). 1991. *Utbildning och produktivitet.* Information om arbetsmarknaden No. 1991:2.

Cuikerman, A. 1992. *Central Bank Strategy, Credibility and Independence.* Cambridge, MA: MIT Press.

Culyer, A. J., et al. 1992. *Svensk sjukvård bäst i världen?* Stockholm: SNS.

Dahl, R. A. 1982. *Dilemmas of Pluralist Democracy: Autonomy vs. Control.* New Haven: Yale University Press.

Dahl, R. A. 1984. "Polyarchy, Pluralism and Scale." *Scandinavian Political Studies* 7(4):225–241.

References

Davis, S. 1992. "Cross-Country Patterns of Change in Relative Wages." *NBER Macroeconomics Annual*. Cambridge, MA: MIT Press.

Democracy Committee (Folkstyrelsekommittén). 1987. *Folkstyrelsens villkor*. SOU 1987:6. Stockholm: Allmänna Förlaget.

Demsetz, H. 1989. *Efficiency and Competition. The Organization of Economic Activity*. Vol II. New York: Basil Blackwell.

ESO. 1992a. *Alternativa verksamhetsformer inom vård och omsorg*. Official Report, Ds 1992:108.

ESO. 1992b. *Anbudskonkurrens vid offentlig produktion*. Official Report, Ds 1992:121.

ESO. 1983. *Produktivitet i privat och offentlig tandvård*. Official Report, Ds Fi 1983:27.

Economic Report of the President. 1993. Budget Baselines, App. F.

Edin, P. A., and Holmlund, B. 1992. "The Swedish Wage Structure: The Rise and Fall of Solidaristic Wage Policy?" Working Paper 1992:13, Department of Economics, University of Uppsala.

Edin, P. A., and Holmlund, B. 1993. "Avkastning och efterfrågan på högre utbildning." *Ekonomisk Debatt* 21(1).

Edgren, G., Faxén, K.-O., and Odhner, C.-E. 1973. *Lönebildning och samhällsekonomi*. EFO report, Stockholm.

Ekonomiska Rådets Årsbok. 1991. Report to the Economic Council. Stockholm: Norstedt.

*Eliasson, G. 1993. "Företagens, institutionernas och marknadernas roll i Sverige." Expert report No. 6 to the Economic Commission. SOU 1993:16. Stockholm: Allmänna Förlaget.

Fägerlind, I. 1991. "Utbildningsstandarden i Sverige 1970–1990 och produktivitetsutvecklingen." Expert report No. 4 to Productivity Delegation. Stockholm: Allmänna Förlaget.

*Fägerlind, I. 1993. "Utbildningen i Sverige och det mänskliga kapitalet." Expert report No. 9 to the Economic Commission. SOU 1993:16. Stockholm: Allmänna Förlaget.

*Feldt, K.-O. 1993. "Förändringens politiska problem." Expert report No. 7 to the Economic Commission. SOU 1993:16. Stockholm: Allmänna Förlaget.

*Flam, H., et al. 1993. "EES-avtalet, ny lagstiftning och konkurrensen i Sverige." Expert report No. 8 to the Economic Commission. SOU 1993:16. Stockholm: Allmänna Förlaget.

Fölster, S. 1990. *Den offentliga sektorn*. Expert report No. 26 to Long-Term Report 1990. Stockholm: Allmänna Förlaget.

*Genberg, H. 1993. "Penningpolitiken efter den 19 november—allmänna principer och internationella lärdomar." Expert report No. 10 to the Economic Commission. SOU 1993:16. Stockholm: Allmänna Förlaget.

Giavazzi, F., and Giovannini, A. 1989. *Limited Exchange Rate Flexibility: The European Monetary System*. Cambridge, MA: MIT Press.

References

Gottfries, N. 1987. "Devalveringarnas effekter på exportindustrins prissättning och marknadsandelar." In Jonung, L. (ed.), *Devalveringen 1982—rivstart eller snedtändning?* Stockholm: SNS Förlag.

Grilli, V., Masciandaro, D., and Tabellini, G. 1991. "Political and Monetary Institutions and Public Financial Policies in the Industrial Countries." *Economic Policy* 13: 341–392.

von Hagen, J. 1992. *Budgeting Procedures and Fiscal Performance in the European Communities*. Commission of the European Communities (DG-II). Economic Papers No. 96, Oct. 1992.

Hall, R. L., and Grofman, B. 1990. "The Committee Assignment Process and the Conditional Nature of Committee Bias." *American Political Science Review* 84(4):1149–1166.

Hansson, P., and Lundberg, L. 1991. "Internationell konkurrens och produktivitetstillväxt." Expert report No. 8 to Productivity Delegation. SOU 1991:82.

Heckscher, G. 1951. *Staten och organisationerna*. Stockholm: KF Förlag.

*Henrekson, M. 1993. "Humankapital, produktivitet och tillväxt." Expert report No. 11 to the Economic Commission. SOU 1993:16. Stockholm: Allmänna Förlaget.

Holmberg, E., and Stjernquist, N. 1980. *Grundlagarna med tillhörande författningar*. Stockholm: Norstedts.

Holmberg, S., and Esaiasson, P. 1988. *De folkvalda: en bok om riksdagsledamöterna och den representativa demokratin i Sverige*. Stockholm: Bonniers.

Holmlund, B. 1990. *Svensk lönebildning—teori, empiri, politik*. Export report No. 24 to Long-Term Report 1990. Stockholm: Allmänna Förlaget.

*Holmlund, B. 1993. "Arbetslösheten—konjunkturfenomen eller systemfel?" Expert report No. 12 to the Economic Commission. SOU 1993:16. Stockholm: Allmänna Förlaget.

*Honkapohja, S., et al. 1993. "The Crisis of the Finnish Economy." Expert report No. 13 to the Economic Commission. SOU 1993:16. Stockholm: Allmänna Förlaget.

IVA (Ingenjörsvetenskapsakademien). 1993. *Företagsledares syn på tillväxt inom svenskt näringsliv*, Stockholm.

*Isaksson, M. 1993. "De svenska direktinvesteringarna i ett internationellt perspektiv." Expert report No. 14 to the Economic Commission. SOU 1993:16. Stockholm: Allmänna Förlaget.

Jakobsson, U. 1992. *Det ekonomiska läget. Industrikrisen i Sverige*. Stockholm: Industriförbundet.

*Jakobsson, U., and Jagrén, L. 1993. "Den underliggande konkurrenskraften." Expert report No. 15 to the Economic Commission. SOU 1993:16. Stockholm: Allmänna Förlaget.

Janlert, U., and Meidner, R. 1992."Vad säger forskningen om arbetslöshetens effekter på individen?" *Ekonomisk Debatt* 6/92:471–482.

Jansson, J. O. 1993a. *Hur välja rätt investeringar i transportinfrastrukturen?* Report to ESO.

Jansson, J. O. 1993b. *Diskussion av trafikverkens inriktningsplaner för investeringar 1994–2003*. NUTEK.

Jansson, J. O., and Nilsson, J.-E. 1989. "Spelar samhällsekonomiska kalkyler någon verklig roll i vägväsendet?" *Ekonomisk Debatt* 2:85–95.

Jernelöv, A. 1992. *Miljöskulden*. Official report, SOU 1992:58.

Johansson, J. 1992. "Det statliga kommittéväsendet: kunskap, kontroll, konsensus." Department of Political Science, Stockholm University.

*Johansson, S-E. 1993. "Bankstödet—Kapitaltäckning—Kreditförsörjning." Expert report No. 16 to the Economic Commission. SOU 1993:16. Stockholm: Allmänna Förlaget.

Jonsson, E. 1993. "Hur bör kommunal skatteutjämning utformas?—Några råd baserade på teori och verklighet." Institute for Municipal Economy, Stockholm University.

Jonung, L. 1993. "Från räntereglering till inflationslån." In L. Werin (ed.), *Det finansiella systemet och rikdsbankens politik 1945 till 1990*. Stockholm: SNS Förlag.

Joskow, P., and Rose, N. 1990. "The Effects of Economic Regulation" in R. Schmalensee and R. Willig (eds.), *Handbook of Industrial Organization, Volume II*. Amsterdam: North-Holland.

*Korpi, W., and Palme, J. 1993. "Socialpolitik, kris och reformer: Sverige i internationell belysning." Expert report No. 17 to the Economic Commission. SOU 1993:16. Stockholm: Allmänna Förlaget.

Krugman, P., and Obstfeld, M. 1991. *International Economics: Theory and Policy*. New York: Harper & Collins.

Landsorganisationen. 1951. *Fackföreningsrörelsen och den fulla sysselsättningen*. Stockholm: LO.

Långtidsutredningen (Long-Term Report). 1990 Official report. Stockholm.

Långtidsutredningen (Long-Term Report). 1992 Official report. Stockholm.

Larsson, U. (ed.). 1990. *Att styra riket: regeringskansliet 1840–1990*. Stockholm: Allmänna Förlaget.

Layard, R., Nickell, S., and Jackman, R. 1991. *Unemployment—Macroeconomic Performance and the Labor Market*. Oxford: Oxford University Press.

Lewin, L. 1992. *Samhället och de organiserade intressena*. Norstedts: Stockholm.

Lichtenberg, F. 1992. "R & D Investment and International Productivity Differentials." NBER Working Paper No. 4161, Cambridge, MA.

Lindbeck, A. 1993. *Unemployment and Macroeconomics*. Cambridge, MA: MIT Press.

Lindbeck, A., and Snower, D. 1988. *The Insider-Outsider Theory of Employment and Unemployment*. Cambridge, MA: MIT Press.

Lindberg, H., Svensson, L., and Söderlind, P. 1993. "Devaluation Expectations: The Swedish Krona 1985–1992." *Economic Journal* 103(420):1170–1179.

Lindgren, R. 1992. "Emittera realobligationer!" *Ekonomisk Debatt* 5/92:395–400.

Lipsey, R., and Swedenborg, B. 1993. "The High Cost of Eating: Agricultural Protection and International Differences in Consumer Prices." NBER Working Paper.

Lucas, R. E. 1990. "Why Doesn't Capital Flow from Rich to Poor Countries?" *American Economic Review* 80(2):92–96.

*Lundström, A., et al. 1993. "De nya och små företagens roll i svensk ekonomi." Expert report No. 18 to the Economic Commission. SOU 1993:16. Stockholm: Allmänna Förlaget.

Maddison, A. 1982. *Phases of Capitalist Development.* Oxford: Oxford University Press.

Magnusson, D. 1993. BRÅ (Crime Prevention Council). "Personal Information."

*Mäler, K.-G. 1993. "Growth and Environment." Expert report No. 19 to the Economic Commission. SOU 1993:16. Stockholm: Allmänna Förlaget.

Mankiw, N. G., et al. 1992. "A Contribution to the Empirics of Economic Growth." *Quarterly Journal of Economics* 107(2):407–437.

Mattsson, N. 1992. "Skatteförmåner och andra särregler i inkomst- och mervärdesskatten." Report to ESO, Ds 1992:6.

Meyerson, P. M., Ståhl, I., and Wickman, K. 1990. *Makten över bostaden.* Stockholm: SNS.

Micheletti, M. 1990. *The Swedish Farmers' Movement and Government Agricultural Policy.* New York: Praeger.

Mincer, J., and Higuchi, Y. 1988. "Wage Structures and Labor Turnover in the U.S. and Japan." *Journal of the Japanese and International Economies* 2(2):97–133.

Ministry of Social Affairs (Socialdepartementet). 1993. *Goda exempel.* Stockholm: Allmänna Förlaget.

Molander, P. 1992. *Statsskulden och budgetprocessen.* Report to ESO, Ds 1992:126.

Murray, R. 1987. "Den offentliga sektorn—produktivitet och effektivitet." Expert report No. 21 to Long-Term Report 1987, Stockholm.

Myhrman, J. 1979. "The Determinants of Inflation and Economic Activity in Sweden." In Assar Lindbeck (ed.), *Inflation and Employment in Open Economies.* Amsterdam: North-Holland.

NUTEK. 1992. *Näringslivets utveckling till 2004—Tillväxt eller stagnation.* Expert report No. 3 to Long-Term Report 1992. Stockholm: Allmänna Förlaget.

Nadiri, M. I. 1991. "Innovationer och teknikspridning." Expert report No. 10 to Productivity Delegation. SOU 1991:82.

National Council for Crime Prevention (BRÅ). 1991. "Åtgärder för att effektivisera kampen mot den ekonomiska brottsligheten." Memo E 39-57/91. Stockholm.

Nilsson, A. 1991. "Influencing the Social Distribution of Higher Education." In I. Persson (ed.), *Generating Equality in the Welfare State.* Oslo: Norwegian University Press.

OECD. 1990. *Education in OECD Countries 1987–88,* Paris.

OECD. 1991. *Taxing Profits in a Global Economy,* Paris.

References

OECD. 1992. *Economic Outlook*, Paris.

OECD. 1993. *Foreign Direct Investment*, Sweden. Paris.

Ohlsson, L. 1992. *R & D for Swedish Industrial Renewal*. Official report, Ds 1992:109.

Olsen, J. P. 1983. *Organized Democracy: Political Institutions in a Welfare State—The Case of Norway*. Bergen: Universitetsförlaget.

Persson, T., and Tabellini, G. 1990. *Macroeconomic Policy: Credibility and Politics*. London: Harwood Academic Publishers.

Persson, T., and Tabellini, G. 1994. "Is Inequality Harmful for Growth?" *American Economic Review* (forthcoming).

Peters, B. G. 1991. *European Politics Reconsidered*. New York: Holmes & Meier.

Petersson, O. 1993. *Svensk politik*. Stockholm: Publica.

Petersson, O., and Söderlind, D. 1992. *Förvaltningspolitik*. Stockholm: Publica.

Petersson, O., Westholm, A., and Blomberg, G. 1987. *Medborgarnas makt*. Stockholm: Carlssons.

Power Delegation (Maktutredningen). 1990. *Demokrati och makt i Sverige*. Main report, SOU 1990:44. Stockholm.

Productivity Delegation (Produktivitetsdelegationen). 1991. *Drivkrafter för produktivitet och välstånd*. SOU 1991:82. Stockholm.

Psacharopoulos, G. 1985. "Returns to Education: Further International Update and Implications." *Journal of Human Resources* 20(4):584–604.

Regional Commission (Regionutredningen). 1992. *Regionala roller: en perspektivstudie*. SOU 1992:63. Stockholm.

Riksbanksutredningen. 1993. *Riksbank för prisstabilitet*. SOU 1993:20. Stockholm.

RRV (Riksrevisionsverket) (Government Accounting Office). 1990. *Vägverkets investeringsplanering*.

Rothstein, B. 1992. *Den korporativa staten: intresseorganisationer och statsförvaltning i svensk politik*. Stockholm: Norstedts.

SAFAD (Statskontoret). 1991. *Statligt föreningsstöd—en kartläggning*. Report No. 1991:6.

*Schaumann, A. 1993. "Dansk Økonomisk politik 1982–1992." Expert report No. 20 to the Economic Commission. SOU 1993:16. Stockholm: Allmänna Förlaget.

*Scherman, K. G. 1993. "En ny socialförsäkring." Expert report No. 21 to the Economic Commission. SOU 1993:16. Stockholm: Allmänna Förlaget.

Schück, H. et al. 1992. *Riksdagen genom tiderna*. 2 ed. Sveriges Riksdag. Stockholm: Stiftelsen Riksbankens Jubileumsfond.

Sigeman, T. 1991. "Arbetsrätt." In *Norstedts Juridiska Handbok*. Stockholm: Norstedts.

Sohlman, Å. 1992. *Hur bra är vi?* Report to ESO, Ds 1992:83.

*Söderström, L. 1993. "Generell eller selektiv välfärdspolitik—om alternativ i socialpolitiken." Expert report No. 24 to the Economic Commission. SOU 1993:16. Stockholm, Allmänna Förlaget.

References

*Ståhl, I. 1993. "Den reglerade arbetsmarknaden." Expert report No. 23 to the Economic Commission. SOU 1993:16. Stockholm: Allmänna Förlaget.

Ståhl, I., and Wickman, K. 1992. *Riv bostadspolitiken*. Stockholm: SNS.

*Steigum, E., Jr. 1993. "Stabilitets- og strukturproblemer i norsk ekonomi." Expert report No. 22 to the Economic Commission. SOU 1993:16. Stockholm: Allmänna Förlaget.

Strömberg, H. 1992. *Kommunalrätt*, 14 ed. Malmö: Ekonomiförlagen.

Swedenborg, B. 1991. "Svenska multinationella företag och produktiviteten." In Expert report No. 8 to Productivity Delegation. SOU 1991:82.

Svensson, L. E. O. 1989. "Finansiell integration, resursfördelning och penningpolitik." Report to 1990 Long-Term Report, Stockholm.

Svensson, L. E. O. 1992. "Växelkursens trovärdighet: Att mäta devalveringsförväntningar." *Ekonomisk Debatt* 2/92:101–113.

Tarschys, D. 1984. *Parlamentet och statsutgifterna: hur finansmakten utövas i nio länder*. Report to ESO, Ds Fi 1984:18.

Tiebout, C. M. 1956. "A Pure Theory of Local Expenditure." *Journal of Political Economy*, 64:1145–1159.

*Urwitz, G., and Viotti, S. 1993. "Det finansiella systemet—Dagens problem och synpunkter på framtiden." Expert report No. 25 to the Economic Commission. SOU 1993:16. Stockholm: Allmänna Förlaget.

*Wadensjö, E. 1993. "Socialförsäkringssystemets okända delar." Expert report No. 26 to the Economic Commission. SOU 1993:16. Stockholm: Allmänna Förlaget.

Westerståhl, J. 1987. *Staten, kommunerna och den statliga styrningen: några principfrågor*. Department of Internal Affairs. Stockholm.

*Wikström, S. 1993. "Företagens förnyelse och tillväxt i Sverige—Finns det några snabba recept?" Expert report No. 27 to the Economic Commission. SOU 1993:16. Stockholm: Allmänna Förlaget.

World Competitiveness Report. 1992. IMD-World Economic Forum, Geneva.

Zetterberg, J. 1989. *Lönestrukturen och den dubbla obalansen*. Report to ESO, Ds 1989:8.

Index

Accommodation policy, 31–34
Adverse selection, 104
Ahrens, 163
Alesina, 164
Andersson, 159, 161
Arvidsson, 122
Association of Local Governments, 143
Aukrust, 25
Austria, 40

Background of Swedish crisis, 31–32, 50–51
Bank Rescue Fund, 67
Banking crisis
 background, 30, 64–67
 solutions, 67–69, 94–95
Barro, 147
Benefit arbitrage, 110–111
Bernanke, 45
Bishop, 118
Björklund, 150, 220
Bolin, 79, 85
Borcherding, 118
Bosworth, 35
Bourdet, 81
Bretton Woods system, 24
Bröms, 153
Brookings Report, 35
Budget process
 automatic budget changes, 187–188
 in parliament, 185–189
 reform proposal, 49, 186–187
 weakness of, 48–49
Bundesbank, 52, 53, 54

Calmfors, 36, 38, 109
Carlén, 142

Cartels, 81
Central bank
 independence, 42–49
 objectives, 191–192
 role, 33–34, 191–192
Central Bureau of Statistics, 149
Citizenship, 172
Civic society, 198–201
 corporatism, 198–200
 mass media, 202
 public debate, 201
Competition
 antitrust policies, 87–88
 food sector, 84–85
 housing sector, 84–85
 merger guidelines, 88
 restrictions on, 77–78, 81–86
Competition Board, 86, 124, 125
Consumer Delegation, 84
Consumption, 57–58
Cost crises, 2–3, 28–30
Cuikerman, 44
Culyer, 122

Dahl, 173
Davis, 151
Debt-to-GDP ratio, 61–63
Deindustrialization, 139–140
Democracy
 active citizens, 204
 monolithic vs. pluralistic, 173
 responsibility and accountability, 174–175
Democracy Committee, 184
Demsetz, 81
Domestic demand, 57–58
Driffill, 36

Index

EC membership, 87
  cost of, 133–134
Economic Report of the President, 167
Edgren, 25
Edin, 150, 151
Education
  incentives, 149–152
  quality, 148–149
  reform possibilities, 152–154
  spending, 148–149
  university systems, 153–155
  wage profiles, 151–152
Efficiency problems, 6–7, 75–77
EMS, 39, 40, 41
Esaiasson, 181
ESO, 117, 124
European Economic Area, 86–87
Exchange rate
  crisis, 40
  ecu system, 40–41
  fixed rates, 23–24, 39–40
  floating rates, 32–35
  overvaluation, 2–3
  policies, 24–28

Fägerlind, 118, 148, 150, 152
Faxén, 25
Federalism
  Swedish style, 196–197
  and taxes, 122–124
Fine-tuning vs. coarse-tuning, 48
Finland, 52
Fiscal policy
  long term, 58–64
  possibilities of, 47–48
  reforms of, 216–217
  short term, 55–58
  trade-offs, 50–51
Flam, 86, 88, 118, 119, 143
Foreign investments of Swedish firms, 139–140
Forward rates, 54
Free-rider problem, 104
Fritzell, 151, 220

Genberg, 32, 40, 45
Giavazzi, 39
Giovannini, 39
Gottfries, 36
Government agencies, 189–191

Government finances
  consolidation of debt, 46–47, 58–64, 125–129, 132–134
  denomination of debt, 46–47
  indexation of debt, 47
  and inflation, 45–47
  and policy autonomy, 46–47, 127–128
Grilli, 44
Grofman, 183
Growth
  and debt, 164–167
  and environment, 167–169
  and equality, 155–156, 160–164
  intergenerational aspects, 165–167
  of multinational firms, 161–162
  proximate sources, 10
  record, 8–12
  of risk firms, 162–163
  wider concept of, 164–167

Hagen, von, 49, 185
Hall, 183
Hansson, 9
Health insurance, 110
Heckscher, 198
Henrekson, 150
Herin, 36
Higuchi, 151
Holmberg, 181
Holmlund, 36, 70, 71, 90, 150
Holte, 25
Honkapohja, 30, 31, 57, 218
Human capital
  importance, 146–148
  externalities, 147–148
  returns, 146–147

Income distribution
  concepts of equality, 222
  difficulties of analysis, 221–222
  effects of stabilization policy, 222–223
  effects of supply-side policies, 223–224
Inflation
  of prices, 4–5
  of wages, 25–26
Infrastructure
  decision making, 145
  interest groups, 141–145
  quality, 144–145
  railroads, 143
  roads, 141–143
  tele, 143

Index   239

Insiders in labor market, 91, 93
Institutional reforms
  budget process, 212
  business environment, 214–215
  need for, 35
  physical and human capital, 215–216
  social security, 213–214
  wage formation, 220
International forces, 2–3, 31–32
Isaksson, 139
IVA, 144

Jackman, 70
Jagrén, 138, 140
Jakobsson, 11, 138, 140
Janlert, 52
Jansson, 142, 143
Jernelöv, 168
Johansson, 67
Jönsson, 122
Jonung, 43
Joskow, 77

Kay, 118
Korpi, 105
Krugman, 27, 32

Labor market
  contracting out, 91
  and new organization of firms, 92–93
  policies, 38
  regulations, 37, 90–94
  seniority rules, 90–91
Layard, 70
Lending rates of banks, 55, 66
Lewin, 198
Lichtenberg, 160
Lindbeck, 70
Lindberg, 30
Lindgren, 47
Lipsey, 79
Local government
  reform proposals, 196–197
  role of local government, 193–198
Lucas, 147
Lundberg, 9, 205

Maastricht Treaty, 39, 41
Magnusson, 132
Madison, 137
Mankiw, 147

Market shares of Sweden, 138–139
Mattson, 188
Meidner, 52
Meyerson, 84
Micheletti, 198
Mincer, 151
Mishkin, 45
Molander, 186
Monetary policy
  country experiences, 45, 54–55
  long term, 38–41
  national autonomy, 41–42
  nonaccommodating, 32–33
  reforms of, 220
  short term, 44–45, 53–55
  trade-offs, 52
Monetary union, 41–42
Moral hazard, 105
Mundell-Fleming model, 27
Myhrman, 36

Nadiri, 158
Narrow banks, 95
National Audit Board, 124
National Council for Crime Prevention, 102
Nickell, 70
Nilsson, 145, 155
NUTEK, 144

Obstfeld, 27, 32
Odhner, 25
OECD, 11, 32
Ohlsson, 139, 162
Olsen, 198
Outsiders in labor market, 91, 93

Palme, 105
Parliament
  role, 181–182
  size, 181
  standing committees, 181–182
Parliamentarianism, 176–178
  role of cabinet, 178–181
  weakness of Swedish, 176–178
Paternalism, 104
Persson, 44, 155
Petersson, 189
Physical capital determinants, 140–141
Pluralism, 173–174
  need for, 95–96

Political system
  reform proposals, 209–212
  relation to private organizations, 211–212
  stability of, 27–28
  weaknesses, 13–14
Price level in Sweden, 78–81
Productivity delegation, 81, 119
Productivity growth
  delayed indicators, 137–138
  record, 8–12
  slowdown, 137–138
Proposals, 49–50, 72–73, 89, 94, 97, 102–103, 115–116, 125, 134–135, 146, 156–157, 160, 164, 169, 192–193, 198, 204
Psacharopoulos, 150
Public consumption
  child care, 122
  competition, 122–125
  consumer sovereignty, 119–121
  costs of, 117–119
  distributional accuracy, 122
  efficiency problems, 116–121
  reform proposals, 121–122
  vouchers, 119–120
Public sector
  characteristics of, 206–207
  expansion, 5, 97–98

Recovery
  easing transition problems, 226–227
  possibilities of, 224–226
  reforms under way, 225–226
Regulations, 76–77, 81
  deregulation, 87
Rents, 81
  control, 84
Riksrevisionsverket, 145
Risk capital market, 96–97
Rose, 77
Rothstein, 198

SAFAD, 130
Sala-i-Martin, 147
Saving
  instability of, 3–5
  private vs. public sector, 11, 96–97
Schaumann, 119
Scherman, 105, 108, 110
Schück, 181
Severance pay, 70–71
Sigeman, 90

Snower, 70
Social contract, 18
Social security system
  basic security, 107–108
  ceiling on benefits, 109
  distributional issues, 112–113
  motives for, 103–105
  poverty traps, 107
  problems, 8, 104–106
  reforms, 105, 112, 129–130
  relation to politics, 108
  selective, 107
  transition problems, 112, 114
Sohlman, 148
Special interest groups, 17, 77, 88–89
Stabilization policy
  long run vs. short run, 207–208
  need for institutional reforms, 35
Ståhl, 84, 85, 87, 93
State's classical role, 14–15
Steigum, 30, 31
Stoltz, 25
Svensson, 30, 39
Swedenborg, 79, 161
Swedish Employers' Confederation (SAF), 200
Swedish model
  characteristics of, 16–17
  crisis of, 17–18
  system failures vs. policy mistakes, 208–209
Swedish Trade Union Confederation (LO), 200
Söderlind, 30, 189
Söderström, 105

Tabellini, 44, 155
Tarschys, 176
Tax system
  double taxation, 101–102
  evasion, 102
  incentives, 100–101
  real taxation, 101
  reforms of, 100–102, 132
  tax credit, 58
  visibility of, 102
Tayloristic work organization, 91–92
Technology
  diffusion of, 11–12
  knowledge as a public good, 158–160
  R & D spending, 158–160
Tiebout, 196

Index 241

Trade-offs
 in fiscal policy, 50–51
 in monetary policy, 52
Transfer payments, 111
 consolidation of, 130–132

Unemployment
 benefits, 38, 56, 110
 development of, 6, 29–30
 and job security legislation, 70–71
 persistence, 70–71, 80
 policies against, 56–57
 social consequences, 52
Urwitz, 95

VAT, 58
Viotti, 95

Wadensjö, 110
Wage formation
 and inflation, 26
 organization, 5, 14, 36–37
 and unemployment, 37–38
Welfare state crisis, 97–100
Wickman, 84, 85, 87
Wikström, 84
Work-injury insurance, 110

Zetterberg, 151